The Seasoned Traveler's Guide to Northern California

The Seasoned Traveler's Guide to Northern California

Edwin Kiester, Jr.
&
William Kiester

Country Roads Press

For Sally—
wife, mom, and our favorite seasoned traveler
and Onie,
companion in the great cities of the world.

The Seasoned Traveler's Guide
to Northern California

©1993 by Edwin Kiester, Jr., and William Kiester.

Published by Country Roads Press
P.O. Box 286, Lower Main Street
Castine, Maine 04421

Cover design by Studio 3, Ellsworth, Maine.
Text design by Genie Dailey, Country Roads Press.

Library of Congress Cataloging-in-Publication Data
Kiester, Edwin.
     The seasoned traveler's guide to Northern California / Ed and Will
  Kiester.
        p. cm.
     Includes index.
     ISBN 1–56626–011–6 : $10.95
    1. California, Northern—Tours. I. Kiester, Will, 1969-
  II. Title.
  F867.5.K54   1993
  917.94—dc20   92–81829

Printed in the United States of America.
10 9 8 7 6 5 4 3 2 1

Contents

Explore one of the greatest cities in the world. Taste fresh crab at
Fisherman's Wharf or dim sum in Chinatown; take in a Mary Cassatt
painting and some priceless blue-and-white porcelain, or watch a shark
in the aquarium at Golden Gate Park; travel through time at the Academy of Sciences; take a walking tour of restaurants, "Painted Ladies,"
or Chinatown; ride the cable cars, sail to Alcatraz, or drive the
Crookedest Street in the World; order pasta in North Beach. And the
restaurants!

Check out the UC Berkeley campus gardens, museums, and bell
tower; ride an old carousel in Tilden Park, explore Jack London's
waterfront, watch dinosaurs in action, pick up a pizza from the
Cheese Board Collective, and enjoy wonderful roses and spectacular views of the bay.

Wander through Filoli with its old mansion and gardens, through Acres
of Orchids, the huge food pyramid at the Coyote Point Museum, or
Sunset magazine's ornamental gardens; applaud as once again Bacall
teaches Bogie how to whistle at the Stanford Theater; stroll the Rodin
sculpture garden at Stanford University.

Contents, continued

Contents, continued

Introduction: Northern California, Here You Come

California is a state. Northern California is a state of mind. Even its residents don't necessarily agree on its geographical limits. Sure, northern California is bounded to the east by the lofty Sierra Nevada, to the west by the Pacific Ocean, to the north by Oregon. But where is the southern cutoff point? Those in the far northern Redwood Empire sniff at the San Francisco Bay Area as central, certainly not northern, California. In fact, the north once mounted an effort to secede from the rest of the state. The Bay Area couldn't agree more. They are definitely northern, certainly not southern, Californians—not to be associated in any way with that vagrant territory they dismiss as La-La Land or Tinseltown.

What probably identifies northern California is an attitude—both liberal and conservative, open to new ideas but protective of old ones, an area that was able to swallow up the many waves that washed over it during the gold rush and after and knit them into one broad outlook. Northern Californians look around at what they see and, for all its difficulties, are proud of it, and proudly tell others about it.

For this book, we have drawn an imaginary line south of Big Sur on the foggy and scenic coast and have extended it arbitrarily eastward to the Sierra Nevada on the other side of the state. Everything north of that is northern California because we said so. That takes in more than enough territory for a first-time, second-time, or repeat visitor to explore and find new sights and delights, or reassess those that he or she (or, most likely, both) may have oohed and aahed over on previous trips with the children in tow. The amazing thing about the Golden State, northern variety, is that it is just what the adjective implies—a treasure trove of riches waiting to be sniffed out and discovered. Like the old miners' contention that more gold lies under the earth than was ever taken from it, just beneath the surface of northern California, many gems remain to be identified and unearthed.

Who would think of trendy, modern, 1990s California as a state with pastoral villages where nothing seems to have changed since dairymen delivered their products by horse and buggy? Or "sunny California" as a place where winter temperatures have dropped to −20° F, and snow depths have exceeded fifteen feet? Or the state of perpetual youth with the oldest living things in the world? All that describes northern California, in spades. California tourist officials like to speak of The Californias, plural, because the state is so diverse. It certainly fits northern California, with its snow-dusted mountains, surf-splashed coast, a long fertile valley that feeds half the country, scenic rolling hills, urban areas contrasted with vast stretches of emptiness, immaculate suburbs, and a world-class city that lures visitors from all over the world.

And a history. Northern Californians like to say that their part of the state created California. Until gold was discovered, the place had only a handful of European settlers. True, English and Spanish explorers had chased each other up and down the coast in the 1500s, and intrepid Spaniards forging north from Mexico had established a chain of missions and small settlements. Then the fortune-seekers came, by the hundreds of thousands. A few got rich. Most didn't. But even those with disappointed hopes liked the place so well that they stayed, sent for the folks back home, and eventually lifted California to be the most populous (and popular) state in the union.

Seasoned travelers may not need an avalanche of advice, but they do need reminders. Northern California is so large and diverse and loaded down with mythology that a nudge here and a bit of new information there and some solid pointers on an ever-changing elsewhere can only be helpful. Here are a few words of advice on how to enjoy northern California and some background on what you'll find—and won't find—in this book.

The weather. There is no such thing as the California climate. The almost daily fog along the coast in midsummer keeps peak temperatures there around 65° to 75°, while the central valley swelters at 120°. Rainfall is scant through the state from April to November—you seldom have to worry about a picnic being postponed—but winter storms can lash the coast intermittently for four months and dump huge amounts of snow in the Sierra Nevada. The winter months along the north coast can be one long drizzle.

Moral: Wear your shorts and T-shirts in Sacramento, but stuff them back in your suitcase and bring out the jacket, slacks, and long-sleeved blouses when you reach San Francisco. (A favorite San Francisco sport in July is to go down to the cable-car turntable and watch the scantily clad tourists shiver.) Bring your raincoat and your parka in winter. Drive an air-conditioned car to Fresno in July.

Earthquakes. Everybody talks about them. The slightest shiver halfway around the world rates headlines in the Bay Area newspapers. Northern Californians have been warned so many times about the imminent "Big One" that they tend to go blissfully on with their lives until joltingly reminded by the Loma Prieta quake of 1989 or the Redwood Empire quake of 1992 that they are straddling some enormously jittery faults. The chances of a quake during your visit, though, are statistically almost zero. However, if you should feel the earth move under your feet or rattle the motel windows, quickly crouch under a strong table or in a doorway as far as possible from windows, bookshelves, or other objects that might topple. But to repeat: don't let worries about earthquakes spoil your visit.

Off-season travel. For most seasoned travelers, the best time to travel anywhere is spring or fall, before or after the family-vacationing summer hordes. That's particularly true in California, when summer can be cool and foggy on the coast and devastatingly hot inland. Spring, which begins in late February or early March in most of the north except the Sierra Nevada, is the season when the hillsides green up and the Gold Rush country, as one example, overflows with blossoms. The waterfalls in Yosemite clear their throats and roar. Fall, believe it or not, is San Francisco's warmest time of year, and the slanting sun glistening across the bay is unforgettable. It's time for the wine harvest in the vineyard country, an event to be both seen and sampled. November 1 ushers in the Dungeness crab. And you may feel the difference in your pocketbook. Rates in the most popular areas drop during the off-season, especially during midweek.

Driving. From north to south, California is the longest state in the union, and the third largest in total area. If transposed to the East Coast, God forbid, it would extend from the top of Florida all the way to New

York City and as far west as Pennsylvania. Northern California is roughly half that size but still large enough to encompass most of the New England states. Unfortunately, mass transportation does not successfully service the state, and the best way to see California is by car.

Superb freeways connect all the major parts of the state. For a quick, high-speed zip from here to there, they are hard to beat. But they are scarcely the visitor's magic carpet. Where possible, avoid them and map out alternate routes. The secondary roads may take longer, but instead of traveling across the often monotonous open spaces, you'll find yourself dipping in and out of small towns, driving past farms or along rivers, and skirting the edges of green foothills. The car trip through the countryside will seem shorter and more enjoyable because you'll be seeing what you came to see, northern California. And unlike the image held by too many people, California is not what lies along the freeways.

Another thing that drivers often forget about sunny California is that the state has snow. Lots of snow. Many tourist destinations lie in the Sierra Nevada where peaks rise above 10,000 feet and hold the largest concentration of ski resorts in the world. It almost never snows in the summer—*almost* never—but from late September through April be prepared for winter driving conditions. I-80, the most commonly used route through the Sierra Nevada, crosses Donner Summit at an elevation of just over 7,000 feet. Winter storms periodically snow-in the road, and the highway patrol closes it except for four-wheel drive vehicles or those equipped with chains or snow tires. "Chain controls" are strictly enforced, so when traveling in the Sierra Nevada carry chains or be prepared to be turned back and wait out the storm. Roadside crews will usually install chains for a fee of about $15. It's important to note that while a few major arteries like I-80 and U.S. 50 across the Sierra Nevada are kept open, many others are simply closed for the winter. It's also important to note that other highways in the state are subject to chain control, especially in the Coast Range and in the area of Mount Lassen.

Another California road hazard is tule fog, a type of haze that occurs primarily in valleys and flat lands, and creeps across the highway late at night and early in the morning. Tule fog, unlike normal fog, is not consistent. It comes in dense clouds that can suddenly deprive a driver of vision 15 feet past the hood. In these conditions, drive slowly and cautiously. If you hit a bank of tule fog, *don't* use your high-beams and *do* stay off the brakes.

On I-5 and I-99, you can occasionally run into visibility problems of a different source. The winds that blow through the arid flat lands sometimes kick up huge clouds of topsoil. These dust storms can engulf the highway and stop traffic. If you see one approaching, simply pull over to the side of the road and wait it out. The dust clouds usually pass in less than five minutes. Otherwise driving in California is a breeze, just like anywhere else. There are few toll highways (no public toll highways), and bridge tolls are a dollar or less (except the Golden Gate Bridge, $3) and are usually collected in one direction only. Rush-hour traffic is the same as in other parts of the country or perhaps worse. Avoid traveling between 8:00 A.M. and 10:00 A.M. or 4:00 P.M. and 6:00 P.M. in any of the metropolitan areas. In the Bay Area, traffic frequently crawls along at a snail's pace, even through sections of freeway with five lanes in either direction.

The outdoors. California is an outdoors state, nowhere more so than in the North. Scratch a northern Californian and you will find a hiker, backpacker, sunbather, camper, or all of the above, or maybe a nature lover. There may be as many birdwatchers as birds. The conservationist/environmentalist voice is nowhere so strong as it is in California.

Bring your plaid shirt, hiking boots, and suntan lotion and join the fun. For those with campers, trailers, or RVs, places are waiting for you deep in the redwoods, by Sierra Nevada streams, overlooking the beaches. California's vaunted state park system combines with national parks and recreation areas and millions of acres of national forest to offer plenty of space. Despite the vastness, however, campground reservations are recommended, especially on busy weekends. Both the state and national parks have centralized reservation facilities with Mistix, a statewide reservation service: national parks, 800-365-2267; state parks, 800-444-7275. While this is not a camping guide, we have tried to lead you to places where tent sites and RV space is available. We have also tried to note roads where RVs and trailers are not advisable.

Shopping. Browsing, window-shopping, and spending rank next to snacking as the traveler's pet pastime. San Francisco's Union Square area offers world-class shopping. The Stanford Shopping Center, on the fringe of the university campus, has been acclaimed both for design and diversity of offerings, but it has close rivals throughout the northern part of the state. Small towns, especially in resort areas, teem with crafts-people, gift shops, and galleries. Some people visit Carmel or Mendocino for the beach; more spend their idle afternoons poring over the merchandise. Again, this book identifies communities noted for their shopping while occasionally pointing a finger at the hokey or tacky. The recent phenomenon of outlet store centers has reinforced an ancient form of tourism: bargain hunting. These gatherings of sometimes more than fifty stores have become so popular that they are springing up on the outskirts of every major and minor metropolis. We have only men-tioned ones near tourist destinations in the sightseeing sections of this book, but here's a complete listing (from largest to smallest) of the big-ger outlet centers in northern California so die-hard shoppers can add them to their itineraries:

VACAVILLE: The Nut Tree, between Sacramento and the Bay Area on I-80. (Take the Nut Tree exit going east and the Monte Vista exit going west.) Over fifty stores. 707-447-5755.

MONTEREY: The American Tin Cannery Outlet, 125 Ocean View Avenue. Forty-six stores. 408-372-1442.

GILROY: The Pacific West Outlet Center, inland from Monterey. (Take State Route 101 and exit at Leavesley Road.) Thirty-six stores. 408-847-4155.

ANDERSON: Shasta Factory Stores, 8 miles south of Redding off I-5 at the Highway 273 interchange. (Take the Deschutes Road exit.) About thirty-five stores. 916-378-1000.

SAN FRANCISCO: At 3rd and Townsend streets. Twenty-four stores. 415-227-0460.

TRUCKEE in Lake Tahoe: At Donner Pass Road and Highway 89. (Take Highway 89 exit off I-80 to Squaw Valley.) Fifteen stores. 916-587-5726.

Eating. This should be every traveler's favorite hobby. You can learn much about the traditions and influences on a society by observing the food, how it is presented and the way it is eaten. Most importantly, in the learning process, you sample more-than-satisfying new entreés. California benefits from the wealth of fresh fruit, vegetables, and meats readily available throughout the state. "California Cuisine" has developed around them. Feta cheese, artichokes, and zucchini are included in the traditional continental dishes to produce this new hybrid of the restaurant food family (although true food snobs do not consider California Cuisine as a specialty of its own). The emphasis is on lighter, fresher fare that better accompanies the warm California climate. And its birthplace is northern California. Chez Panisse in Berkeley, where the new taste is said to have originated, has become something of a hallowed shrine. Being comprised of polyglot communities, California has a diverse cuisine. Every kind of cookery from Asia can be found within a few blocks of Clement Street in San Francisco. In the Gold Rush country, Cornish pasties, the meat-and-vegetable pie of the hard-rock miners' lunchboxes, has become a household staple, sold from carts on the street. With hundreds of miles of coast, northern California preceded the rest of the country in its love affair with seafood. The opening of the Dungeness crab season in San Francisco has all the importance of a religious festival.

Senior rates. Northern California is just as welcoming and hospitable toward senior travelers as other parts of the country—maybe more so. Many attractions have senior rates, as do many of the restaurants and lodging places. A few wineries in the grape-crushing country of Napa and Sonoma counties even offer senior discounts on their reds and whites. At Alpine Meadows in the Sierra Nevada, you can ski free if you are over 75 (and a surprising number of skiers take advantage of it). If you are over 62, be sure to pick up a Golden Age Pass that gives you free entry into any of the national parks, which normally charge about $5 per admission. (Request one at the ranger station of any of the national parks.)

Where possible, we have noted establishments that advertise senior rates. The enterprises differ on whether senior status begins at 60, 62, or 65, so be sure to bring your identification. And always inquire about senior discounts. Many places agree to them, but simply don't advertise the discount.

What this guide includes. *The Seasoned Traveler's Guide to Northern California* certainly covers the basics. It includes the main tourist attractions of each area. However, it delves deeper into these sights than the average guide, exposing myths or legends or historical background about them when interesting and relevant. But the Eiffel

Tower-type tourist sights, while they always entertain, do not stand out as the most intriguing aspects of northern California. The standard attractions suggest the direction or background of a people, but the small museums, eccentric tours, and local hangout restaurants fill in important details about the region's character, explaining differences in attitude or lifestyle and exposing new ideas.

We searched for an array of museums for each area that, together, would paint a full picture of the area's upbringing: its art, history, and natural history as described through artifacts and displays. This background information shows the visitor what to look for and explains why the culture is the way it is, therefore allowing a more in-depth appreciation of it.

We felt that seasoned travelers would explore with greater appreciation and patience, and would be more likely to take time to stop and enjoy nature. And California has plenty of it. State parks and national parks are sprinkled across the northern half of the state. Short hikes are mentioned for both outdoor types and city slickers, taking you through rugged natural terrain, relatively unmarked by human footprints. Most of nature found in the heart of metropolitan areas— flower gardens, bird sanctuaries, aquariums, and zoos—have also been included.

What we have omitted. We chose the restaurants, hotels, and occasionally the sights listed here based on local advice and personal preferences. Sorting through the volume of restaurants, we attempted to include a good selection of different cuisines. We searched for local specialties and restaurants having a unique ambience or food that you might not encounter anywhere else, evenly spread across the price range. Avoiding the trendy, we selected restaurants that have and will endure the waves of fashion. We found that the notable restaurants tended to charge higher prices and that expensive restaurants sometimes dominated the eating section. Northern California abounds in inexpensive and predictable fast-food restaurants, but it did not seem much of a service to a seasoned traveler to lead him or her to the nearest McDonald's.

Hotel listings follow a similar philosophy and a similar pattern. We included economy hotels but emphasized the bed and breakfasts, sensing that many seasoned travelers prefer the friendliness and hospitality of a family-run B&B to the hustle and bustle of a commercial hotel. The traveler on a budget should splurge for a night and enjoy the luxury of an old Victorian and a friendly breakfast, but we also included an economical standby, either a chain hotel or a recommended inexpensive accommodation. We concede that the most highly rated may not be the most practical. Anyway, it's always fun to walk through the lobby of a deep-pockets hotel, or press your nose against the window of a five-star restaurant, even if you have no intention of staying or dining there.

Both the restaurants and lodging places are identified as Inexpensive, Moderate, or Expensive. In general, we have used the yardsticks shown in the accompanying box.

Of course, we could not include everything. Our criteria for selection, prices, and space considerations forced us to cut out some good but standard accommodations and restaurants. We feel, however, that our selections fit the needs of a wide variety of travelers, from the high to low budget, from the quietly adventuresome to the enthusiastic.

Restaurants—A meal for one person with tax and tip:
  Under $10—Inexpensive
  $10 to $20—Moderate
  Over $20—Expensive

Hotels—A double room (including breakfast, in a B&B):
  Under $60—Inexpensive
  $60 to $100—Moderate
  Over $100—Expensive

A few exceptions and caveats: (1) These estimates do not include senior or other discounts, which can range up to 25%. (2) We have largely been guided by the local price scale. For instance, both eating and sleeping in the Napa Valley tend to be pricey. A double room that might qualify as Expensive elsewhere is only Moderate here. (3) Some municipalities levy a tax on hotel/motel rooms, occasionally as high as 10%. (4) Most B&Bs charge by the room, on grounds that although two breakfasts may be eaten, only one room is occupied. On the other hand, some follow the European model, charging by the person, since there are often two people eating. Always ask beforehand. Also, remember that B&B prices may be misleadingly high because breakfast is included. And one final note about B&Bs: most prefer multinight occupancy and do not like to rent for overnight stays.

A final word. We did not write this book for the traveler who visits a new place, or even a familiar one, and does little more than he could comfortably do at home, insulating himself in a hotel in front of the television set or eating at a familiar chain restaurant. It is written for the adventurous, those willing to experiment and explore, those who thirst for knowledge and education—those who wish to jump into a culture and take in its nuances and intricacies. Our vision is that the seasoned traveler is just that person.

Now head for northern California and enjoy.

Ed & Will Kiester

Chapter 1

San Francisco–By Foot, Cable Car, and Automobile

The fog thrusts through the Golden Gate in midafternoon, licking along the waterfront, creeping over the hills, shrouding the city with mystery and dreams. The cable cars clatter and ding, chunking slowly up the old streets. On the ruffled bay, sailboats tack under the forbidding monolith of Alcatraz. Chinatown grandmothers haggle in Cantonese over the price of fish. No wonder Tony Bennett left his heart in San Francisco.

Locals refer to San Francisco as "The City," as if there were no other worthy of the name. Travel promotions pitch their cliché, "Everybody's Favorite City," and with reason. Certainly San Francisco is at the top of every list as a northern California travel destination. It is a must to see if you have never been there, a place to go again as a seasoned traveler. San Francisco's charm never fades.

To begin with, the setting is magnificent. Built on forty hills and crammed on a narrow neck of land, the city huddles around a bay that is one of the great sheltered harbors of the earth. The majestic Golden Gate Bridge dramatizes the port's welcoming arms to the world, the swooping Oakland Bay Bridge its link to the continent beyond. The climate is legendary. Romantic fog alternates with crystalline sunshine. Pleasantly cool temperatures keep gardens in bloom year-round. Houses of pastel stucco and brightly painted gingerbread open to breathtaking vistas. It's a compact city where nothing is far from anything else. A tolerant city where weirdos and wackos are accepted and enjoyed, but the emphasis is on culture and community spirit.

Oddly, the early explorers and conquistadores missed the place.

Spanish galleons plied the coast in the 1500s. Sir Francis Drake arrived in 1579. Perhaps because of the concealing fog or the narrow entry of the Golden Gate, the harbor lay hidden from them. It wasn't until 1769 that Gaspar de Portola and a Franciscan missionary band reached the bay by an overland route. A settlement grew up around Mission Dolores, but San Francisco remained a far-flung outpost of first the Spanish Empire and then the Mexican republic. In 1846, when California became part of the United States, San Francisco's population numbered only 900 souls. Then gold was discovered on the American River.

"The World Rushed In," one recent account of the gold mania was entitled. Overnight, the sleepy settlement mushroomed into a wild, brawling frontier community of 20,000, fortuneseekers scrambling over each other en route to the El Dorado of gold nuggets, impromptu merchants and scalawags piggybacking on the mother lode of commerce. San Francisco became the gateway to gold as ship after ship fought its way around Cape Horn to dump its cargo, human and otherwise, on the city's wharves.

The gold fever subsided, but by then San Francisco had matured into a major city, the chief port of the West and the jumping-off place for the Orient. The transcontinental railroad cemented its role as the commercial and financial center of the Pacific Coast.

The second epochal event in San Francisco history occurred a half century later. On April 18, 1906, San Franciscans were rocked from their beds by the strongest earthquake ever recorded in the lower forty-eight states. The disastrous quake shook down many of the city's frame buildings, but, more devastating, touched off raging fires that firemen were powerless to quench because the quake had broken water lines. Four-fifths of the city was destroyed before the fire burned itself out. But the city's spirit and atmosphere survived. San Francisco doggedly rebuilt itself from the ashes into the appealing city it had been before—and remains today.

Because of its topography and history, San Francisco continues to be a relatively easy city to get around in, on foot or via an efficient public-transportation system. An automobile allows easier access to some outlying attractions. Choose your own method of locomotion or better still, use both. There is plenty to see and enjoy, in a day, a week, or a lifetime.

San Francisco by Foot and Cable Car

The highlights of San Francisco are as diverse as its landscape. Chinatown's architecture and people contrast with the neighboring Italian community of North Beach; Union Square offers upscale department stores; Fisherman's Wharf sells fresh crab. The different pageantry dispersed across the city attracts visitors from all over the world. However, it is the broad range of activities, tailored to each of the San Francisco neighborhoods, that keeps visitors coming back. At Ghirardelli Square, sample different chocolate desserts and shop in boutiques and gift stores. Relax at a sidewalk cafe in North Beach, sip espresso and watch the Italian-American waiter frantically wave his arms as he expresses political opinions or simply gives you directions. San Francisco brings sightseeing to a new level, from passive awe to active participation.

The activities can sometimes monopolize your attention. Be sure to look up from your diligent tourist work—having a drink at the Top of the Mark or eating dim sum in Chinatown—to enjoy the vistas only available in San Francisco. Bring your camera and prepare yourself for the most spectacular bay views, pleasantly interrupted by brightly colored Victorian-style apartments, bay windows and all. Choice photo opportunities unveil themselves as you travel from neighborhood to neighborhood. For the best pictures and the least headache, avoid the snapshot through the car window.

San Francisco literally has its ups and downs, and locals would assert that one of its downs is parking. They do not refer to burning out the car's clutch trying to parallel park on a 20 percent grade—you should be so lucky. They refer to the near impossibility of finding a spot. In the center of this compact city, a car is a liability. Cable-car lines connect the main attractions. On this unique public transportation that travels hills so steep that some say they climb halfway to the stars, you can ride from the Financial District in the south, to Fisherman's Wharf at the north tip of the city, or over swanky Nob Hill. The Municipal Railway, or Muni, as the system is nicknamed, takes you everywhere else. Take Muni buses from Washington Park in North Beach up to the Coit Tower for a convenient ride to spectacular views.

Another way to get around San Francisco is by the oldest form of transportation, walking. Because the city is so small geographically, go by foot between some of the attractions. Trek from the heart of Chinatown to Washington Square (the heart of North Beach) in under ten minutes and arrive at Fisherman's Wharf in another fifteen to twenty minutes.

A good place to start a visit is the **Visitor Information Center,** located on the lower level of Hallidie Plaza at the corner of Powell and Market streets. The multilingual staff can answer most questions, from weather to directions. Free brochures suggest tour opportunities, lodging, restaurants or cultural events. You can also buy single-day or multi-day Muni Passports. These tickets give unlimited access to San Francisco's public transportation, including the cable cars. Use the passport to travel comfortably throughout the city without the hassle of digging in your pocket for change. Buses normally cost 85¢, exact change, seniors only 15¢, transfer valid for any direction for two hours. Cable cars cost $2. Muni Passports cost $6 for a one-day, $10 for a three-day and $15 for a seven-day pass. You can also purchase Muni Passports on Stockton Street at Union Square, at the Cable Car Museum, and at the corner of Washington and Mason streets. Route information is published in the Yellow Pages or call 415-673-MUNI.

Whether you go to the Visitor Information Center for advice or a Muni Passport, join the crowd. Record numbers of travelers come through San Francisco each year, and the Visitor Information Center is a popular starting place. Be prepared to wait at least five to ten minutes in summer (sometimes longer on weekends). The line of tourists often extends out the door. The center is open weekdays 9:00 A.M. to 5:30 P.M., Saturday until 3:00 P.M., and Sunday 10:00 A.M. to 2:00 P.M. You can also call the 24-hour Events Hotline at 415-391-2001 for a recorded message listing seasonal events and cultural happenings.

Market Street runs just south of the **Financial District,** the core of the tall temples of money that make up San Francisco's skyline. You need not visit this area to see it—its buildings are visible from Union Square to Telegraph Hill. The tallest and most distinctively San Francisco building is the **Transamerica Building** at 600 Montgomery Street. The narrow pyramid was the first skyscaper in the city, standing 853 feet tall and looking as if it was the end of a gigantic nail hammered through from China.

The **Old Mint Museum**, a couple of blocks from the Visitor Information Center, has an exterior as rich in history as the interior but definitely not worth more on the open market. First opened in 1874, it unarguably represents the finest example of Federal classic revival architecture in the West. Its proud columned façade and granite walls proved solidly constructed, surviving the 1906 earthquake while most neighboring buildings crumbled. You can see the old etching and coin stamping machines in action and even have your own coin stamped with the Old Mint insignia (bronze blanks cost $1). The highlight of the Old Mint lies well protected in the Gold Vault. The glittering pyramid of twenty-eight gold bars, 999.9 fine, with a total weight of 10,642.9 ounces and worth over a million dollars, will hypnotize the innocent visitor with greed. The Old Mint is open Monday to Friday 10:00 A.M. to 4:00 P.M. Admission is free. It is located at Fifth and Mission streets.

It has been said that many travelers prefer shopping to almost all other visitor activities. While this may be a slight exaggeration, a stroll through the local department stores can be a cultural experience, especially in **Union Square**. San Francisco's top retailing names encircle the well-manicured square: Saks Fifth Avenue, Burberry's of London, Macy's, Bally of Switzerland, I Magnin, Neiman Marcus, and the list goes on. Smaller shops with equally well-known names crowd the adjoining blocks: Gucci, Tiffany and Co., Brooks Brothers, and Gump's, a San Francisco tradition that specializes in oriental-designed crafts, to name just a few. San Francisco's retail core ranks fourth in the nation in total sales volume, and you can see why. Millions of shoppers pour through the stores—an excellent opportunity to find that perfect wedding gift or birthday present. The selection is outstanding.

The green centerpiece, boxed in by four of San Francisco's large arteries—Geary, Powell, Post, and Stockton streets—conceals a large underground public parking lot (although you can hardly notice) and hosts an ecletic population. Amid barbered shrubs and towering palm trees, shoppers, strollers, brown baggers, sunbathers, orators, chess players, and street entertainers share the grassy plot with a large community of pigeons and a towering pedestal commemorating Admiral George Dewey's victory over the Spanish fleet in Manila Bay in 1898. Sit on a bench, watch the fun, and listen to the soapbox political speeches. Politics, in fact, have been part of the park since it received its name. The park was dubbed Union Square during the Civil War. It was the battleground for a series of violent pro-Union demonstrations. Today the political role has been reduced, although the square occasionally serves as the stage for a rally.

Midway on the Stockton Street side, **Maiden Lane** cuts away from the square and heads east. Before the 1906 quake, it was considered San Francisco's raunchiest red-light district. Those heady days have passed, and the fair maiden has grown and has cleaned up her act. This quiet two-block mall, closed to automobiles from 11:00 A.M. to 4:00 P.M., offers a pleasant stroll past art galleries and boutiques. You can also see the Circle Gallery, designed by Frank Lloyd Wright in 1949. This yellow-brick building with its internal spiral ramp became the prototype for his Guggenheim Museum in New York.

SAN FRANCISCO VIEWS BY GLASS ELEVATOR

San Francisco's luxury hotels do more than bathe the affluent in extravagance. They also take advantage of spectacular views. So should you. Many of the hotels whisk their guests to the top via exterior glass elevators. Instead of staring at your feet while ascending, you can look out across the San Francisco skyline and the bay. And the list of advantages continues: rides cost nothing, you stay warm in the glass enclosure, and you get aerial views of the city from within the city.

As you might expect, Nob Hill boasts one of the most spectacular exterior elevator rides. The **Fairmont Hotel,** at the top of the hill, added its glass lifts in 1961 to allow its guests to admire the dazzling lights of the city. For the best view, ride the skylift to the Fairmont Crown, twenty-four stories above street level, and look down on brightly lighted Chinatown, the looming buildings of the Financial District, and the choppy waters of the bay. On your left you will see the Coit Tower, one of San Francisco's perpetual symbols, and on the right you will look over the bohemian South of Market (So-Ma) area and down the South Bay Peninsula. The hotel is located at the corner of California and Mason streets.

The **Westin St. Francis,** in Union Square, features five glass elevators that catapult you upward thirty-two stories in thirty seconds at an ear-popping rate of 1000 feet per minute (by comparison, the Fairmont elevator runs between 100 and 200 feet per minute). The laminated solar glass allows unobstructed views of Union Square with the Financial District and the bay as background. The hotel is located at 335 Powell Street.

Nob Hill, the residential equivalent of Union Square, has always been a bastion of luxury, wealth, and high class, from its original settlers to its name. (You can get there from Union Square on both the Powell-Mason and the Powell-Hyde cable-car lines.) Nob, a contraction of the Hindu word nabob or nawwab, means "a very wealthy or powerful person." San Francisco nobs made their wealth in the mid-1800s on gold, silver, and the Central Pacific Railroad. After the 1848 gold discovery, miner rapscallions flooded the San Francisco lowlands. The rich, primarily the Big Four railroad barons, needed an escape, and they found it

The asymmetric shape of the **Hyatt Regency San Francisco,** in the Embarcadero Center, boasts glass elevators with a different outlook. While you get quick glimpses of the bay, your most interesting scene is of the interior: the atrium lobby with its greenery, perpetual waterfall, sculpture, shops, and open-air restaurants. For an added bonus, the elevators take you up twenty floors to the city's only revolving restaurant, the Equinox. You'll find the hotel at 5 Embarcadero Center.

The **Mark Hopkins Intercontinental,** on Nob Hill, brings new meaning to the term restaurant ambience. Emphasizing the "high" in high society, the hotel houses the Top of the Mark, a five-star restaurant with a tremendous view of San Francisco and the bay. It is famous for dancing and elegance and a good place to spot the high fashion in this normally dressed-down city (long trousers and collar shirts required). Even if the grandeur of society dining does not meet your budget, you can enjoy the outlook over a couple of afternoon or evening drinks. To make reservations call 415-392-3434 and ask for the Top of the Mark. The hotel is located at 999 California Street at Mason Street.

Fisherman's Wharf seems an unlikely spot for a glass elevator. Most of the buildings are only two stories tall, but who says a glass elevator must go any higher? For a short but enjoyable ride, take the glass elevator at the Cannery giving you a second-story view of the east end of the wharf. The Cannery is located at the corner of Leavenworth and Beach streets.

376 feet up on Nob Hill. The mansions of Charles Crocker, Leland Stanford, Mark Hopkins, and Collis Huntington graced the hill. Today, elegant hotels have replaced the showplace personal dwellings. Accommodations like the prestigious Huntington Hotel continue the spirit of luxury, hosting such notables as Alistair Cooke and Luciano Pavarotti or royalty like Princesses Margaret and Grace and Prince Charles. The 600-room Fairmont Hotel and Tower also attracts celebrities but in a different way. While stars stay in their $6,000-a-day penthouse suite on the roof, film crews use the lobbies. Many movies and television shows, from Alfred Hitchcock's thriller, *Vertigo,* to the scene of the prime-time soap "Hotel," have been filmed there.

The only remaining mansion on Nob Hill, an imposing brownstone structure that James Flood built at 1000 California Street in 1886, now houses the Pacific Union Club, an exclusive men's organization that caters to the modern-day San Francisco magnate. Directly behind the P-U Club (as scornful plebians irreverently refer to it) lies Huntington Park, a pleasant green park brightened by tended flower beds. Carefully groomed poodles slowly lead their properly postured human counterparts through the park, waiting to see or be seen.

The benches of Huntington Park offer a resting place to appreciate the grace of **Grace Episcopal Cathedral** just across the street. Although from the outside the surrounding hotels dwarf the church, once inside, the towering ceiling detailed by narrow arches makes you appreciate this gigantic work of architecture, the largest example of Gothic architecture in the West. Be sure to see the gilded bronze doors, created by Lorenzo Ghiberti for the baptistry of the Duomo in Florence, called La Porta del Paradiso (The Gates of Heaven). A cast of the notable piece of Italian Renaissance art stands as the cathedral's east entrance.

The Orient touches all of America's big cities. New York has its Chinese enclave, as have Chicago, Boston, and even Los Angeles. None of these compare to San Francisco's **Chinatown,** two blocks wide and eight blocks long, a narrow strip between Kearny and Stockton streets on the east and west and Bush Street and Broadway on the north and south. This area makes up the most populated Chinese settlement this side of Taiwan. Cars crowd the narrow hilly streets, drivers yelling (probably Chinese insults) at gridlocked motorists. And the traffic on the sidewalks can be worse than on the roads. Packs of camera-toting tourists dodge Chinese locals carrying their groceries home. However, do not be scared away by the chaos. Chinatown's many intriguing features make the pedestrian traffic worth daring.

This area taps all your senses with new and exotic inputs. Your ears will ring with the sing-song twang of the (usually) Cantonese dialect, you will smell the mouth-watering aroma of glazed duck, and you will see everything from roasted pigs hanging in restaurant windows to pagoda roofs to lobsters, crabs, and carp being sold out of common fish tanks. Signs bear Chinese characters, golden lion statues guard the bank entrances, the stores close for different holidays, and even the lighting system has an Oriental influence. The dragon entwined, lantern-style street lamps have become the colony's icon. You leave with the impression that a different set of laws rules this tightly packed Chinese community.

St. Mary's Park is an oasis in the middle of bustling Chinatown. Its green lawns sit above the hectic streets (atop a parking garage), sheltered from the street noises. Young men and women relax on the park benches and watch old men do Tai Chi, a martial art in which one uses complete muscle control to move the body very slowly through a pattern of Karate-type punches, blocks, and kicks in a gracefully choreographed exercise. It is particularly dramatic at dawn when most of the masters perform. A 12-foot, brightly colored statue of Sun Yat Sen stands in the park, created by local artist Beniamino Bufano and placed in 1937 to honor the founder of the Republic of China.

The market places of Chinatown are completely different from your average supermarket. The Chinese grocers fill their stores with exotic products that often spill out of the stores and onto the sidewalks in the street stalls that sell everything from Chinese magazines to skyline postcards to gingerroot and Chinese cabbage. Little markets prescribe herbal medications. You must see them to appreciate the immense volume of Oriental goods stuffed onto the short shelves of these little stores. The best concentration of food markets has moved west a block to Stockton Street between the 1000 and 1200 blocks, just north of the heart of Chinatown (and some Chinese markets have spilled into the Italian quarter of North Beach). At these markets you can buy anything from chicken feet to shark fins, seahorses, lichee nuts, or glazed ducks.

Be sure to look up occasionally (when you are out of the traffic pattern, or you may be trampled by a herd of Chinese grandmothers rushing home from market). The majority of the store fronts are simple

Western architecture but the rooftops are pure Chinese. Arched eaves, carved cornices, and filigreed balconies give this area an Eastern flavor, a reminder of the Chinese community's perseverance in building this area from the ground up. Some buildings preserve the full pagoda-style architecture, from the roof down. The **Bank of Canton,** at 743 Washington Street, occupies the oldest Oriental-style edifice in the quarter, rebuilt after the 1906 earthquake. This traditional three-tiered temple formerly housed the Chinatown Telephone Exchange. Called the China-5, twenty operators worked the switchboard, using their fluency in five dialects and their phenomenal memories to link hundreds of Chinese subscribers who disregarded phone numbers and demanded their parties by name. The switchboard operated until 1949 when the dial system took over.

The **Chinese Historical Society of America,** at 17 Adler Place just off 1140 Grant Avenue, provides a detailed overview of Chinese history in a pocket-size museum. It explains the Chinese immigrants' important role in the development of the West's mining, rail, and fishing industries.

William A. Richardson, an English explorer, staked out San Francisco's first European habitation (a canvas tent) in 1835. The site lies right in the heart of Chinatown at 837-827 Grant Avenue between Clay and Washington streets. As you walk by, wave to the memory of the city's humble beginnnings.

Broadway acted as the boundary between Chinatown and North Beach until 1965 when the government liberalized the federal immigration laws, and Chinatown burst at its seams and flooded into the Italian quarter. Now Stockton Street (and some of Vallejo Street) holds an odd conglomeration of businesses where the Antonellis mix with the Changs–where Chinatown overlaps North Beach. This is not Broadway's only strange mix. On Broadway past Columbus, North Beach's main drag, fine Italian cafes and eateries sit next to strip joints and discos. Club Fugazi, featuring the comic revue, "Beach Blanket Babylon," is in this neighborhood near Broadway and Kearny Street at 678 Green Street (mentioned in Chapter 3). Broadway represents an eclectic, ethnic, wild, yet harmless area uniting a North Beach that has no beach and a Chinatown in the West.

San Francisco Italians have come a long way, and their home, **North Beach,** has seen several transformations. But one thing about North Beach restaurants has always stayed the same: ravioli, tortellini, lasagna, and garlic, garlic, garlic. Some embrace this sweet pungent herb to the point of the outrageous, serving pizza with cloves of garlic resting on the cheese to be eaten as if they were pepperoni. While the strong garlic perfume pervades the air, those opposed to this fruit of life need not despair. Many fine Italian restaurants use it sparingly, a dab here on the fettucini alfredo and a dab there on the roast rabbit, and you can request that the garlic content be toned down.

Washington Square is the heart of North Beach, bordered by Columbus Avenue and Powell, Filbert, and Stockton streets. Like an authentic Italian piazza, this square is dominated by the tall spires of the Church of Saints Peter and Paul. The lush lawn makes for a pleasant resting spot where you can ponder why the statue of Benjamin *Franklin* stands in *Washington* Square, and join the old Italian men sunning themselves on the benches.

At one time, a finger of the bay extended four blocks farther inland in the vicinity of Francisco Street on the north and fronted Montgomery Street on the south—the beach of North Beach. A year after the discovery of gold in 1848, the face of this area slowly began to change. Landfill dried this inlet of the bay, covering the hulls of a hundred abandoned ships whose crews had stampeded for the mother lode. People coveted flat land in San Francisco so locals rapidly settled the landfill areas that today make up the Marina District and parts of North Beach.

The fire resulting from the 1906 earthquake destroyed much of North Beach and would have taken the houses of Telegraph Hill, too, had it not been for the ingenuity of the Italian community. Lacking water, the Italians supposedly broke open reserve barrels and fought the flames with wine-soaked blankets and buckets of vino. The Italian community then rebuilt rapidly, transforming North Beach into a little Italy. In the late forties, artists and writers converged here attracted by the low rents. A decade later Bohemian turned into Beat as tattoo parlors sprouted on Columbus Avenue and characters like Jack Kerouac, Allen Ginsberg, and Lawrence Ferlinghetti frequented local bars such as **Vesuvio's Cafe** at 255 Columbus Avenue, 415-362-3770; the **Cafe Trieste** at 601 Vallejo Street, 415-392-6739; or the **Bohemian Cigar Store** at 566 Columbus Avenue, 415-362-0536. Tours took busloads of sightseers to stare at the free-spirited beatniks. To relive the life of the beat poet (or at least sample it), spend the night in these local haunts and the day at the **City Lights Bookstore,** 261 Columbus Avenue, collecting conversation material from the cramped shelves that still contain literature on theater, art, politics— anything that would feed a starving artist.

One day the locals plotted their revenge. They piled into chartered buses that read "Beatnik Tour of Squaresville." Thumping their bongos, they invaded Union Square and entered many of the upper-class establishments including the St. Francis Hotel where they examined the upstanding clientele with mock curiosity.

Today, North Beach still preserves its culture even though it shares space with Chinese markets, ex-hippies, and reformed beatniks. The whole neighborhood has taken on a trendy, upscale atmosphere, propelled by the fine Italian restaurants.

Telegraph Hill rises impressively to the east of Washington Square, with **Coit Tower** sitting on its lofty perch. The tower lacks a glass elevator but definitely not a view. Just from the base you have a sweeping vista across the bay. Take the enclosed elevator up 210 feet to the top for $3, $2 for seniors, and witness arguably the most engaging panorama of the city. Lillie Hitchcock Coit (1843–1929), one of San Francisco's most avid fans and active citizens, participated in many of the roughest activities around. She gambled in North Beach, smoked cigars, and publicly ice-skated in shortened skirts, but she is best known for volunteer civic duty as a fire fighter. After being named the mascot of the Knickerbocker Hose Company #5 in 1863, she rarely missed a blaze. She left a $125,000 bequest to the city to be used "for the purpose of adding beauty to the city which I have always loved." Coit Tower, a monument to her devotion to the city, stands as a proud example of classicism and Art Deco architecture, although to some the tower looks like a fire hose nozzle, a more befitting symbol of Lillie Coit's legacy.

Murals, painted by twenty-five San Francisco artists, cover the interior of the tower. The murals represent various scenes from California life. The tower is an easy bus ride from Washington Square. Just take #39 directly to the base, although in the summer tourist season cars wait in line for parking spots, slowing all traffic.

Markets, gift shops, T-shirt shops, museums, street entertainers, harbors, huge piers, and even sea lions populate San Francisco's famed **Fisherman's Wharf.** The waterfront hums with activity from camera-aiming tourists to crab-toting fish market workmen. The wharf began as a seafood-lover's heaven, and for all today's hustle and bustle, it remains that way. On one side of the covered walkway, fronting on the harbor, seafood restaurants established by the old fishing families entice diners with fish dishes and views to match. The tiny booths along the curbside specialize in the walkaway cocktail, a paper cup of crab or shrimp that you can consume bite by bite while inspecting the souvenir abalone shells. The big day of the year is the beginning of the Dungeness crab season when the ill-tempered creatures plucked from the cold Pacific waters begin to appear in the restaurants and markets. Fresh (not frozen and thawed) Dungeness crab and sourdough bread is said to be the ultimate San Francisco dining experience.

As for the wharf's street entertainers, they rise above the everyday subway guitar strummer or harmonica player. You get quality performances from mimes, rappers, jugglers, magicians, singers, or one-man bands. All of them take kindly to donations. The San Francisco Art Commission regulates the acts, forcing them to adhere to the relatively simple guideline that keeps the entertainment above board—all shows must "contribute to the favorable impression visitors get of the city." A trip down Fisherman's Wharf will verify this.

At the east end of Fisherman's Wharf, Pier 39 was once a docking bay for large freight ships but now serves as a bustling shopping center. Clothing and shoe stores share the boarded walkway with face painters and hot-dog stands. On the west side you should check out the sea lions basking in the sun on a network of abandoned harbor berths. These fat and lazy sunbathers have become a star attraction of the pier. At the very end of the pier you get an unobstructed view of the sailboats heeling precariously as they crisscross in front of Alcatraz.

In fact, the Red and White Fleet launches boats for the infamous island from right next door, at Pier 41. With all the attributes of an island resort—water, peaceful surroundings, lush vegetation, and views of the city skyline—**Alcatraz,** or "The Rock," as both inmates and the public called it, once brought new meaning to the word "vacation." A trip to The Rock, during its years as a maximum security federal prison, meant that the authorities from another slammer had deemed that you were "incorrigible," too much of a troublemaker to reform. It also meant years of confinement, just across the bay from beautiful freedom, in one of the toughest prisons in the U.S.

Attorney General Robert Kennedy ordered Alcatraz closed in 1963 due to its high cost of maintenance. Before its closure, Alcatraz incarcerated the most notorious convicts in America, from Al Capone to Robert "the Birdman" Stroud and George "Machine-Gun" Kelly, men who were considered incorrigible and then some. Alcatraz received the

GUIDED WALKING TOURS

One way to really see San Francisco, its nooks and crannies and hidden haunts, is by guided walking tour. Most of the tour groups specialize in specific neighborhoods revealing small alley or historic spots that you might otherwise miss. A guided trip through residential areas like North Beach and Chinatown fills in the details of local lore and gives you an in-depth impression about the culture.

The variety of tours fits every interest and need. You can take a culinary tour of North Beach and Chinatown or wander through antique shops all over the city or visit the scenes of famous San Francisco crimes. Just put on your comfortable walking shoes, and the area will come to life through the explanation of your host. Advance reservations are required for most tours. Guided walking tours cost from $15 on up for two hours; with food they start at about $20 per person.

To gain insight into the foreign world of Chinatown, hook up with Linda Lee of **Chinatown Discovery Tours.** Her comprehensive behind-the-scenes tour takes you through a private Buddhist temple, an herb shop, a fortune cookie factory, a tea room, and more. The tour ends with a Chinese luncheon or dinner. Call 415-982-8839.

Shirley Fong-Torres, a television chef, cookbook author, and restaurant critic, leads the **Chinatown Walking Tours with the "Wok Wiz,"** giving you a chef's perspective of Chinatown. You will meet colorful characters and and see unusual businesses. The brush painting ceremony, private tea ceremony, and visit to a Chinese rice noodle factory highlight the tour that ends with a Chinese luncheon. Call 415-355-9657.

Ruby Tom, a graduate of the California Culinary Academy,

worst of the worst, and the prison was well equipped for the job. Between 1909 and 1912, army engineers rebuilt what had originally been a Spanish fort and then a Civil War outpost into a jail that at that time was the largest reinforced concrete structure in the world. Barbed wire and sometimes up to 100 guards secured the prisoners. While Alcatraz could hold 336 prisoners, it never reached capacity. The average convict population of 260 kept the guard-to-prisoner ratio at about one guard to every three prisoners.

helps food lovers sort through the different San Francisco restaurants in her **Glorious Food Culinary Walks.** You can take a Chinatown Culinary Walk in the morning and a North Beach Culinary Walk in the afternoon, visiting produce markets, a microbrewery, a charcuterie, and a coffee-roasting house, and sampling dim sum and all kinds of noodles. Call 415-441-5637.

Some people say that you do not know a city until you see its antiques. If you subscribe to this doctrine you must join **Antique Amblings,** a guided tour of the city's top antique shops led by a former dealer. Call 415-435-5036.

Those who like to get an early start on their sightseeing (or tourists from back East who haven't adjusted yet to Pacific time) should take **A.M. Walks.** Author John McCarroll divulges San Francisco's notorious past: lust, crime, and foolishness in Chinatown, Union Square, and along the piers. Enjoy San Francisco in the early morning while the commuters and more importantly their cars remain at home—the city hardly stirs. Call 415-928-5965.

To learn about early dirty dealings late in the afternoon, hitch onto the **Frisco Tours and Productions' Crime Tour** led by local author Mark Gordon. You visit the scenes of infamous crimes from the Patty Hearst bank robbery to the murder of Sam Spade's partner in *The Maltese Falcon.* Actors are employed to portray some of the city's great personalities. Call 415-681-5555. Friends of the San Francisco Public Library offer many free tours, called **City Guides,** that cover most parts of the city. Tour themes range from Art Deco Marina to Walk the Waterfront. The lively hosts tell many interesting anecdotes. Call 415-557-4266.

For the visitor, Alcatraz offers a unique angle on San Francisco's skyline. For the prisoner, it was a torturing reminder of his captivity. On New Year's Eve, one prisoner recalled, inmates could hear parties and women's voices carrying across the water. Freedom was so close and yet an impossible dream.

Coaxed on by the proximity of the San Francisco shore, some prisoners tried to escape. There were thirty-six attempts in all, but only five prisoners reached the boundaries of the island to face the challenge of the cold bay and the strong currents. Most authorities believe that the would-be escapees drowned in the forty-five-to-fifty degree water, and the current swept away their bodies. However, nobody knows for sure.

Learn about the prison, its prisoners, and the escape attempts via the award-winning audio tour. When you arrive at the cell block, a host will issue you a walkman and a cassette and off you go into the world of the most notorious criminals. The voices of former prison guards and actual inmates not only describe the interior but also give you the sense of gloom that filled the prisoners' lives. You see the cell block with its rows of small bare cells, each outfitted with a bed and a latrine. Not much more could fit into them. The prisoners occupied these cells for an average of ten to fifteen years. Alvin Karpis (the only man personally arrested by J. Edgar Hoover) had the longest stay of twenty-six years.

You can experience the horror of solitary confinement and walk into one of the dark cells. Sound effects add dimension to the entire presentation, especially the prison escape stories. The audio tours guide you around the cell block for about thirty-five minutes after which you return the walkman and cassette to the special deposit area. The whole trip takes an average of two to two and a half hours. The Red and White Fleet ferry ride to Alcatraz (from Pier 41) costs $8.50 with the audio tour and $5.50 without it. Advance reservations are strongly suggested. Seniors receive a discount. Be sure to bring a jacket even in summer; the temperature on the island is much cooler and often breezy. Also bring your comfortable walking shoes. You need to walk up a steep hill to the cell block. Call 415-546-2700 for reservations.

Pier 45 harbors the USS *Pampanito,* a World War II submarine that you can tour. It made six patrols during the war, sinking six Japanese ships and damaging four others. The self-guided audio tour takes you from the forward torpedo room to the after torpedo room, ducking through steel water-tight doors as you make your way through the living quarters, the control room, and the engine room. The front desk will issue you a radio that explains each room as you enter. The self-guided tour costs $4 and lasts about twenty minutes but you can go at your own pace. To find the sub, look for the USS *Pampanito* signs on Pier 45. It is open 9:00 A.M. to 9:00 P.M. daily.

At the west end of the wharf, an easy walk from Pier 41 or Pier 39, the **Cannery** houses a variety of boutiques in an old brick canning factory. You can have a drink in open-air cafes or grab a bite to eat while watching street entertainers delight a crowd of children huddled around the stage in the middle of the big courtyard. On the third floor, check out **The Museum of the City of San Francisco,** which recounts the infamous 1906 earthquake through old photographs, paintings, and artifacts. Admission is free, and the museum is open Wednesday through Sunday, 11:00 A.M. to 4:00 P.M. Call 415-928-0289.

Across the street and half a block west of the Cannery, the **Hyde Street Pier** docks several antique vessels. You can walk around the deck and through the lower levels to experience the seamen's cramped living quarters. Check out the *C. A. Thayer,* a three-masted schooner that remains one of two sailing ships from a fleet of 900 that carried lumber from the Pacific Northwest around the turn of the century. The *Eureka,* a side-wheeler ferry, hauled as many as 2300 passengers and 120 cars at a time across the bay from 1922 to 1941. You can still see the massive four-story steam engine that powered the ferry, the largest built in her day. An antique car collection is now housed in her main auto bay.

Balclutha, the largest sailing ship on the pier, represents the typical vessel that called yearly in San Francisco from Europe. Launched in Scotland over a century ago, this square-rigged vessel holds a hoard of nautical equipment displayed in a museum-like arrangement on its lower deck. The pier is open from 9:30 A.M. to 5:00 P.M. and guided tours through the different boats leave daily. Call for specific times. The pier is located at the foot of Hyde Street and entry onto it costs $3. Call 415-556-3002.

A short walk across the beach from the Hyde Street Pier, the **Maritime Museum** displays models, paintings, and parts of old ships, from the whaling days to post-World War II battleships. Here you can see huge mast sections and painted figureheads that adorned the sailing craft over 100 years ago. Walk around the ten-foot glass-encased model of the battleship USS *California* that was commissioned in 1921. The museum is open from 10:00 A.M. to 5:00 P.M. Admission is free.

The **Aquatic Park,** separating the Hyde Street Pier from the Maritime Museum, makes a perfect spot to rest and relax. You can sit on the three steps that lead down to the sandy beach and look out into a secluded section of the bay, protected by the municipal pier on your left and the Hyde Street Pier on your right. You can often see swimmers weathering the cold water and swimming laps between orange buoys set in the water.

Ghirardelli Square stands on Beach Street between Polk and Larkin streets a block up the hill from the Aquatic Park. The red-brick square that originally housed the Ghirardelli Chocolate Factory was the first such old factory reconverted into a yuppie shopping center. Grouped around a courtyard dominated by a clock tower, the square's buildings are of eclectic shapes and varying levels. Here you can buy anything from gadgets at Sharper Image, to clothes at Ann Taylor, to, of course, chocolate from the special Ghirardelli chocolate shop and restaurant. Or browse from shop to shop and applaud the musicians and street jugglers.

Below the square, at Hyde and Beach streets, is one of the best shows in town. This is the terminus of the Hyde Street cable-car line, where, in the old-fashioned way, passengers disembark and push the cable car to rotate it on the turntable so that it can be launched in the other direction. At San Francisco's insistence, that feature of the cars was maintained during the renovation. You don't have to be a passenger to join in the pushing.

San Francisco by Automobile

With its compact terrain and intimidating hills, San Francisco may seem like a place to leave the car at home or in a parking garage. Rely on your Reeboks, the cable cars, and the Muni for exploring the heart of the city, but use your own wheels for travel to many other attractions scattered throughout the area. A car enables you to appreciate some of the city's parks and museums, its beaches, and its great views.

There a few simple rules about driving in San Francisco, however. When parking on the street, curb your wheels—you'll find reminder signs everywhere—by wedging them against the curb. Also, set the hand brake and move the gearshift into the "Park" position, or into gear in a stick-shift car. This law to prevent runaways is strictly enforced. Also, when stopping on an upgrade, allow the driver ahead plenty of space. As he starts out, he may drift backward as the gears engage. Use the engine, rather than the brakes, to control speed by shifting to a lower gear on steep downhills. That's for your own peace of mind. Also, if a sign warns Hill or Steep Grade, believe it. Such designations may indicate as much as a 31.5 percent plunge. And, even though San Francisco is safer than most major cities, don't leave possessions visible in a parked car, especially overnight. Lock all doors and the trunk.

As of autumn 1992, city traffic still had not totally recovered from the Loma Prieta earthquake three years before. Several freeways damaged by the quake had been demolished, to the immense delight of residents whose views had been blocked by the concrete monsters; others were still under repair. The result was additional congestion on already-crowded streets. Finally, the center of the city is crisscrossed by one-way streets with four-way and two-way stop signs. Street parking space is rare.

The well-marked **49-Mile Drive** is an excellent way to get a vehicular overview of the entire city. Simply look for the red, white, and light blue signs, carrying a seagull, that designate the route. The drive was laid out at the time of the Golden Gate Exposition of 1939, winding around the city and eventually bringing motorists to the exposition site on Treasure Island. President Franklin D. Roosevelt dedicated the drive before the opening of the exposition and was one of the first motorists to travel around it. The 49-mile designation, incidentally, not only represents the miles covered and the year of the gold rush that put San Francisco on the map, but signifies how compact the city is. The Treasure Island terminus has been eliminated, but the drive still connects the city's major attractions, from the Financial District to Chinatown to the Golden Gate Bridge and the Great Beach. And as a bonus it introduces you to the city's multiple neighborhoods, each of which has its own personality, diverse ethnic mix, cultural and commercial features, and miniclimate. The inappropriately named Sunset District shivers in the summer fog while the Mission District basks in warmth.

The **Golden Gate Bridge** spans the choppy waters between the Pacific Ocean and San Francisco Bay, but that stark fact says little about the romantic legends, engineering-wise and otherwise, that have grown up around it. It was regarded as the "bridge that could never be built," because it needed to withstand 100 mph winds and to be constructed in a channel where the tides were merciless, with sufficient clearance for oceangoing vessels—not to mention the little matter of possible earthquakes. The task took four years and cost several lives but was finally completed in 1937. Its suspended central span is nearly a mile long. The towers—among the largest ever built—loom 750 feet above the angry whitecaps. Devoted fans consider this engineering marvel one of the wonders of the world. However, sheer size is only one of its attributes.

The bridge has been a backdrop for so many movies, TV shows,

CABLE CARS AND BUSES

San Francisco's famous and beloved **cable cars** elicit amusement park-type enjoyment from the most stoic traveler, startling riders with their sudden bay vistas as well as rapid right-angle turns and quick descents. The cable cars entertain to the point that visitors forget their original purpose—a vital transportation link specially designed to navigate the steep San Francisco hills. Although local commuters rarely hop onto the cable cars today, opting for the faster and less expensive bus system, these motorless trolleys beautifully serve the visitor's transportation needs with enjoyable rides between most of the main tourist attractions in the city.

The **Cable Car Museum, Powerhouse, and Car Barn** contains the complicated winding gears that play out and reel in the cable car's towing line—eleven miles of wrapped steel rope that can haul up to twenty-six cars at a time. You can watch the gears rotate just fifteen feet below you as the cable threads its figure-eight route through the fourteen-foot winders, a type of gear that powers the cable. Placards explain the function of the different machinery and give interesting tidbits about the system. You can read about cable replacement and the complicated process of splicing a new one. The museum is open daily 10:00 A.M. to 5:00 P.M., in summer 10:00 A.M. to 6:00 P.M. The museum is located at 1201 Mason Street (at Washington Street), two blocks north from the top of Nob Hill and two blocks west of Chinatown (up the hill).

Andrew S. Hallidie, a London-born engineer and metal rope manufacturer, developed the cable car after he supposedly witnessed a team of four horses struggling to haul a heavily loaded horsecar up a steep San Francisco street. One horse slipped on the rain slicked cobblestones, and the car rolled backward, dragging the four beasts behind it. Reportedly, Hallidie vowed to put a stop to this kind of cruelty. Dubbed "Hallidie's Folly," the first cable car took its maiden voyage in the early morning of August 2, 1873, from the top of Clay Street down Nob Hill's precipitous east side. To the astonishment of all present, it worked very well.

Hallidie's engineering had overcome the main obstacle of hill climbing for early transportation, the engine. Engines at that time were far too heavy and too weak to carry large loads successfully up steep hills. Cable cars eliminated the burden of a motor. A cable that ran continuously beneath the street at a steady rate could act as the propulsion; the car simply grabbed the cable to be towed uphill and downhill. When the car needed to stop, the gripman released the cable, and the coasting car was brought to a halt by its own braking system. The light, motorless carriage scaled hills with much greater ease. Today the system works in the same manner as it did over 100 years ago.

The cable-car system was renovated—but not modernized—in 1982, and you will truly appreciate the renovation. While 9½ miles per hour does not seem to be a breathtaking speed, it seems like you are breaking the sound barrier when you take a ninety-degree turn or plunge down a near-vertical hill. Instinctively you grab for the nearest handrail and thank the heavens that the system has been upgraded for safety. The gripmen and conductors, vintage San Francisco characters in their own right, give sage advice. Heed them. "Curve, hold on!" they will holler in the exaggeratedly low showman voice, or "Heeeeere we go!" they will playfully bellow with the ding of the bell before the first roller coaster descent down Powell Street (a 17 percent grade) or California Street (a 21.3 percent grade).

Three cable-car lines cut across San Francisco. Both the Powell-Mason line and the Powell-Hyde line start at the corner of Market and Powell streets at the San Francisco Visitor Information Center. These lines take you up Powell Street, through Union Square. To enter Chinatown, get off on Washington or Jackson street and walk down the hill two blocks. The Powell-Mason line splits off, taking you past North Beach, on the way down to the east end of Fisherman's Wharf, while the Powell-Hyde line climbs over Russian Hill and passes Lombard Street on its way to the west end of Fisherman's Wharf. Be sure to buy a ticket before boarding. You can board at any of the stops with a cable-car transfer (good also for buses) or a Muni Passport. For tickets, look for the self-service machines at all the terminals and major stops: Powell and Market streets, Powell and California streets, California and Drumm streets, California Street and Van Ness Avenue, Bay and Taylor streets, and Hyde and Beach streets at Victorian Park.

and photographs that it seems as familiar to out-of-towners as their own back gardens. Yet there is nothing like seeing it for yourself. Many of the city's great views—and San Francisco is a city full of great views— are either *of* the bridge or *from* the bridge. Views *of* the bridge are every- where—its towers suddenly pop up above buildings or hilltops at the most unexpected times. But the most memorable views are in midafter- noon, from vantage points along the Marina and the waterfront, when the fog swoops in, completely shrouding the roadway and piers while the towers still rise majestically above the fog layer, clearly visible and seemingly resting in midair.

For the best views *from* the bridge, leave your car at the Doyle Drive parking area and head across the span on foot. It's a brisk walk, with stiff ocean breezes often swirling through the Gate. A jacket with sleeves is recommended. The sidewalk stands 200 to 250 feet above the water, high enough for daredevil pilots to fly under it and bungee-jump- ers to dive from it. From this perch you can see far across the bay to the piers and hills of Oakland and look out west through the Gate to the Farallon Islands. Closer at hand lie Alcatraz and sailboats scudding about the bay. You may see a container vessel or a tanker heading under the bridge out to sea or returning from a Pacific voyage. From the vista point on the Marin County side of the bridge are dynamite views of the San Francisco skyline—the stuff of picture postcards. Bring your cam- era and binoculars. The bridge toll for cars is $3, paid on the southbound trip. There is no charge for pedestrians.

Beneath the bridge on the San Francisco side, **Fort Point** is a shrine to the days when coast artillery installations bristled around the gate to protect San Francisco from attack by sea. Constructed before the Civil War, the fort was equipped with 149 cannons that could throw a shell two miles. None was ever fired in anger. The National Park Ser- vice periodically cuts loose with one in a cannon demonstration. A mu- seum at the old fort is filled with military memorabilia from more than a century as an active post. National Park Service guides in Civil War uniforms conduct regular tours of the now-peaceful installation. It is open daily from 10:00 A.M. to 5:00 P.M. Admission is free. Call 415- 556-1693.

The fort is part of the historic **Presidio of San Francisco,** deacti- vated by the military and being returned to civilian use. A handsome green enclave of eucalyptus trees, parade grounds, old barracks, and family housing, its future for peaceful purposes is still being debated.

(One possibility is to turn the fort into a headquarters for an international foundation headed by Mikhail Gorbachev.) Meanwhile, its beaches, drives, and grounds are open to visitors.

Drive through the Presidio on the 49-Mile Drive for some of the best views of the Golden Gate on the Pacific side. From the turnout at Land's End, you can see the Gate, the bridge, the beaches along the water, and the Marin headlands across the way. At Lincoln Park, admire the **California Palace of the Legion of Honor.** The building, modeled on the Legion of Honor in Paris, is closed until 1994 for earthquake proofing, and much of its collection of French Impressionist and other paintings are on loan to other institutions. Massive sculptures by Auguste Rodin and Anna Huntington are still on view in the entrance courtyard, however, and the view of the city from the courtyard is smashing.

The **Cliff House** beyond Lincoln Park perches on rocks above the sea with sweeping views down the four-mile-long Ocean Beach and the Great Highway along the western edge of the city, where San Francisco meets the sea. The Cliff House is actually the third of that name. The first, a gingerbread, six-story structure erected by the mining millionaire and ex-mayor Adolph Sutro, was destroyed by fire in 1907. The Cliff House balcony and terrace overlook Seal Rocks, where a large colony of sea lions takes its leisure in the sun (when there is any), sharing the space with a flock of shore birds. Coin-operated telescopes allow you to peep at the creatures. You can also watch them from the picture windows of the Cliff House dining rooms.

Along the Great Highway, a huge Dutch windmill dating back to 1902 is surrounded by the Queen Wilhelmina Tulip Gardens, which blaze with color during spring. The windmill marks the entrance to **Golden Gate Park,** the one-time wasteland of scrub and sand dunes that has been transformed into the city's thousand-acre jewel. It's a carpet of green, of rhododendron bowers, flowers, and lakes, with horseback riding and Sunday concerts, and is home to the city's major museums.

The **M.H. De Young Memorial Museum** is particularly noted for its twenty-two galleries of American art including the acclaimed Rockefeller collection with works by Whistler, Copley, Sargent, Homer, Mary Cassatt, and other painters of the nineteenth and early twentieth centuries. There is also a grand gallery of American landscape paintings, many of them of western scenes, and an outstanding display of decorative arts and period furniture. Pottery, basketry, sculpture, and carvings from Africa, Oceania, and the Americas are shown in the Traditional Gallery, and tapestries, sculpture, and religious paintings in the classical sections. The museum is open 10:00 A.M. to 5:00 P.M. but closed Monday and Tuesday. Admission is $5, $3 for seniors. It is located on Tea Garden Drive. Call 415-750-3600.

The **Asian Art Museum,** adjoining the DeYoung, is internationally renowned for its collection of arts from China, Korea, Japan, India, Tibet, Nepal, and Pakistan. The artworks were gathered by Avery Brundage, the long-time leader of the Olympics Committee, and a special museum was built to house them in 1966. The Chinese permanent collection galleries have recently been refurbished and enlarged and now contain more than 500 works, many of them being displayed for the first time. In particular, see the collections of carved jade and the priceless blue-and-white porcelains. The museum is open 10:00 A.M. to 5:00 P.M. Wednesday to Sunday. Admission is $5, $3 for seniors. Free docent tours are given daily; you can also rent a self-guiding audio tape. It is located on Tea Garden Drive. Call 415-668-8921.

If you want to experience an earthquake and go back home to tell the folks about it, visit the **California Academy of Sciences,** across the Music Concourse from the DeYoung and the Asian Art museums. The Space and Earth Hall "earthquake floor" lets you ride out a simulated tremor and walk away afterward. One of America's top natural history museums, the Academy of Sciences also boasts a planetarium and the nation's oldest aquarium. Stroll through the diverse habitats of California wildlife in the "Wild California Hall," or follow the evidence for evolution in the newly opened "Life Through Time" exhibit.

The **Steinhart Aquarium** exhibit that draws the most crowds is the 100,000-gallon Fish Roundabout, where 14,000 fish and their friends circle swiftly through the water at visitor eye level. The new coral reef exhibit features sharks, giant clams, and living hard and soft coral. In the lobby you can look down on alligators, crocodiles, and turtles cohabiting in the Reptile Tank. The **Morrison Planetarium** has daily showings throughout the year and Laserium light shows at scheduled intervals. The academy is open 10:00 A.M. to 5:00 P.M. daily, in summer until 7:00 P.M. Admission is $6, seniors $3. The academy is located on Tea Garden Drive. Call 415-221-5100.

Like many of California's gold miners, the **Conservatory of Flowers** came around Cape Horn, and thus qualifies as the park's most venerable institution. Copied from London's Kew Gardens, the intricate glass structure was crated and shipped in pieces from England and reassembled in 1879. Featured is a tropical garden and elaborate seasonal displays of flowers. Open daily 9:00 A.M. to 5:00 P.M. Admission is $1.50, seniors 75¢. The conservatory is located on John F. Kennedy Drive. Call 415-617-7017.

Strybing Arboretum and Botanical Gardens, world renowned, boasts more than 6,000 species of plants; it emphasizes those that thrive in a Mediterranean climate similar to San Francisco's. Flowers burst into bloom year-round on a seasonal basis. A remarkable section is the Garden of Fragrance, especially for the visually impaired. There's a towering grove of California redwoods, one of the few within the city limits. An excellent guided tour leaves the bookstore daily at 1:30 P.M., but you are free to wander through the gardens and greenhouses on your own. The gardens are open weekdays 8:00 A.M. to 4:30 P.M., weekends 10:00 A.M. to 5:00 P.M. Admission is free. The arboretum is located on Ninth Avenue and Lincoln Way. Call 415-661-1316.

The **Japanese Tea Garden** is a pleasant, quiet oasis next to the Asian Art Museum. A five-acre, meticulously landscaped plot of arched bridges, ponds, small waterfalls, combed gravel walkways, and statuaries, it was created for the 1894 Midwinter Exposition. The best time to visit is in the spring when the cherry trees blossom and the garden bursts with color and fragrance. Tea is gracefully served in the teahouse from 10:30 A.M. to 5:00 P.M.; the garden is open from 8:30 A.M. to 5:30 P.M. Admission is $1, seniors half-price. The tea garden is located on Tea Garden Drive. Call 415-558-4268.

Note: For $10, you can buy a Culture Pass that admits you to the Academy of Sciences, the DeYoung and Asian Art museums, the Japanese Tea Garden, and the Conservatory of Flowers. You can visit them all in one day, or return as you choose—the pass is good for one year. Each admission is for one time only.

Everyone has heard of San Francisco's Chinatown; **Japantown** is more of a secret, quite different and worth a visit. It sits on the hillside beneath Pacific Heights, bordering the Western Addition, and is roughly bounded by Geary Boulevard and Fillmore, Laguna, and Sutter streets. Nihonmachi, the Japanese name for the district, thrived during the 1930s, with temples, Japanese markets, and shops, but virtually disappeared when Japanese Americans were "relocated" during World War II. It was revived after the war, but many of the city's 12,000 citizens of Japanese descent now live elsewhere. Nonetheless, the area retains its

HAIGHT-ASHBURY

The 1967 "Summer of Love" finalized the youthful transformation of one of San Francisco's prettiest neighborhoods, Haight-Ashbury—the cultural center for the free thinking, the free spirited, and those with "good Karma." The hippies had arrived in full force searching for peace, love, the ultimate high, and a way to stop the Vietnam War. Today, some remnants of this counterculture still can be seen in the form of wildly dressed locals perusing the used-clothing stores on Haight Street. You should go just to count how many odd hair colors cap youthful heads: orange and day-glow green have been recent favorites.

Slowly, however, Haight-Ashbury has become more gentrified, making it a safe place for an afternoon stroll through the neighborhood and its side streets full of Queen Anne Victorians. Or bring a picnic to the lush lawn of the Golden Gate Park Pan Handle. For more tranquility, try Buena Vista Park on Haight and Lyon streets, and catch some shade under one of the many eucalyptus trees.

Japanese character, and the April Cherry Blossom Festival is a lustrous event, two weekends of street performances featuring dancing, martial arts, taiko drumming, and calligraphy demonstrations.

The cobblestoned **Japan Center Mall** is the heart of the new Japantown. This block-long pedestrian mall has been designed to resemble a Japanese village, dominated by an entry gate and with shops and small noodle restaurants and sushi bars behind shoji screens. Its centerpiece is a fountain sculpted by the Japanese-American artist Ruth Asawa.

The three-block-long **Japan Center,** across Post Street, comprises an elegant complex of theaters, restaurants, sushi bars, and shops, many of them displaying the fruits of modern Japanese electronic wizardry while others offer screens, prints, vases, and lacquerware in the more ancient Japanese tradition. Connoisseurs say the city's best sushi is served here. The **Kabuki Hot Spring** is a renowned Japanese traditional spa and shiatsu massage center, a tempting place to relax after a hard

ENTERTAINMENT TONIGHT

San Francisco boasts a world-class symphony orchestra, opera company, and ballet company with performance halls to match. In the Civic Center, bounded by Van Ness and Golden Gate avenues, and Hayes and Hyde streets, the cultural facilities cluster around the French Renaissance City Hall, built in 1915 with a dome higher than the U.S. Capitol. The striking semicircular Louise M. Davies Symphony Hall, remodeled in 1992 to improve the orchestra's sound, is the symphony's home. Across the street, the War Memorial Opera House houses the San Francisco Opera and Ballet. The Beaux Arts San Francisco Main Library lies across Civic Center Plaza.

The city's theater district stretches along Geary Street, a few blocks west of Union Square. Touring companies play the theaters regularly; the American Conservatory Theater (ACT) was one of the first urban repertory companies and is nationally known. Many prominent stage, film, and television stars served their apprenticeships here.

Music from jazz to rock can be found throughout the city, in hotels and small clubs, along with improvisational theater, comedy houses, and small theater groups. The strip shows of Broadway have largely disappeared, although a few survive. A complete listing of what's in town during your visit can be obtained from the Visitor Information Center, or by consulting newspapers. A 24-hour "What's Happening" recording also fills you in on current events and activities. Call 415-391-2001. Or check out the free *San Francisco Guardian,* which has a complete listing of regional events.

For the quintessential San Francisco experience, however, seek out "Beach Blanket Babylon." This irreverent cabaret revue has been running for nearly twenty years, steadily updated to include more topical and audacious sketches. Among recent targets have been the Addams Family, Justice Clarence Thomas and Anita Hill, and Snow White; obviously, nothing is sacred. Performances are Wednesday and Thursday at 8:00 P.M., Friday and Saturday at 8:00 P.M. and 10:30 P.M., and Sunday at 3:00 P.M. and 7:30 P.M. Reservations are recommended. You'll find the revue at the Club Fugazi, 678 Green Street, North Beach. Call 415-421-4222.

day's sightseeing. The center was designed by the noted Japanese-American architect Minoru Yamasaki. He had the frazzled touring motorist in mind. There is a 600-car parking garage under the building, eliminating parking hassles and allowing you to explore the area on foot. The center is located at 1520 Webster Street. Call 415-922-6776.

To see how the upper crust lives (or at least used to), travel a few blocks uphill from Japantown to **Pacific Heights.** The city's grandest mansions are found along this hilltop with its magnificent views of the Golden Gate and across the bay to the hills of Marin. A few of the show-place homes are still owned by wealthy families (the Gordon Getty family, for instance), but others have been converted into consulates, convents, and private schools; some have been razed to make way for condominiums. Except for social events and special occasions, none are open to the public, but awestruck viewing is free.

Broadway between Webster and Lyon streets is the place to start. Several of the most stately mansions are found along this bluff, commanding a breathtaking view of the bay. They include the three-story mansion at 2220 Broadway, built in the Italian Renaissance style for the silver-mine heir James Flood, and the baroque Grant House next door. Both are now occupied by the Convent of the Sacred Heart. Another of the Flood family's baronial homes, at 2120 Broadway, houses the Hamlin School. Around the corner, at 2550 Webster Street, is the Georgian mansion designed by architect Willis Polk for the William B. Bourn family. Bourn, whose fortune was based on the rich Empire gold mine near Grass Valley, obviously had a thing for opulent living. His Filoli estate (see Chapter 3) was the showplace of the peninsula, and his "cottage" at the Empire mine rivaled it in the Mother Lode. The handsome stone dwelling at 2090 Jackson Street, occupied by the California Historical Society, was once the Whittier home.

At 2080 Washington Street, the Spreckels mansion, built for the sugar heir and his family, is perhaps the most elegant of all. The French-style mansion fronts on Lafayette Park. The Spreckels family liked it so well that they commissioned the architect to design the California Palace of the Legion of Honor, in Lincoln Park, in the same style, and donated money for it. A map of the Pacific Heights mansions is available from the Hallidie Plaza Visitor Center.

Below Pacific Heights, Union Street runs through **Cow Hollow,** once the city's dairy area but now an upscale shopping district, lined with craft shops, gourmet stores and cappuccino bars. It's a pleasant browsing and window-gazing stroll down Union Street from Gough to Fillmore streets, with many galleries and antiquaries and other enterprises courting the tourist dollar. The Victorian structures along the street have been converted into shopping compounds. Be sure to venture into the passageways and courtyards which often hold some of the most intriguing shops.

The Palace of Fine Arts, a pinkish, domed Greco-Romanesque structure, pokes its head up amid the trees a few blocks off Cow Hollow. Built for the 1915 Pan-Pacific Exposition, it now houses the **Exploratorium,** a children's hands-on science museum that has been widely acclaimed as the best of its kind. While its primary audience is ten to twelve year olds, the scientific exhibits actually appeal to all ages. The gardens and swan-filled lagoons make it an appealing place for a rest stop or a picnic. The Exploratorium is open Tuesday to Sunday 10:00 A.M. to 5:00 P.M., Wednesday 10:00 A.M. to 9:30 P.M. Admission is $8, $6 for seniors. The palace is located at Baker and Beach streets, in the Marina District. Call 415-563-7337.

How better to wind up an auto tour of San Francisco than a hair-raising plunge down the **Crookedest Street in the World?** The 1000 block of Lombard Street with its eight switchbacks is a favorite tourist destination; at the height of the visitor season, cars may be lined up for two blocks down Lombard Street waiting their turn for the downhill drive. Actually, the drop down the face of Russian Hill is a molehill by San Francisco standards. It's "only" an 18 percent grade. At least ten other hills in San Francisco surpass 25 percent. The maneuvering isn't that difficult. Nonetheless, test your brakes and keep both hands on the wheel. The drive passes some handsome hillside homes and flower gardens, so let your passengers look.

Restaurants

San Francisco is said to have more restaurant tables per capita than any city in the country. The number probably reflects hungry tourists as well as San Franciscans' love for good—and innovative—cuisine. The only-fresh-ingredients school of cookery got its start here; so did the melding of American and ethnic cooking. And certainly San Francisco has more, and a wider range of, ethnic eateries than anywhere else you

THE PAINTED LADIES

San Francisco is the land of bright-colored gingerbread. Much of the city was built between 1860 and 1900, when Victorian-style architecture was in vogue. Columns, fretwork, friezes, stained-glass and fanlight windows, carved entries, and other decor in the Addams family style adorned homes and office buildings all over the city. Many of these frame structures were destroyed in the raging fire that swept the city following the 1906 earthquake. But others survived west of Van Ness Avenue, known as "the street that saved the city" because the flames did not jump this broad thoroughfare. In recent years, many have been restored and beautified even beyond their earlier elegance.

There are two ways to see these architectural gems, apart from an occasional rubbernecking glimpse as you drive by. The Convention and Visitors Bureau outlines a 6.5-mile loop that includes some of the most colorful examples. The Foundation for San Francisco's Architectural Heritage sponsors a two-hour conducted "Heritage Walk" of Victorians in the Pacific Heights area on Sunday at 12:30 P.M. Admission is $3, $1 for seniors. Tours meet at the Haas-Lilienthal House, 2007 Franklin Street. Call 415-441-3000.

San Francisco Victorians came in three basic designs: Italianate, built between 1850 and 1875, with bay windows, pipe-stem col-

---

can pick up a pair of chopsticks. With such a sea of choices, any recommendations are bound to be somewhat arbitrary and personal. A fuller list is available in the *The San Francisco Book,* distributed by the San Francisco Convention and Visitors Bureau.

- **Jack's** is something of a shrine, having operated in the same Financial District location since 1863. It offers nominally French cuisine, but with its own distinctive touches left from years of appealing to San Francisco palates. Regulars go for the steak, chops, and fish dishes. Moderate. 615 Sacramento Street. 415-421-7355.

- **Ernie's** has elegance and silk walls to match, right out of San Francisco's classiest days. The French menu has won five-star umns, and flat crowns; Queen Anne, patterned after an English style, with shingled siding, hooded domes, and tall, narrow windows; and Stick, or Eastlake, a later version of Italianate most easily distinguished by horseshoe arches.

The Haas-Lilienthal House, an imposing 1886 Queen Anne, is the queen of San Francisco Victorians, and the only one open for public visits (although others have been modernized and turned into bed and breakfasts.) Designed for a prominent family whose wealth was built on Levi-Strauss jeans manufacture, and which is still active in community and philanthropic affairs, the grand house maintains many of the original family furnishings. Its crowning glory is a cone-shaped turret and observation platform with a view of the bay. Intricate carvings decorate the roofline, cornices, and entry porch. Tours are offered Wednesday 12:00 noon to 3:30 P.M., Sunday 11:00 A.M. to 4:30 P.M. Admission is $4, $2 for seniors.

Alamo Square, at Hayes and Steiner streets in the Western Addition, is known as "Postcard Row" because its line of colorful restored Victorians, with the city's skyline in the background, has been a favorite of photographers. The Victorians include several bed and breakfasts and the Archbishop's Mansion at 1000 Fulton Street, originally a residence built in 1904 for San Francisco's Catholic prelate.

awards for more than twenty-five years in a row. Expensive. 847 Montgomery Street. 415-397-5969.

- **Stars** and its noted chef-restaurateur Jeremiah Tower do everything with style and accompany it with piano background music. Offering excellent food, it is a place to see and be seen. 150 Redwood Alley in the Civic Center. Expensive. 415-861-7827.

- **Square One** features the innovative dishes of another noted chef, Joyce Goldstein. Mediterranean-type dishes are prepared with fresh-from-the-farm ingredients and given a special California twist. The menu changes daily. Moderate to expensive. 190 Pacific Avenue. 415-788-1110.

- **Fog City Diner** started the fad for 1950s-type dining car decor and simple regional dishes—"gourmet diner fare"—and it is still one of the city's trendiest and most popular eating places. Reserve well ahead of time. Moderate. 1300 Battery Street. 415-982-2000.

- **Washington Square Bar and Grill,** a.k.a. "The Washbag," is the writers' and critics' hangout, specializing in pasta, calamari, cioppino, and versions thereof, along with the hamburgers and other lunch fare you might expect. Moderate. 1707 Powell Street. 415-982-8123.

- **Tadich's Cold Day Grill,** another old-timer, dishes out excellent seafood dishes at a counter and in private booths. Inexpensive to moderate. 240 California Street. 415-391-2373.

- **The Waterfront** features dramatic views of the bay from every table (the best are from the upstairs picture windows, reserve well ahead of time) and excellent seafood. Crab Louie, shrimp salads, and ceviche are popular choices. Moderate. Pier 7, Embarcadero. 415-391-2696.

- **Scoma's** overlooks the fishing fleet at Fisherman's Wharf, where it has been serving petrale sole and the "catch of the day" for decades and decades. The seafood is prepared with an Italian touch. Moderate. Pier 47, Fisherman's Wharf. 415-771-4383.

- **Capp's Corner** is in a great old North Beach tradition, alas rapidly disappearing in these days of light and healthful eating. You sit elbow to elbow at long tables and eat family style—six courses of hearty Italian dishes, washed down with the house red, served in water tumblers. Inexpensive. 1600 Powell Street. 415-989-2589.

- **Golden Dragon** is a personal choice as the best of the dim sum restaurants. Neither as glitzy nor as colorful as some others, it offers a vast variety and is operated in the old style, with carts wheeled by your table and the bill tallied by counting the used plates. A clue to its quality: favored by

Chinese families for their weekend lunch. Inexpensive. 816 Washington Street at Grant Avenue. 415-398-3920 or 415-398-4550.

- **Fior d'Italia** is said to be San Francisco's oldest Italian restaurant. "Withstanding the taste of time" is its slogan. The food is Northern Italian. Moderate. 601 Union Street, North Beach. 415-986-1886.

- **Little Joe's and Baby Joe's** brings traditional Italian cooking to life and Italian food prices down to earth. The kitchen is right in the dining room and you can watch the showmenchefs flip your real veal cutlet gracefully in the air, then catch it without looking as they drop your pasta in to boil. Inexpensive to moderate. 523 Broadway. 415-982-7639.

- **Salamagundi** serves gourmet soups, salads, and sandwiches cafeteria style, a few blocks from Union Square. The onion soup and the Caesar salad are notable. Open until midnight for after-theater snacks. Inexpensive. 442 Geary Street. 415-441-0894.

- **Sam Woh** offers a great, noisy show in the heart of Chinatown. Three narrow floors of booths, with dumbwaiters carrying the food between floors, Woh's specializes in noodle dishes in more tasty varieties than even a noodle freak can possibly imagine. If you order soup, do not plan on eating a second course. Inexpensive. 813 Washington Street. 415-982-0596.

- **Empress of China** is one of several upscale Chinese restaurants (others are Tommy Toy and Kan's) appealing to visitors who like quiet, elegant service and don't mind paying for it. It features Mandarin specialties, gilt and brocade surroundings, and great views. Moderate to expensive. 808 Grant Avenue. 415-434-1345.

- **Greens at Fort Mason** serves vegetarian dishes, but what dishes! Owned and operated by the Tassajara Zen Center in Carmel Valley, it is the ultimate in creative vegetarian cooking that satisfies the devoted meat eater. Meals are served with crusty homemade breads. A price-fixed meal is served Friday and Saturday nights. Building A, Fort Mason Marina. Moderate to expensive. 415-771-6222.

• **Clement Street.** What San Franciscans call "The Avenues" (those with numbers extending out to the western edge) bristle with as much ethnicity as the United Nations. Within a few blocks on Geary Street, you may find Singaporean, Cambodian, Burmese, and Laotian restaurants; parallel Clement Street has Peruvian, Japanese, Danish, and Thai rubbing elbows, along with sub- and sub-sub specialties, like The Oceans, which specializes in seafood prepared the Chinese way; the Bali, with an Indonesian rice table, and several places that concentrate on Hakka dishes, the food of the Hong Kong rickshaw drivers. A personal favorite is the **Narai,** 2229 Clement Street, 415-751-6363, whose cuisine stems from the Chinese community in the waterfront areas of Thailand, mingling the best of two nationalities. But the fun is to restaurant-hop from window to window, studying the menus and trying to make a choice—then deciding where you'll return for tomorrow night.

Lodging ————————————————————————

"The San Francisco Lodging Guide" is 44 pages long and lists 380 B&Bs, inns, luxury hotels, and budget accommodations. Here is a range of recommendations:

• **Hotel Bedford.** A small, European-style hotel within walking distance of Union Square, the Bedford has recently been renovated. It is popular with visitors from abroad. Moderate. 761 Post Street. 415-673-6040.

• **Fairmont Hotel** is for those with deep pockets. It is elegant, with old-style class and one of the most magnificent lobbies anywhere. It sits atop Nob Hill with views from its Crown Room to everywhere. Very expensive. 950 Mason Street. 415-772-5000.

- **Bed and Breakfast Inn** claims to have been first to bring the B&B concept from Europe to America, about 1966. If not the first, it is certainly one of the most pleasant and comfortable, encompassing three connected ivy-covered Victorians off Union Street. Expensive. 4 Charlton Court. 415-921-9784.

- **TraveLodge at the Wharf** is nothing spectacular, but convenient to the tourist meccas of the wharf and Ghirardelli Square and to cable-car lines. Rooms on the high floors have good views of the Golden Gate and Alcatraz. Moderate to expensive. 250 Beach Street. 415-392-6700.

- **Columbus Motor Inn** is another convenient location, within walking distance of Fisherman's Wharf and North Beach. It has large, comfortable rooms. Moderate. 1075 Columbus Avenue. 415-885-1492.

- **Cow Hollow Motor Inn** is one of the best of the modern motels along "Motel Row" on Lombard Street (U.S. 101 North.) It has been recently renovated and upgraded. There is free parking under the building. 2190 Lombard Street. Moderate. 415-921-5800.

- **Archbishop's Mansion** is in an old, comfortable Victorian built for San Francisco's Roman Catholic archbishops and is part of "Postcard Row" on Alamo Square in the Western Addition. It is decorated with antiques; many rooms have fireplaces. Moderate to expensive. 1000 Fulton Street. 415-563-7871.

- **The Cartwright** is another small, family-owned hotel close to Union Square and popular with European visitors. It has brass beds and antique furnishings and is recently renovated. Moderate. 524 Sutter Street. 415-421-2865.

Watering Holes and Landmarks ——————

- **The Garden Court of the Sheraton Palace Hotel** with its stained-glass dome and glittering crystal chandeliers has recently been reopened after a restoration to bring back its old-time elegance, and the restoration was, to say the least, successful. Once the gathering spot for society ladies in white gloves meeting for tea, it's now a place where the younger movers and shakers meet for Calistoga water and chardonnay. Expensive. 2 New Montgomery Street. 415-392-8600.

• **Buena Vista,** or the "Bee Vee," is where they invented Irish coffee and the Ramos fizz. Try one of each, and if your eyes still focus, gaze out across Aquatic Park, the cable-car turntable to Alcatraz. This is a good place for a rest stop after Ghirardelli Square shopping or window-shopping. Inexpensive. 2765 Hyde Street. 415-474-5044.

• **Cliff House Seafood and Beverage Company** is the place to sit by the window and watch the antics of the sea lions and the seagulls on Seal Rock. They feature seafood dishes, too. This is a favorite spot for a Sunday brunch by the sea. Moderate. 1000 Point Lobos. 415-386-3300.

• **Top of the Mark** is the locale of many romantic farewell and homecoming scenes in World War II movies and just as stately as ever. It still has the greatest views in town. Expensive. The Mark Hopkins Hotel, 999 California Street. 415-392-3434.

• **Perry's** is a popular spot in the Union Street yuppie ghetto, with a long bar, a small garden out back, and lots of conviviality late into the evening. Moderate. 1944 Union Street. 415-922-9008.

Chapter 2

The East Bay–
Berkeley, Oakland,
and Benicia

The communities across the Bay Bridge from San Francisco, an area collectively known as the East Bay, are often overshadowed by their more glamorous neighbor and neglected by visitors. Too bad. Oakland, Berkeley, Alameda, and their neighbors combine an attractive mix of historic sites, venerable architecture, elegant homes, wooded hillsides (partly decimated, alas, by a devastating fire in 1991), spectacular water views, bustling streets and ethnic quarters, cultural attractions, and one of the world's most renowned universities.

Berkeley

The bay, mountains, and academics power the vitality of Berkeley, a city with many faces. College students, leftover hippies, and political radicals intermingle along the edges of the 45,000-student UC Berkeley campus, which, for all the "Berserkeley" media image, enjoys a towering reputation for its large number of Nobel Prize winners and great achievements in scientific research and wide-ranging scholarship. The city itself lies cradled between San Francisco Bay and a sharply rising line of foothills. From Tilden Park you get breathtaking views of the Golden Gate Bridge, the Bay Bridge, and the San Francisco skyline. The fresh bay breeze adds to the city's energetic ambience and complements the scenic drives of the foothills.

The **UC Berkeley campus,** at the heart of the city, is the obvious starting place for a visit. (Student-led walking tours of the campus are

37

conducted Monday, Wednesday, and Friday. For information, call the university Visitor Center, 510-642-5215. There is also a free leaflet outlining a self-guided tour.)

Sproul Plaza, the campus gateway, opens up at the end of bustling Telegraph Avenue, lined with palm readers, craft stalls, and taco and T-shirt vendors. Sproul is constantly filled with aspiring engineers, scientists, and politicians debating, lounging, soliciting signatures on petitions, distributing literature, or simply hurrying from class to class. **Sather Tower,** known as the Campanile, is the campus's most visible and enduring landmark. Designer Galen Howard modeled the 327-foot tower after the famous campanile in the Piazza San Marco in Venice, Italy. The Italianate structure was completed in 1913, a few years after the 1906 earthquake; Howard designed it to survive future earthquakes, and it has. Views and bells are the campanile's main attractions. For less than a dollar, you can take an elevator ride to the top (weekdays 10:00 A.M. to 3:30 P.M., Sundays 10:00 A.M. to 1:45 P.M.) for a dramatic 360-degree panorama of the bay and its surroundings. The 61-bell carillon serenades students and visitors daily at 7:50 A.M., noon, and 6:00 P.M. and at a special performance on Sunday from 2:00 to 2:45 P.M.

Along the southern edge of the campus, on Bancroft Way, stand three museums diverse in character but similar in the richness and depth of their collections and exhibits.

The **Pacific Film Archive,** housed in the University Art Museum at 2625 Durant Avenue, has been deemed one of the most complete collections of classic films in the country; go here to see Garbo, Gable, and John Gilbert in their early triumphs, as well as experimental films from the cutting edge of cinematography. (Shows change weekly; admission is $5.50, $3.50 for seniors. 510-642-1412.) Upstairs, the **University Art Museum** boasts a concentrated selection of contemporary art, centered around the permanent exhibitions of paintings of the internationally famed Hans Hofmann, a former Berkeley faculty member. Across Bancroft Way, the small **P.A. Hearst Museum of Anthropology** in Kroeber Hall is like an iceberg; what you see in its exhibit halls represents only a tiny portion of the museum's vast million-item collection of archaeological treasures from the ancient civilizations of Egypt and Peru and anthropological artifacts from Asia and Oceania. Exhibits rotate every three to four months, admission is $1.50, 50¢ for seniors, free on Thursdays. Call 510-643-7648.

The **Bancroft Library,** located smack-dab in the center of campus, holds the original nugget that launched the 1848 gold rush, along with early California paintings, rare books, and manuscripts. Admission is free.

Berkeley is also a mecca for flower lovers. Along the scenic South Park Drive, the **UC Berkeley Botanical Garden** exhibits more than 10,000 species and varieties of plants and flowers—the largest horticulture collection of any university in the country. Note the Coming Events board at the garden entrance, which directs you to specimens in bloom. Stroll through the plant spectrum from misty greenhouses of ferns to desert cactus gardens. The botanical garden is a wonderful spot for a lunch al fresco. The **Berkeley Rose Garden,** a half-mile north of campus on Euclid Avenue, features 250 varieties of roses, many of them older varieties seldom seen elsewhere. The garden is carefully pruned in January to be at its peak for Mother's Day, but it's worth a visit anytime from May to October. Admission is free at both gardens.

The **Lawrence Hall of Science,** also on South Park Drive, is a first-class science museum, and it features a great view of the glistening bay from its terrace. Hands-on exhibits and scientific toys lead you through basic lessons in astronomy, biology, physics, and computer science. The museum is named for Berkeley Professor Ernest O. Lawrence, a pioneer in atomic research. Summers, the place is surrounded by dinosaurs—an outdoor display of mechanical brontosauruses and tyrannosauruses that move, eat, and stomp with all the realism of eons ago. The spectacular planetarium shows dramatize the heavenly world above us. For information on show times and displays, call 510-642-5132.

Special events and fairs fill the Berkeley streets almost all year long. They feature arts and crafts, street performers, and always a wide variety of diverse food vendors. The Juneteenth Festival (second or third weekend in June) celebrates the arrival of news of the Emancipation Proclamation. Its highlight is a rambunctious parade along Adeline Street between Ashby and Alcatraz avenues. The Solano Avenue Stroll and Parade in September runs along Solano Avenue; more than eighty floats roll through the street, interspersed with a band and a variety of other street entertainment. For two weekends in March, Telegraph Avenue is closed to vehicular traffic and is solely devoted to displays by artisans from throughout the West. More than 250 vendors set up stalls

SCENIC DETOUR

For the best views, a taste of Berkeley living, and a pleasant outdoor lunch, pick up a pizza at the Cheese Board Pizza Collective and head up Grizzly Peak Boulevard into Tilden Park. The twisting panoramic road winds steeply uphill amid fragrant eucalyptus groves and elegant (and sometimes funky) homes overlooking the city and the bay. The best views are from the turnouts at the summit.

Quiet natural settings are the norm in Tilden Park. The park reserves 2,078 acres to shelter wildlife and preserve the natural beauty of the Berkeley hills. Secluded picnic tables and short hiking trails encourage both eating and exploring. Deep in the park, a scaled-down steam train snakes along the scenic ridge; for information, call 510-548-6100. Deeper yet, an antique merry-go-round still enchants children, their parents, and grandparents as it has for nearly seventy years. The carousel's carved menagerie is led by a glorious white horse. His brightly painted followers include a giraffe, a sea monster, and an ostrich. Harry Perry, an original owner, still runs the concession stand next to the carousel. For directions and information, call 510-524-6283.

along Telegraph Avenue, between Dwight and Bancroft ways. For street fair information, call the Berkeley Convention and Visitors Bureau, 510-549-7040.

For theater lovers, the award-winning **California Shakespeare Festival** presents four of the bard's plays each summer, outdoors in the Bruns Amphitheater, Gateway Boulevard. For ticket information, call 510-548-9666.

Restaurants ──────────────────────────

The city of Berkeley's embrace of the new and different includes its restaurants. Berkeley menus range from Afghan specialties to fresh seafood to five-star gourmet dishes. Don't forget the coffeehouses where students sit until the wee small hours debating everything from Aristotle to Zoroaster. (A selected list of eating places is available from the Berkeley Convention and Visitors Bureau, 1843 University Avenue, Berkeley, California 94703. 510-549-7040.)

- **Spenger's Fish Grotto,** a venerable, bustling seafood house on the western edge of Berkeley just off the University Avenue exit of I-80, specializes in fresh fish at reasonable prices. A short distance away, on the bay front, the more upscale **H's Lordship's Restaurant** offers more formal seafood dining combined with a spectacular view of the bay. 199 Seawall Drive. 510-843-2733.

- Coffeehouses are clustered around the campus, mainly along Telegraph and University avenues. Caffé Strada, on the corner of Bancroft Way and College Avenue, is a student favorite. It offers a wide range of Italian coffees including the specialty, Cafe Latte (one-quarter espresso coffee, three-quarters milk—available decaffeinated, too). It's a nice place to sit on the shady terrace and soak up the student atmosphere. 2300 College Avenue. 510-843-5282.

- Small, diverse restaurants—most of them within range of the average pocketbook—are sprinkled along Shattuck Avenue between Rose and Cedar streets. The aromas of garlic, curry, coffee, and fresh bread tantalize the nostrils and lure the passerby to lunch.

- **The Cheese Board Collective,** on Shattuck Avenue, could be considered quintessentially Berkeley. It offers delicious California-cuisine-influenced pizza but strictly according to its own highly individualistic schedule. You can buy pizza on Monday and Friday after 4:30 P.M., Tuesday, Wednesday, and Thursday between 11:30 A.M. and 1:30 P.M., and Saturday from noon to 2:00 P.M. A loyal clientele conforms to these hours to enjoy pizza topped with feta cheese, lemon, garlic, and/or artichoke hearts, with a crisp sourdough crust that gives a light and subtle tang. 1512 Shattuck. 510-549-3187.

- **Chez Panisse,** 1517 Shattuck Avenue, qualifies as a historic shrine. Its renowned chef-owner, Alice Waters, developed the California Cuisine with its unique blend of fresh ingredients from local farmers, simply prepared in previously unheard of combinations. A typical Monday night prix fixe dinner might consist of Tuscan lamb stew with fava beans and artichokes, or red-wine fish and shellfish soup with aioli. Its cuisine is widely copied, but (its fans like to say) never surpassed, which is why gourmands fight to pay $45 to $65 per dish. Reservations must be made one to two weeks in advance for weekday lunches and a month or more in advance for dinner. However, an adjoining, more moderately priced cafe offers same-day reservations for lunch and serves dinner without reservations. There's a thirty- to forty-five-minute wait and long lines, but a Chez Panisse dinner is worth it.

Lodging ————————————————————————

Berkeley's accommodations cater to parents visiting their aspiring undergraduates, as well as to sightseeing travelers with a spectrum of budgets.

- The **Berkeley City Club** offers fine rooms and secure dwellings as well as a heated indoor pool and central location. Its grand Gothic architecture designed by Julia Morgan (see box, page 43) provides a classy atmosphere at moderate rates. Rooms include a full breakfast. Call ahead. Payment is due upon arrival. 2315 Durant Avenue. 510-848-7800.

- The **Shattuck Hotel,** also centrally located, has moderately priced rooms in an old-fashioned setting. The building itself is a historic landmark built in 1910. A senior discount, validated overnight parking, and a continental breakfast are included. 2086 Alliston Way. In-state call 800-SHATTUCK; out-of-state, 800-BERKELEY.

- Just out of the way on Ashby is the **Claremont Hotel Resort,** an immense white structure set into the side of the Berkeley hills. It is the East Bay's premier luxury resort, including

A WOMAN'S PLACE IS AT THE DRAWING BOARD

Until Julia Morgan came along, architecture was a man's field. The Berkeley-educated architect changed that. Morgan is best known for the Hearst Castle at San Simeon, California, the publisher's self-indulgent hilltop mansion that is a popular tourist attraction. Morgan's earlier and equally pioneering works dot Berkeley. Visit the Berkeley City Club at Bancroft Way and Durant Avenue with its Gothic doorways, arched windows, and high ceilings. Other examples are the Greek Theater on the UC Berkeley campus, where she served as assistant to designer Galen Howard and initiated the use of reinforced concrete, and St. John's Presbyterian Church, her first independent commission, as well as numerous private residences. A guide to Morgan's works is available from the Berkeley Convention and Visitors Bureau.

tennis courts, swimming pool, workout room, and hot tubs. Located at Ashby and Domingo streets on the border of Berkeley and Oakland. 510-843-3000.

- Less expensive lodging is available at the **Golden Bear Motel.** It's clean and cheap for all ages, located in the west side of Berkeley. 1620 San Pablo Avenue. 510-525-6770.

- Berkeley also offers a moderately priced bed and breakfast network that spans into Oakland. For information call 510-540-5123.

Oakland

The poet Gertrude Stein is alleged to have gibed about Oakland: "There is no *there* there." It is a canard. There is plenty of "there" in Oakland, which some call the most ethnically diverse city in California. With this diversity has come some social unrest, and a few outlying areas of Oakland should be avoided. However, the downtown remains very safe and full of cultural intrigue. From its inception, the city has served as a vital seaport connection for the Bay Area, and it remains an important shipping link. In Oakland, history still runs through the streets.

Three major neighborhoods appeal to visitors—Chinatown, Old Oakland, and Jack London's Waterfront, named for the Oakland-born novelist whose books still rank with the most gripping tales of the sea. Each area exudes its own distinctive feel. The best way to sample each is on foot. The Oakland Tours program provides maps of six recommended walking tours. Call 510-273-3234.

San Francisco's Chinatown is larger and more famous, but Oakland's **Chinatown,** an area roughly bordered by Ninth, Seventh, Webster, and Alice streets, may be more authentic. The Oakland Chinese community dates back to the gold rush, but Chinese has been recently augmented by a babel of other voices from Vietnam, Cambodia, the Philippines, and India. The Chinatown streets are a noisy hodgepodge of small groceries advertising exotic spices and herbal remedies where the scents of fried noodles and smoked pork waft across the bustling sidewalks.

Old Oakland adjoins Chinatown. Incorporating the city's old business district of the 1870s, the district ranges along Eighth and Tenth streets, between Broadway and Jefferson Street. The original architecture is little changed; behind the original storefront façades of the past lie boutiques, groceries, and restaurants of the present. Many of the original brick hotels have been converted into shops or offices, yet hints of Old Oakland's history remain. This area is made for a leisurely afternoon of window-shopping, eating well, and people-watching.

G.B. Ratto's International Grocers at 821 Washington Street has a century-old reputation as one of the leading markets in the region, a "one-stop store to satisfy the craving for Old World cuisine," according to its brochure. The market sells spices, grains, rice, and such luxuries as olives imported from southern France, jelly imported from England, and a selection of sauces from India. G.B. Ratto's is a great place to browse and pick up exotic picnic fare or unusual gifts for epicurean relatives.

Jack London's Waterfront, redeveloped between the old docks and Embarcadero in the 1970s and 1980s, appeals to strollers, browsers, shoppers, and diners—a far cry from the brawling Barbary Coast of the London stories. The waterfront has been transformed into a walking park lined with craft and antique shops, seafood restaurants, and historic sites to stroll while seagulls wheel and cry overhead. Located on the water at the foot of Broadway.

The Oakland Museum is a must-see for any visitor who wants to understand what California is all about. This little gem of a museum, an architectural delight, tucked into a residential neighborhood at Tenth and Oak streets, is completely devoted to California's history, culture, people, arts, topography, and nature. The displays are arranged chronologically and vividly bring to life all aspects of this multifaceted state. The history section, for example, traces the ever-changing face of California from an authentic gold rush assay office to contemporary windsurfers and skateboarders. The ecology section profiles the state from west to east as it was before colonists came, from the tidal pools of the coastline to the wildlife of the high Sierra to the desert's cacti. The collection of works by California artists is highlighted by an impressive wall-size stained-glass window by Arthur and Lucia Mathews depicting the westward view from Oakland across the bay to the hills of Marin County. Museum admission is free; guided tours are available through the docent center. Senior groups are given a free tea and tour service. For information call 510-238-3514. Afternoon visits are suggested to avoid school tours in the morning.

Restaurants ————————————————————

- **Ratto's** dining room, adjoining the International Grocers at 821 Washington Street, offers moderately priced lunches featuring sandwiches, salads, or pasta and traditional Italian cuisine at dinner. Go on the weekend if you can, when waiters serve operatic arias along with the fettucine. Call in advance for weekend dinner reservations. Moderate to expensive. 510-832-6503.

- **Pacific Coast Brewing Company** brews its own beer on the premises. The varieties of hoppy suds range from a medium-body beer to rich stout and hard cider. The inexpensive meals are based on workman's fare *a la* British pubs and include bangers and mash and Cornish pasties. The

small kitchen can make service slow, but beer drinkers may
not notice. 906 Washington Street. 510-836-2739.

- **Kincaid's Bay House** grills up fresh seafood. Its waterfront
  location provides a bayside view to Jack London Square.
  Moderate to expensive. 510-835-8600.

- **Tsing Tao House** is a personal favorite among Chinatown's
  many restaurants. Its authentic Cantonese cuisine includes a
  lengthy list of noodle dishes. 200 Broadway. Inexpensive to
  moderate. 510-465-8811.

Lodging

The **Washington Inn** in Old Oakland, characterized by deep mahogany details, marble pedestal sinks, and antique furniture, was once
the home-away-from-home for visiting baseball teams but now generally caters to a corporate clientele. On weekends, however, the inn offers a special deal for tourists. If you mention Ratto's, rooms are reduced to $50 a night, double occupancy, and they will even get you
reservations at Ratto's for Italian food and opera singing. Rates normally are moderate to expensive. 495 Tenth Street. 510-452-1776.

Benicia

Benicia is a quaint, overlooked village tucked between the East
Bay Hills and the waterways of the delta. It holds a wealth of only-in-
California-type history, along with a striking number of antique shops.
Originally Benicia's harbor was considered deeper and more protected
than San Francisco's. The city held promise of strong growth both com-
mercially and politically. Early settlers called the area "Francisco,"
naming it for the bay when what is now San Francisco was known as
"Yerba Buena." But in 1847, Robert Semple, Thomas Larkin, and General Mariano Guadaloupe Vallejo (leader of the Mexican forces in California) founded the city and dubbed it "Benicia," after the general's
"charming and beautiful wife." In 1848, the discovery of gold in the
Sierra Nevada foothills halted the expansion of the region. Locals are

proud to point out that, after California achieved statehood, Benicia had a brief but historic role as the capital of California, one of this area's claims to fame. Benicia's present-day city hall served as the capitol building for thirteen months until, in 1852, Sacramento lobbyists convinced the government to move its home.

From Benicia Point, at the foot of First Street near the municipal pier, you can see another high spot in Benicia's checkered history. A few yards beyond the beach was the location of the Corbett-Choynski heavyweight title bout in 1878. Both San Francisco and Marin counties forbade boxing in those days, so the ring was built on a barge anchored just offshore in San Pablo Bay. The contestants bobbed and weaved for a grueling twenty-seven rounds before Corbett emerged as the victor by a knockout.

Even Benicia's architecture testifies to its unusual history. Many of the early houses are Cape Cod saltboxes with their distinctive sloping roofs, a style rarely found in California and brought here by original Massachusetts settlers. Some of them were actually dismantled in New England, shipped around Cape Horn, and reassembled in Benicia.

The **Benicia State Capitol and Historic Park** at First and G streets, has been painstakingly restored, down to the spittoons at every senator's desk (smoking was outlawed in Benicia) and the original supporting columns made from the masts of old San Francisco ships. Here you can see the chambers of the fourth California legislature dating back to 1853. Admission is $2.

The **Camel Barn Museum** is a monument to Benicia's historic role as a U.S. Army arsenal and to one of the oddest experiments in U.S. military history. During the late 1850s, Secretary of War Jefferson Davis, later to become president of the Confederacy, developed a plan to import camels to transport military supplies across the desert between Arizona and California. Thirty-five of the beasts of burden were brought into the U.S. The start of the Civil War cashiered the project, and the camels were brought to Benicia to be sold. After the auction, several of the animals broke free and wild camels roamed through the fields around Benicia. The sandstone barn itself (which actually never held camels) traces the history of the camel experiment as well as other aspects of Benician history.

Constructed of sandstone in 1859, the **clock tower** first served as a fortress to protect against Indian attacks and then as a watchtower to control shipping. Today it provides visitors with panoramic views of the bay.

Restaurants

The small downtown of Benicia has a surprisingly large number of restaurants. Some of the eateries take advantage of their seaside location, boasting fresh, catch-of-the-day fish as well as sweeping bay views.

- **Captain Blyther's** upscale, casual restaurant prepares the best seafood in town and also has the best view. The dining room with floor to ceiling windows sits right on the water near the Benicia Municipal Pier at the end of First Street. Moderate. 123 First Street. 707-745-4082.

- At the **Union Hotel Restaurant,** brass rail decor replaces the ocean view, and steak specialties are added to seafood cuisine. Steak lovers will rejoice over the Aged New York Steak gently matured in Jack Daniels and green peppercorn marinade. Moderate. 401 First Street. 707-746-0105.

- **Mabel's** provides the traditional diner setting with a '90s California twist. Here art deco and modern art adorn the walls above booths with red vinyl benches and Formica table tops. Great for a casual gourmet lunch. Be sure to get dessert. Their menu boasts a wide selection of homemade sweets. Inexpensive (but costlier than normal diner food). 635 First Street. 707-746-7068.

Vallejo

Vallejo, another former capital of California, adjoins Benicia along the Carquinez Straits. It was also the original home of the Mexican leader General M.G. Vallejo. But most visitors come here not for history, but for wildlife. Marine World Africa USA, a 160-acre nonprofit animal kingdom, is a wild animal theme park where visitors can mingle with elephants and giraffes and watch aquatic shows featuring gigantic killer whales. The park is at 2001 Marine World Parkway. Call 707-643-6722.

Chapter 3

Down
the San Francisco
Peninsula

Those who consider California freeways all smoggy gridlock should point their cars down I-280 from the city the locals never call Frisco. The multilane highway, which once won an award as America's most scenic highway, runs along the spine of the San Francisco Peninsula. To the west lie the hills and woodlands of the San Francisco Fish and Game Refuge and the Crystal Springs Reservoir; beyond those lie the Santa Cruz Mountains, sometimes wearing a skullcap of fog. To the east roll hills dotted with sprawling estates; between the lanes bloom bank on bank of red and white oleander. Meanwhile, out of sight beyond the mountains to the west, two-lane State Highway 1, the Cabrillo Highway, threads along the Pacific shore alternating between dramatic cliffs and scimitar-shaped beaches at the edge of artichoke and pumpkin fields. U.S. 101, a more bumper-to-bumper conveyor belt, hugs the San Francisco bay shore on the east. In the triangular area bounded by these roads lies not only handsome scenery and secluded mansions but also splotches of history, rolling horse country, remarkable small museums, a world-class university, and flowers, flowers, flowers.

Filoli sounds like the name of an Italian villa, but in fact was coined by William Bourn, Jr., owner of the Empire gold mine, for his baronial estate tucked into the hills at Woodside. It is derived from Bourn's slogan, To FIght, LOve, LIve = Filoli. The 42-room, 36,000-square-foot Georgian mansion is maintained by the National Trust for Historic Preservation and is considered a classic example of country-house architecture. Of particular interest are the formal dining room with a table half the length of a football field, the massive vault where

49

the silver collection was stored, and the grand ballroom. Many of the furnishings are antique pieces brought over from Europe by the Bourn family, who also owned a castle in Ireland, then retained by the second owners, the Roth family of the Matson shipping line. Soak up the era of opulence in the paneled library where the gentlemen retired after dinner for brandy and cigars or in the French provincial drawing room where the ladies waited for the cigar smoke to clear.

Sixteen acres of formal gardens surround the estate, carefully planned and planted to be in bloom year-round. Literally hundreds of species are lovingly tended in the brick-walled gardens; the list of rose species alone covers four single-spaced pages. If there is a single best season, it is probably late spring when the gardens burst with dogwood, lilacs, tulips, iris, tree peonies, wisteria, and on and on.

After touring the gardens, you can sip tea in the cozy teahouse, designed in Italian Renaissance style, or browse in the cupolaed carriage house, another architectural jewel converted into a gift shop. Plants from the gardens are for sale in the courtyard between the two buildings. The mansion and gardens are open from mid-February to the first week in November, Tuesday through Saturday. Docents conduct tours of both. Admission is normally by advance reservation only; however, unreserved self-guided garden tours are allowed each Friday and several other days a month (more in summer.) The mansion is located on Canada Road, Woodside. Take the Edgewood Road exit off I-280, turn north on Canada Road, and watch for the unobtrusive, easily missed small sign directing you to the mansion and gardens. For information and reservations call 415-364-2880.

Acres of Orchids is just that—row on row of the delicate blooms in white, wine-red, deep purple, golden yellow, green—orchids with spots, stripes, and figures. The million square feet of greenhouse ships four million flowers a year. One-hour tours at 10:30 A.M. and 1:30 P.M. include a visit to the hybridizing laboratory where new plants are cloned. You'll find roses and gardenias, too. This floral extravaganza is located at 1450 El Camino Real, South San Francisco. From I-280, take the Hickey Boulevard exit east, turn south one block on El Camino Real and follow the flower fragrance. Call 415-871-5655.

More flowers can be seen on a tour of *Sunset,* the Magazine of Western Living. Three acres of formal gardens, designed by the noted landscape architect Thomas Church, display the flora of the Pacific Coast, from the cacti of Baja California to the rhododendrons and camellias of the Pacific Northwest. *Sunset*'s gardening staff explains the plantings. The one-hour tour also includes a visit to the magazine's test kitchens narrated by *Sunset*'s cooks. Tastings are not offered. *Sunset* is located at 80 Willow Road, Menlo Park. Call 415-324-5479 or 324-5481.

Coyote Point Museum is a small natural history museum built around an ecological theme. Located on a dramatic point overlooking San Francisco Bay, it emphasizes the interrelationships of wildlife, marine animals, insects, plants, and the geology and natural resources of the Bay Area. A unique exhibit is the huge food pyramid. Burrowing owls, badgers, river otters, red-legged frogs and snakes are shown in their natural habitats. On windy days, go out by the water and watch the brightly colored windsurfers skimming across the ocean in every direction. The museum is open Tuesday to Saturday 10:00 A.M. to 5:00 P.M. and Sunday 12:00 noon to 5:00 P.M. Admission is $3, $2 for seniors. It is located at 1651 Coyote Point Boulevard, San Mateo, off U.S. 101 at the Dore Avenue exit. Call 415-342-7755.

Sanchez Adobe Historic Site is a restored adobe bungalow originally built in 1842 for Don Francisco Sanchez in return for his service as commandante of the San Francisco Presidio during the Mexican era. Earlier, the site was the "support farm" for San Francisco's Mission Dolores. During Prohibition, it became a speakeasy known as Adobe House. The restoration, furnished with antiques of the Mexican period, is the only adobe open to the public on the Peninsula. The site is open Tuesday and Thursday 10:00 A.M. to 4:00 P.M., Saturday and Sunday 1:00 P.M. to 5:00 P.M. It is located at 1000 Linda Mar Boulevard, Pacifica. Call 415-359-1462.

The **Woodside Store** dates back to 1854 and the days of heavy redwood logging in the Santa Cruz Mountains. It was the first store between San Jose and San Francisco. Owner Robert Orville Tripp was not only a storekeeper but also a dentist; when not pulling teeth he sold calico, great wheels of cheese, coffee, and boots. Much of the merchandise is still on display in the carefully preserved store, along with his adjustable dentist's chair, an innovation for those days. The store is open Tuesday, Thursday, Saturday, and Sunday 12:00 noon to 5:00 P.M. Admission is free. It is located at King's Mountain and Tripp roads, Woodside (off I-280, Woodside Road exit). Call 415-851-7615.

The **Stanford Theater** in Palo Alto is a refurbished, gussied-up showplace out of the cinema's glory days of the 1930s, complete with a monster pipe organ, a red plush lobby, and a popcorn machine, too. The theater specializes in films from the silent era and from the golden days

SCENIC DETOUR

I-280 and State Highway 1 share a roadway from San Francisco to the Pacifica exit, where State Highway 1 branches west to the coast. At Pacifica, the road begins its climb over Devil's Slide, a right-of-way cut out of Montara Mountain, 2000 feet above the crashing surf. The views of cliff, rocks, white water, and open sea are spectacular. The road then follows the coast through the seaside communities of Montara, Moss Beach, El Granada, Princeton, and Half Moon Bay.

Stop at Princeton, a small commercial fishing port, to watch fishermen selling their catch right off the boat. Small markets and souvenir shops also operate on the pier. Birders can hop a boat for a trip to the offshore Farallon Islands to visit gulls and pelicans in their offshore rookeries. The fish markets specialize in unusual specialties such as sea urchin.

Continue to Half Moon Bay, at the junction of State Highways 1 and 92, another old fishing port now better known as an agricultural center (and mushrooming residential area for those willing to tackle the daily commute over Devil's Slide or the Santa Cruz Mountains). The main cash crop is flowers, fields of them stretching between the sea and the foothills. Crop Number 2 is pumpkins. The event of the year is the Pumpkin Festival when Halloweeners by the thousands pour into town to pick their own jack-o'-lanterns and sample pumpkin wine. Turn east on State Highway 92 to return to I-280.

of the 1930s and 1940s. Catch up with (or see again) the old Cary Grant comedies or Bacall teaching Bogie how to whistle. Admission is $5, $4 for those over 65. You'll find the theater at 221 University Avenue, Palo Alto. Call 415-324-3700.

Stanford University

Even its archrivals across the bay in Berkeley acknowledge that Stanford is one of the premier educational institutions in the world. Home of twenty Nobel Prize winners and counting, it has gained an international reputation in scientifc and medical research, psychology, economics, education, law, business, and on and on. Oh, yes, while amassing this record it also gave birth to Silicon Valley, bastion of the computer industry.

The university was founded by railroad magnate Leland Stanford and his wife, Jane Lathrop Stanford, in memory of their only son, Leland Jr., who died tragically of typhoid fever on a European trip at age sixteen. (Hence the official name is Leland Stanford Junior University.) The family's 10,000-acre farm became the campus. Laid out by Frederick Law Olmsted, who designed Central Park, it is surprisingly compact, architecturally unified around the original concept of buff sandstone buildings with red tile roofs, and the campus center has been rigidly kept free of automobiles (but watch out for bicycle traffic between classes, which can resemble the running of the Tour de France.) Much of the original farm has been left as open space; other property has been leased for the Stanford Shopping Center and Silicon Valley headquarters which provide a buffer around the campus proper. Student-guided tours of the campus begin from the visitor information kiosk at the campus's main entrance on Palm Drive daily at 11:00 A.M. and 3:15 P.M. Campus maps and leaflets are also available.

Hoover Tower, named for the former president who was a Stanford alumnus, is the campus's 285-foot-high landmark. A fourteenth-floor observation platform allows sweeping views all across the campus and up and down the Peninsula. The building and an adjoining low-rise house the Hoover Institution and its treasure trove of priceless documents related to war, revolution, and peace, begun by Hoover after World War I. (It owns an original copy of *Pravda,* the Communist party newspaper, and other materials related to the Russian Revolution of 1917.) An exhibit of materials from the collection and its history is on display in the lobby. The building is open daily 10:00 A.M. to 5:00 P.M.; the observation platform is open 10:00 A.M. to 4:30 P.M.

The **Memorial Church,** dedicated by Mrs. Stanford to her husband after his death, was damaged in the 1989 earthquake and reopened only in late 1992. (It had also been damaged in the famous 1906 earthquake, which toppled a steeple that was never replaced.) Its luminescent frescoes on the main façade were fortunately spared. The interior reminds one of a European cathedral, with sunlight filtering through stained glass, a massive altar, and dark wooden pews. It is a favorite place for campus weddings.

The **Art Museum,** housing Mrs. Stanford's collections and other works, also was closed for repairs after the 1989 earthquake; it is to be reopened in 1994. Most of the paintings, however, are temporarily exhibited in the art gallery adjoining Hoover Tower. The Rodin Sculpture Garden, with many sculptures by the famous creator of *The Thinker,* adjoins the museum and continues to be open to visitors. Docents conduct tours both of the garden and the art gallery.

Restaurants —————————————————————

The Peninsula boasts so many fine restaurants you might think residents did nothing but eat. The selection ranges through ethnic cuisine of every stripe to eat-with-your-fingers ribs joints to classic continental with candlelight to California cuisine at its trendiest. Following are a few selections. A fuller list is available from San Mateo County Convention and Visitors Bureau, 111 Anza Boulevard, Suite 410, Burlingame, California 94010. For sure, no one goes away from the Peninsula hungry.

- The **Oasis** has been the student hangout since time immemorial. Generations of Stanfordites have gathered here to carve their names in the tables, throw peanut shells on the floor, and sing "Come Join the Band," the Stanford anthem. The menu runs to hamburgers, beer, and boisterousness. Inexpensive. 241 El Camino Real, Menlo Park. 415-326-8896.

- **Kincaid's Bayhouse**, near the San Francisco International Airport, poses a difficult choice: "catch of the day" seafood or select beef. Enjoy the great view of the bay through floor-to-ceiling windows. Moderate to expensive. 60 Bayview Place, Burlingame. 415-342-9844.

- The **Shore Bird** appears to have been transplanted from Cape Cod, but the view of Pillar Point Harbor is pure Pacific. Fresh seafood, naturally, is the specialty. Moderate to expensive. 390 Capistrano Road, Princeton. 415-728-5541.

- **China Lion** is one of a number of small Peninsula Chinese restaurants favored by the Chinese-American community and other locals—and one of the best. Mandarin and Szechuan cuisine are the specialties. 3345 El Camino Real, Palo Alto. 415-424-8168. **Chef Chu's** is operated by the same family. 1067 N. San Antonio Road at El Camino, Los Altos. 415-948-2696.

- **Maddalena's** features continental French and Italian cuisine in a candlelight restaurant and adjoining cafe-bar with pianist and chanteuse. Dining in the restaurant is expensive; light dishes in the cafe-bar are budget priced. 544 Emerson, Palo Alto. 415-326-6082.

- **Frankie, Johnny and Luigi Too** claims to serve the best hand-tossed New York-style pizza anywhere—at least, anywhere west of Mulberry Street. Go and evaluate for yourself. Anyway, how can you resist the name? Inexpensive. 919 West El Camino Real, Mountain View. 415-967-5384.

- **Castaway** features a weekend brunch that would stagger Henry VIII. Perched amid eucalyptus groves on a hilltop in Coyote Point Park, it offers great views of the bay. Moderate to expensive. 1631 Coyote Point Drive, San Mateo. 415-347-1027.

Lodging ————————————————————————

Motels and full-service hotels, many of them national chains, are more common than inns and B&Bs on the Peninsula although there are plenty of both. The former tend to cluster around the San Francisco Airport and along U.S. 101. Inns and B&Bs are found in residential neighborhoods and in the coastside communities.

- **Old Thyme Inn** is a restored Queen Anne Victorian with individually decorated rooms, two of which have whirlpool baths. The name isn't a pun. It's named for a carefully tended herb garden. Expensive. 799 Main Street, Half Moon Bay. 415-726-1616.

- **San Benito House**, is an old inn within walking distance of the ocean. It is decorated with European antiques. Moderate. 356 Main Street, Half Moon Bay. 415-726-3425.

- **Cowper Inn** is a restored old Victorian a short distance from Stanford and the Palo Alto shopping district. Moderate. 705 Cowper Street, Palo Alto. 415-327-4475.

- **Hyatt Rickey's** traditionally was the home-away-from-home for Stanford visiting families, but is now upgraded to a full-service hotel. It is large and sprawling but comfortable. Moderate to expensive. 4219 El Camino Real, Palo Alto. 415-493-8000.

- **Days Inn** is near the airport and offers special rates for seniors who are members of its September Days Club. It is comfortable. Moderate. 777 Airport Boulevard, Burlingame. 415-342-7772.

- **Best Western Sundial Motel** is in the heart of everything. Inexpensive to moderate. 316 El Camino Real, Redwood City. 415-366-3808.

- **Holiday Inn Belmont** is one of a number of Holiday Inns in the airport-Peninsula area. It caters to commercial travelers. Moderate. 1101 Shoreway Road, Belmont. 415-591-1417.

Chapter 4

Silicon Valley and All That

Exactly where Silicon Valley begins and ends is a matter of disagreement. It grew up on the fringes of the Stanford campus (actually on open land that was part of the original Stanford farm) and has been relentlessly moving southward since, chewing up the cherry and apricot orchards that once flourished through the then-named Santa Clara Valley. Laptop computers and laser printers are turned out from Palo Alto to San Jose and points in between. But there's more to this area than chips and semiconductors. High tech is here, but so is some surprising low tech. An example for sippers and sniffers: Santa Clara County is home to more than fifty wineries, putting it right up there with the Napa Valley.

San Jose

San Jose (slurred into "Sanazzay" by the locals) is the eleventh largest city in the United States. Surprised? So are some northern Californians, who still tend to think of the place as an overgrown crossroads surrounded by prune orchards. In fact, San Jose has not only advanced to the unofficial capital of Silicon Valley and a sprawling metropolis, but also its downtown has been spruced up into a major business-visitor destination, featuring a convention center, a performing arts center, major hotels, shopping centers, and a showpiece light-rail transit line. At the same time, San Jose has retained some of the offbeat charm of its agricultural past while developing a necklace of ethnic settlements that have added a spice of Vietnamese, Cambodian, Filipino, and Eastern European to the old Hispanic and Anglo flavor.

San Jose was actually a farm town from the start. Soldiers under Spanish explorer Gaspar de Portola discovered the fertile Santa Clara Valley in 1769, and El Pueblo de San Jose de Guadalupe was officially established in 1777, as an agricultural community to raise crops and cattle for the garrisons at the presidios of Monterey and San Francisco. The original colony numbered sixty-six men, women, and children and earned the distinction of being the first Spanish colony with families. Prior to that time, only the Franciscan clergy under Father Junipero Serra had accompanied the Spanish military.

The **San Jose Historical Museum** in Kelley Park is a good place to start a visit because it provides a benchmark for San Jose as it used to be and where it is today. Here the San Jose of 1900 has been faithfully reproduced around a central plaza, with a print shop, a bandstand, an ice cream fountain, a doctor's office, a firehouse and a post office, dominated by a 115-foot early electric-light tower. You can walk through the Umbarger House, a meticulously restored Victorian home that looks like the family has just gone down the street to the ice cream social and will be back any minute, or visit the appropriately named Dashaway Stables with its blacksmith shop and collection of antique carriages and buggies. The Bank of Italy, forerunner of the Bank of America, demonstrates what deposits and withdrawals were like in 1910. The community's development from Native-American days to the present is traced in the Pacific Hotel. The museum is open Monday to Friday 10:00 A.M. to 4:30 P.M., Saturday and Sunday 12:00 P.M. to 4:30 P.M. Admission is $2, $1.50 for seniors. It is located at 1600 Senter Road. Call 408-287-2290.

The **Japanese Friendship Gardens,** also in Kelley Park, highlight San Jose's multicultural character. Okayama, Japan, one of San Jose's four sister cities, worked with San Jose to design the gardens, making generous donations for cultivation and landscaping. Winding paths around pools, over tiny knolls, and across arched footbridges lead to a peaceful Japanese teahouse where you can sip tea (or soft drinks) and watch the brightly colored Koi (carp) idling in the pools.

The **Tech Museum of Innovation** is Silicon Valley's latest jewel. Opened only in 1990, the new museum answers every question you ever had about the high-tech world, from robotics to microchips, and many you haven't thought of. It's an interactive museum where a robot will draw your picture or play games with you, or you can guide your simulated spaceship over the surface of Mars looking for clues to life. A spectacular biotechnology exhibit unlocks the mysteries of DNA, explaining not only its role in all life but also how it can be used to eliminate disease or develop better-tasting tomatoes. An intriguing exhibit demonstrates the blending of high tech and low tech, showing how Space Age technological breakthroughs have redesigned the bicycle. There's even a computer-aided design station, where you can fashion your own wheels. And, though it sounds like an oxymoron, a giant microchip shows you how silicon makes possible many of the everyday products we all take for granted. In the hands-on laboratory, you can even make your own superconducting wafer. The museum, temporarily housed in a building affectionately known as "the garage," (after the garage where Steve Jobs and Stephen Wozniak launched Apple Computer and the personal-computer business) is to be moved in the mid-1990s to a new building. The museum is open Tuesday to Sunday 10:00 A.M. to 5:00 P.M. Admission is $6, $4 for those over 65. It is located at 145 West San Carlos Street. Call 408-279-7150.

The **Rosicrucian Museum** is at the other end of the time scale. Inspired by the Temple of Amon, at Karnak, Egypt, the museum houses the largest collection of artifacts from ancient Egypt in the western United States. Many of the items date back more than 6,000 years, including human and animal mummies, funerary boats, precious jewelry, and ancient pottery. There's a detailed model of King Zoser's Step Pyramid built in the Third Egyptian Dynasty. You can walk through a full-scale replica of a noble's stonecut tomb adorned with images of daily life in the Nile Valley. In the surrounding Rosicrucian Park you'll find an obelisk, a sphinx, and early statuary. There is also an affiliated planetarium and science center. The museum is open daily 9:00 A.M. to 5:00 P.M. Admission is $4. The planetarium shows are $3. It is located at 1342 Naglee Avenue. Call 408-287-9171.

Quilts and coverlets are an art form that goes back centuries. In the **American Museum of Quilts and Textiles** colorful examples from nineteenth- and twentieth-century America are on display. Docents explain not only the needlework but also the lives of the makers and the cultural traditions associated with quilt making. Exhibits change regularly. The museum is open Tuesday to Saturday 10:00 A.M. to 4:00 P.M. The suggested donation is $2. It is located at 766 South Second Street. Call 408-971-0323.

How to characterize the **Winchester Mystery House**? Weird? Zany? Supernatural? Bizarre? This 160-room Victorian-era mansion, bedecked with turrets and cupolas and furbelows, is all of the above. Built by the heiress to the Winchester rifle fortune, Sarah Winchester, a woman with millions of dollars and an equal number of superstitions, the house was under construction for thirty-eight years. Many of its features can only be explained by the wealthy widow's obsession with the occult. Staircases end abruptly at the ceiling, a window is built into the floor. A brick chimney has no outlet. Doors open onto blank walls. And Mrs. Winchester was in thrall to the number thirteen: there are thirteen cement blocks in the carriage entrance hall, thirteen blue and amber stones in a spider-glass window, thirteen windows and doors in the old sewing room, thirteen lights in the chandeliers—and those are only a few examples.

The heiress kept the carpenters at work around the clock, apparently convinced by a medium that continuous building would appease the evil spirits of people killed by "The Gun That Won the West," the basis of her $20-million nest egg. While they were at it, they constructed a home that was a marvel for its time, with modern heating and sewer systems, gas lights that operated at the touch of a button, and three working elevators. Hand-inlaid parquet floors combine with gold and silver chandeliers and Tiffany glass windows.

Regular guided tours cover 110 of the mansion's 160 rooms. A self-guided tour covers the six acres of elaborate plantings, which kept busy a full-time staff of eight gardeners. Mrs. Winchester brought in plants from all over the world and interspersed them with statues from mythology and Indian lore. Not surprisingly, the driveway leading to the front entrance is lined with exactly thirteen California fan palms.

Since the family fortune was based on guns, the tour also includes an **American Firearms Museum,** featuring the Winchester 1873 but also including B. Tyler Henry's 1860 repeating rifle that Oliver Winchester adapted into the Winchester 1866 and then "The Gun That Won the West." Also on display are custom-made rifles carried by Teddy Roosevelt and John Wayne. The adjoining **Winchester Antique Products Museum** reflects another little-known chapter of industrial history with contemporary overtones. When World War I ended, Winchester converted its military production facilities to civilian needs, just as the defense industry is being asked to do in the 1990s. At one time 6,300 hardware stores carried Winchester-made products, including cutlery, flashlights, wagons, lawn mowers, roller skates, and garden tools. The museum is open daily. Admission to the house, gardens, and museums is $12.50, $9.50 for seniors. It is located at 525 South Winchester Boulevard, San Jose. Call 408-247-2101.

San Jose's new light-rail system, connecting the Almaden Valley in south San Jose with the Great America theme park in Santa Clara, is ultramodern. Downtown, however, it's strictly nostalgic with five refurbished trolleys dating back to the early 1900s circling at twenty-minute intervals around the shops, restaurants, convention center, and other attractions. Lovingly restored to their original reds, greens, and golds with lustrous polished mahogany interiors, the cars are open to the air with wide platforms for the sightseeing standees. The antique trolleys operate weekdays 9:00 A.M. to 3:30 P.M. and weekends and holidays 11:00 A.M. to 6:00 P.M. Adult fare is 25¢, 10¢ for seniors.

Overfelt Botanical Gardens contain another gift from a San Jose sister city. In this case the donor is the city of Tainen, Taiwan, and the gift is the Chinese cultural garden. A massive, ornate gate stands at the entrance to the garden, and paths lead to a statue of Confucius set by a reflecting pool. Best views are from two pavilions on either side of the statue. Much of the remainder of the thirty-seven acres has been left in a natural state as a wildlife sanctuary; it's an excellent place to watch migratory waterfowl.

Lick Observatory at Mount Hamilton, twenty-five miles south of San Jose, is an astronomical research station operated by the University of California-Santa Cruz. It's reachable by a narrow, winding mountain road up the 4,209-foot summit; campers and trailers are not advised. Guides explain and demonstrate the observatory's 120-inch telescope, once one of the major stargazing instruments of the world; tours also cover the main building. Night viewing programs are intermittently offered during the summer. Admission is free. The observatory is on Mount Hamilton Road, Mount Hamilton. Call 408-274-5062.

Santa Clara and Vicinity

The **Ames Research Center** of the National Aeronautics and Space Administration (NASA) has played a prominent role in the history of flight and in human exploration of space. Much pioneering work in aeronautics has been conducted here; it is the center for the life-sciences experiments conducted aboard the space shuttle. The center touches all aspects of experimental aeronautics and space travel, from computation to flight.

A two-hour, two-mile walking tour, led by trained guides knowledgeable in aeronautics and space technology, covers much of the facility. It begins with a half-hour orientation followed by an exterior view of the center's huge wind tunnels used for testing aerodynamics, a visit to an aircraft hangar to inspect research aircraft, and a demonstration of a flight simulator. The trained guide also explains experimental aircraft

SCENIC DETOUR: WINERIES

Wine growing in the Santa Clara Valley literally traces its roots back to the 1770s when the Franciscan fathers planted grapes for sacramental wines at the Santa Clara Mission. Commercial wine making began in the mid-1800s; several century-old wineries still operate today. The Santa Clara Valley Wine Growers Association furnishes a free listing and map showing winery locations and information on tastings and tours; on the first Saturday in May, the association holds a wine festival for all member wineries at Hecker Pass Winery near Gilroy. For information write Santa Clara Valley Wine Growers Association, P.O. Box 1192, Morgan Hill, California 95037. Call 408-779-2145.

Mirassou Vineyards is operated by America's oldest winemaking family, Pelliers, who established the winery in 1854 with cuttings brought from France. The fifth generation now operates the winery, one of the largest in Santa Clara Valley, which is noted for its white wines in the French tradition. Tastings are offered daily 10:00 A.M. to 5:00 P.M. 3000 Aborn Road, San Jose. Call 408-274-4000.

Mirassou Champagne Cellars makes sparkling wine in the century-old caves of the former Novitiate Winery. The cellars are near Los Gatos's Old Town. 300 College Avenue, Los Gatos. 408-395-3790.

Byington Winery, one of the newest and most acclaimed wineries in the valley, operates from an Italian-style chateau tucked into designs and methods used for studying the atmosphere and observing the planet from the air.

A self-guided tour also is available at the visitor center where continuous videos describe the latest developments in space research and Ames's role in them. A gallery of photographs shows views of the earth from space. Outside the center, visitors can explore a one-third size model of the space shuttle, a "retired" U-2 high-altitude spy plane, a Titan 1 rocket, and an oblique-wing aircraft.

Tours are conducted Monday, Wednesday, and Friday 9:30 A.M. and 1:30 P.M. in groups of twenty persons or more. Reservations are necessary and should be requested several weeks in advance. The visitor

---

the Santa Cruz Mountains. Although the winery is new, the eighty-two-acre vineyard is one of the valley's oldest grape-growing areas. The winery is known for excellent chardonnays. A pleasant picnic area is equipped with barbecues. Tastings are offered daily, 10:00 A.M. to 5:00 P.M. 21850 Bear Creek Road, Los Gatos. 408-354-1111.

Pedrizzetti Winery, family owned and operated, began with Barbera cuttings brought from Italy in 1913 and still specializes in that brambly red. It also makes fruit and dessert wines. Tastings are offered daily, 10:00 A.M. to 6:00 P.M. 1645 San Pedro Avenue, Morgan Hill. 408-779-7389.

Congress Springs Vineyards is nestled among the redwoods in the Santa Cruz Mountains above Saratoga. The hundred-year-old winery, revived in 1976, is built around hundreds of old oak barrels and casks; its estate vineyard goes back eighty years. Tastings are offered daily, 11:00 A.M. to 5:00 P.M. 23600 Congress Springs Road, Saratoga. 408-741-2930.

Hecker Pass Winery offers tasting in a rustic lounge with a twenty-foot redwood bar overlooking the vineyards and picnic area. Established by the Italian Fortino wine-making family, Hecker Pass specializes in premium varietal and dessert wines. Tastings are offered daily, 10:00 A.M. to 6:00 P.M. 4605 Hecker Pass Highway, Gilroy. 408-842-8755.

center is open daily 8:00 A.M. to 4:30 P.M. Admission to both guided and self-guided tours is free. You'll find the center at Moffett Field, Mountain View, ten miles north of Santa Clara on U.S.101. Call 408-604-6497.

The **University of Santa Clara** is the oldest private university in California, founded in 1867 by the Jesuit order. It is still one of the premier religious institutions of higher education in the U.S., especially in the fields of law and engineering .

The **Mission Santa Clara de Asis** on the campus was founded in 1777. The present building is an enlarged replica of the third mission built in 1825. A self-guided tour of the mission, the eighth in the series of twenty-one California missions, is available through the mission office. Call 408-544-4023.

De Saisset Museum on the campus was established in 1955 and houses many notable paintings by California artists. It also includes artifacts from the precolonial residents of the area, the Ohlone Indians, and relics from the early mission and colonial days. Revolving exhibits display African, American, European, and Oriental art. Call 408-544-4528.

Saratoga

Tucked in the hills west of Santa Clara, this suburban community boasts many fine homes and scenic surroundings. State Highway 9 is a particularly scenic drive.

Hakone Gardens is another small formal garden in the Japanese style, donated by a wealthy benefactor and designed in 1917 by a member of the Emperor's garden staff. The gardens are open weekdays 10:00 A.M. to 5:00 P.M., weekends 11:00 A.M. to 5:00 P.M. A donation is suggested. They are located at 2100 Big Basin Way, Saratoga. Call 408-867-3438.

Villa Montalvo once was the summer home of San Francisco mayor and U.S. Senator James D. Phelan. The Mediterranean-style structure is now an arboretum and center for the performing arts. Art exhibits and arts festivals are held throughout the summer and fall; the landscaped gardens boast more than 400 species of plants and 85 species of birds. The villa is open Monday to Friday 8:00 A.M. to

6:00 P.M., Saturday and Sunday 9:00 A.M. to 5:00 P.M.; gallery hours are Thursday and Friday, 1:00 P.M. to 4:00 P.M., and Saturday and Sunday, 11:00 A.M. to 4:00 P.M. Admission is free. It is located on Montalvo Road, off State Highway 9, Saratoga. Call 408-741-3421.

Restaurants

- **Gordon Biersch Brewing Company** makes its own beers and serves them with California-type light cuisine, with an occasional sausage dish thrown in for bierstube purists. Moderate. 33 East San Fernando Street, San Jose. 408-294-6785.

- **Hochburg von Germania** represents one of those ethnic groups large in numbers but little noticed in Silicon Valley. More than a century old, decorated in the best Bavarian style and serving the traditional German specialties like veal shank and jagerschnitzel. Moderate. 261 North Second Street, San Jose. 408-295-4484.

- **Golden Chopsticks,** one of the pricier Vietnamese restaurants that have recently sprung up around San Jose, features "roasted crab" and other Southeast Asian specialties. (Smaller, budget-priced Vietnamese restaurants are found elsewhere in San Jose, especially in so-called "Little Saigon" south of San Jose State University). Moderate. 1765 South Winchester Boulevard, Campbell. 408-370-6610.

- **Henry's World Famous Hi-Life** has been barbecuing ribs and chicken for the locals for more than three decades, to great popularity. It is also known for quality steaks. Moderate. 301 West St. John Street, San Jose. 408-295-5414.

Lodging

- **Days Inn Santa Clara** is the local outpost of the popular chain, with special rates for members of its September Days

Club. Convenient to the Ames NASA Research Center and (for those traveling with grandchildren) the Great America theme park. Moderate. 4200 Great America Parkway, Santa Clara. 408-980-1525.

- **Sundowner Inn** is a comfortable, convenient motel near the northern end of Silicon Valley. Complimentary continental breakfast is served in your room. Moderate. 504 Ross Drive, Sunnyvale. 408-734-9900.

- **La Hacienda Inn** is tucked into the hills near Los Gatos, surrounded by landscaped gardens and decorated in American southwestern style. Complimentary continental breakfast is offered. Expensive. 18840 Saratoga-Los Gatos Road, Los Gatos. 408-354-9230.

- **Hotel DeAnza** is San Jose's grande dame, an Art Deco historical landmark completely redone as part of the San Jose downtown restoration. It is walking distance from the shops and cultural center. The hallmark is personal service, down to the chocolate on the pillow, the turned-down beds, and the terrycloth robes. Expensive. 233 West Santa Clara Street, San Jose. 408-286-1000.

- **Budget Inn** is simple, no-nonsense and comfortable. It is located in the area south of San Jose, near the Mirassou Winery. Inexpensive. 2460 Fontaine Road, San Jose. 408-270-7666.

Chapter 5
Santa Cruz

Locals call Santa Cruz the "first surfing town." Those not looking for the giant wave praise its beautiful and isolated setting between the breakers of Monterey Bay and the Santa Cruz Mountains. Regardless of how you look at it, the atmosphere and the location make the small beachside community an exciting place to visit for both the young and the nostalgic. Here surfers paddle next to seals, the funky old boardwalk and amusement park are a few steps from the beach, and ex-hippies go to school when they are not producing ceramics and tie-dyed T-shirts. Clustered along the coast are tiny resort towns and agricultural communities, each with its distinctive personality. The combination spawns an equally entertaining mixture of attractions from vineyards where you can sample local award-winning wines to the Mystery Spot where you seem to defy gravity. Santa Cruz's intense and youthful energy will wake up the most reserved and invigorate the energetic.

Nature purists and relaxation-seeking vacationers, do not despair. Santa Cruz is surrounded by state parks dedicated to preserving the abundance of seaside and beautiful wilderness. The Santa Cruz area also offers a host of museums, a beautiful flower garden, and an aquarium/research facility where you can experience the region through its history and wildlife.

The **Santa Cruz Beach-Boardwalk** is the epicenter of the rocking Santa Cruz lifestyle—the real epicenter of the 1989 Loma Prieta quake that shook the whole San Francisco Bay Area and interrupted the World

Series was located in the Santa Cruz Mountains, just east of the town. Here, beach meets amusement park. This is not an average beach but a clean, golden sand beach that stretches for a mile along the northern-most perimeter of Monterey Bay. And not an average amusement park, but a park that has been entertaining visitors for more than eighty-five years, has survived several earthquakes, and offers more than twenty-five rides.

Amusement parks are an endangered species these days so Santa Cruz is a time warp back to olden times. It's pure entertainment, whether you watch shrieking adolescents as they roar around on the Giant Dipper, swing above the calliopes and carousels on the Sky Glider, or simply stroll along and smell the caramel popcorn. Buzzers, flashing lights, cotton candy, penny-pitch games, and bumper cars—everything but a kissing booth—line the boardwalk.

The immense wooden frame that immediately grabs your attention at the east end of the park is the Giant Dipper, a roller coaster built in 1924. The Giant Dipper still dives down steep plunges and zooms around curves and thrills riders just as it did more than sixty-five years ago. It still rates among the ten best roller coaster rides in the world. Even if you choose not to ride it, admire it. The track structure was an awesome architectural feat for the 1920s and contributed substantially to the engineering history of the U.S.

For an aerial view of the park, take the 1,000-foot-long Sky Glider. Suspended from cables like a ski lift, the Sky Glider gives you a bird's-eye view of the boardwalk, a good way to survey the scene without being caught in the youthful mayhem on the ground. Admission is free but you have to buy tickets for the rides at one of the special ticket booths along the Boardwalk.

The Santa Cruz Beach is for sun lovers and people watchers. Hop off the Boardwalk and onto the beach where California bathing beauties park on the sand and soak up the rays, prance at the edge of the cold water, or jump around on the volleyball courts. Join them for an afternoon and bring your suntan lotion, but remember that, like much of California's coast, Santa Cruz can be cool, and the sea breeze some-times drops the temperatures. Bring a light jacket just in case.

Monterey Bay views and seafood attract the visitor onto the **Santa Cruz Municipal Wharf**. Here, fishermen lean their poles over the edges, occasionally pulling in a rock cod or perch but more often bask-ing, reading, or gazing across the bay at the fishing boats, parasailers, and sunbathers. Fish markets and seafood restaurants along the wharf offer the catch of the day. Calamari (squid) in all its forms is a specialty. You can drive out onto the wharf almost to the restaurant door and park your car in one of the metered stalls (if you can find a vacant one). After lunch, walk to the end of the wharf and peer over the edge to watch the harbor seals and sea lions playing aquatic games for the tourists.

The **McPherson Center for Art and History** opened in January 1993 to reveal the artistic side of Santa Cruz life and its background history. Rotating displays of art range from regional exhibits featuring Bay Area and Monterey area artists to traveling shows with art from all over the world. You can also see special design demonstrations that showcase artistic and functional products like kite designs, combining aerodynamics and aesthetics. Open daily. 408-429-1964.

The history section outlines the area's chronology from the Native Americans in the region to the Spanish explorers to present-day Santa Cruz life. Artifacts from each era give dimension to the history. You can study a model of the Powder Works, the region's only producer of blasting powder, which supplied the railroad construction in the late 1800s, or send a telegram in a recreated Wells Fargo office. Check out the fifteen- to twenty-minute film made up of spliced-together home movies including old footage of the boardwalk. Admission runs under $4. Call 408-429-1964.

For those who like a natural history overview to orient themselves in unfamiliar territory, Santa Cruz offers the **Santa Cruz City Museum.** In this small museum, you can see baskets, seashell necklaces, and bone knives used by the original inhabitants of the coast, the Ohlone Indians, or examine a fossilized tooth of a Colombian mammoth who roamed the region some 100,000 years ago. The museum includes displays about the current regional wildlife. Museum hours are Tuesday to Saturday 10:00 A.M. to 5:00 P.M., Sunday noon to 5:00 P.M. Admission is free although a $1 donation is requested. The museum is located at 1305 East Cliff Drive. Call 408-429-3773.

Many of the region's most alluring attractions lie on the outskirts of Santa Cruz or in the surrounding seaside towns, including Aptos, Capitola, Soquel, and Watsonville. Approximate times from downtown Santa Cruz are given, but unfortunately no natural link or route can be easily identified. However, driving from one site to the next is not difficult with the help of a map.

Flower lovers should not miss the **Antonelli Begonia Gardens** located near the border of Santa Cruz and Capitola. Rows and rows of colorful flowers fill the tables and the planters of this nursery. The fresh,

SCENIC DETOUR

West Cliff Drive runs west of the wharf and winds above the rocky shore around the Santa Cruz residential area, right along the coast. Roller bladers, bikers, casual walkers, and surfers clad in wet suits and carrying boards crowd the sidewalk overlooking the beach and the ocean. A fifteen- to twenty-minute drive will take you around the most scenic Santa Cruz coastline to the Long Marine Laboratory and Aquarium at the Santa Cruz city limits .

Lighthouse Point on West Cliff Drive offers ocean views with added attractions. You get a sweeping panorama of Monterey Bay, seals snoozing on Seal Rock, and surfers riding the large waves of the infamous Steamer's Lane. The lighthouse is home to the **Santa Cruz Surfing Museum,** a one-room exhibit stuffed with early redwood surfboards, some more than ten feet long and one complete with a shark bite. The photo gallery features early surfers in full-length wool bathing suits, the precursor to the wet suit. Surf videos run continuously. It is a good place for a quick dip into California surfing history. Museum hours vary. It is located on 1305 East Cliff Drive. Call 408-429-3429.

Natural Bridges State Beach, located where West Cliff Drive turns away from the coast, is home to the largest colony of monarch butterflies in the U.S., outdoing the population across the bay at Pacific Grove. The Monarch Trail takes you for a short one and one half-mile loop through clouds of fluttering orange monarchs who gather there for a winter sojourn, September through March. A wooden boardwalk protects your feet from the trail's rough and rocky terrain as you dodge the graceful insects.

sweet perfume from the blossoms almost overwhelms your olfactory system. Be sure to catch the internationally famous begonia displays. Begonia season peaks in August and September. The garden is located at 2545 Capitola Road, about fifteen minutes from downtown Santa Cruz. Keep an eye out for the understated wooden sign, which is easy to miss. The gardens are open daily 9:00 A.M. to 5:00 P.M. Call 408-475-5222.

The **Mystery Spot** seems to defy those basic natural laws we all learned in grade-school science. Here, you find yourself appearing to

For those who like to get right down into seaside ecology, walk out on the beach and around the park's remarkable number of tide pools. Here you can pick up and examine starfish, close sea anemones (by lightly sticking your finger into them), and watch little crabs scamper into the water. It's a fine place for a picnic combined with a nature walk. Park admission is $6 per car, $5 for seniors.

The **Long Marine Laboratory and Aquarium** on the western edge of Santa Cruz consists of a small exhibit room displaying marine life and a large research facility. The aquarium holds sixteen tanks, including an up-close view of large sea anemones and an open, waist-high tank inhabited by a mean, big-toothed ling cod accompanied by a sea bass. Keep your fingers out of the water. The aquarium also displays a model of the Monterey Bay submarine canyon, fossils, and marine skeletons including one of a blue whale.

The research facility, affiliated with the University of California at Santa Cruz, studies marine mammal biology—sea lion cognition and pinniped (seals, walruses, and sea lions) diving physiology. Docents conduct interesting and informative tours around the facility every fifteen to thirty minutes and explain the research in progress. They will be happy to show you the sea lion rescue tank where students train orphaned sea lions to survive in the open ocean as well as explain what pinniped diving physiology actually is and how you research it. Hours are Tuesday to Sunday 1:00 P.M. to 4:00 P.M. Admission and tours are free. The research facility is located near Natural Bridges State Park off Delaware Avenue. Call 408-459-4308.

lean at precarious angles while balls seem to be rolling uphill. Guides perform demonstrations and offer possible explanations during a thirty-five-minute walking tour. The site is open daily 9:30 A.M. to 5:00 P.M. Admission and tours cost $3 for adults. It is located about ten minutes northeast of downtown Santa Cruz at 1953 Branciforte Drive. Call 408-423-8897.

To learn about one of the original industries in the Santa Cruz mountains, go to **Roaring Camp & Big Trees Narrow-Gauge Railroad,** a recreated 1880s logging town nestled into the Santa Cruz Mountains. The town includes a covered bridge, an old-time general store, and an old-fashioned lithography shop. Country and western music and a chuckwagon barbecue complete the frontier scene. From here, you can take the historic narrow-gauge steam train through the redwood forest to the summit of Bear Mountain or take another route on a standard-gauge diesel that will carry you down to the Santa Cruz Beach boardwalk past spectacular vistas of the San Lorenzo River. Trains to Bear Mountain travel four times a day (five times on weekends and holidays); the boardwalk train departs on weekends twice a day, morning and early afternoon, with return trips around noon and 5:00 P.M. Train rides are under $14. Admission to Roaring Camp is $3 for parking. The depot is located twenty minutes north of downtown Santa Cruz on Graham Hill Road and Roaring Camp Road in Felton. Call 408-335-4484 or 335-4400 for specific trip times and other information.

Sequoia sempervirens redwoods, among the tallest trees in the world, reach for the sky in the **Henry Cowell Redwoods State Park,** adjoining Roaring Camp. This is one of the southernmost stands of redwoods, which grow in a very limited area of the California Coast Range. Expect to develop a stiff neck as you walk through the deep shade of the redwood groves with your head tilted back trying to find the tops of these mammoth trees. Do not miss the redwood circle known as the "cathedral," a popular wedding location. This park is full of short hikes and picnic grounds, good for an afternoon getaway in the woods. Day use costs $5 per car. It is located off Graham Hill Road on State Highway 9 in Felton. Call 408-335-9145.

There are seals and seals, but the biggest of all hang out at **Año Nuevo State Reserve,** on the coast north of Santa Cruz on State Highway 1 (actually across the line in San Mateo County). Elephant seals can weigh in at three tons and measure sixteen feet in length—a snug fit in the average living room. At one time Año Nuevo's herd was down to seventeen seals; now, thanks to protective measures, there are 740 of the monsters and counting. A bull elephant seal can sire fifty pups in a single year. You have to walk into the park and view them from a respectable distance, which is just as well, since you wouldn't want one to step on your foot. The males can be quite belligerent, especially during the mating season. Males fight loud and vicious battles to protect their harems. They don't seem to mind, though, when humans watch their somewhat clumsy and raucous breeding efforts, their main reason for coming ashore. When elephant seal bulls are not in residence, other less cumbersome seals also hang out at this reserve. Visits are by reservation only, although you can drop by the Año Nuevo entrance and hope to replace a no-show. Call 415-879-0227.

Watsonville is berry land, not to mention lettuce, peas, apples, and artichokes. In this rich agricultural area south of Santa Cruz you can pick loganberries, ollallieberries, raspberries, blackberries, boysenberries, blueberries, and especially strawberries, for which the region is particularly noted. Bring your own container or eat as you pick. The largest concentration of you-pick farms is along Route 152 east, or, in season, watch for signs.

Wine-loving travelers often overlook the wines produced in Santa Cruz County. Although the area has been overshadowed by the better-known Sonoma and Napa valleys, many wine enthusiasts cite Santa Cruz County as a premium-quality wine-producing region. Santa Cruz has approximately two dozen **family-owned wineries.** According to locals, the small size of these operations allows the wine makers the opportunity to handcraft each of their wines at every vintage. The predominant varieties grown in the area today are chardonnay, cabernet sauvignon, and pinot noir.

Bargetto Winery has been producing award-winning wines since 1933. It is one of the oldest wineries in the county. Although best known for its traditional wines, the winery also produces a line of unique fruit wines—raspberry, ollallieberry, apricot—made from fresh fruit, and mead, which is made with honey. Free wine tasting is offered in a courtyard right along Soquel Creek. The winery is open Monday to Saturday 9:00 A.M. to 5:00 P.M., Sunday 11:00 A.M. to 5:00 P.M. It is located at 3535 North Main Street, Soquel. Call 408-475-2258.

Roudon-Smith Winery specializes in Santa Cruz-grown wines, featuring their estate chardonnay. Some picnicking space is available among the redwood trees around the winery. The winery is open Saturday and Sunday 11:00 A.M. to 4:00 P.M. for free wine tasting. It is located at 2364 Bean Creek Road, Santa Cruz. Call 408-438-1244.

Hallcrest Vineyards, in Felton, offers free tasting daily 11:00 A.M. to 5:30 P.M. and tours of the winery by appointment. Its picnic area overlooks the vineyard and surrounding Henry Cowell State Park. The winery is located at 379 Felton Empire Road, Felton. Call 408-335-4441.

Storrs Winery creates handcrafted wines from the Santa Cruz Mountains, using traditional Burgundian methods to producing barrel-fermented chardonnays. In addition they produce limited quantities of Santa Cruz Mountain white riesling and zinfandel. Tasting is daily, 12:00 P.M. to 5:00 P.M. Old Sash Mill, 303 Potrero Street #35, Santa Cruz. Call 408-458-5030.

Restaurants

Santa Cruz area restaurants counterbalance its way of life. The region boasts many good restaurants with a variety of atmospheres ranging from the classic diner to the ultimate in romantic ambience. Extravagantly wild food or restaurants are not the norm; instead the people of Santa Cruz seem to prefer the basic and traditional, possibly as a break from their hectic youthful life. However, you can find the new-generation influence, especially in restaurants specializing in vegetarian dishes.

• At **Aldo's Harbor Restaurant,** the main dining room is the back deck overlooking the Santa Cruz Harbor entrance

SCENIC DETOUR

Big Basin Redwood State Park lies hidden deep in the Santa Cruz Mountains. In reaction to the ever-growing logging industry around the turn of the century, some of California's first environmentalists fought to protect this area which was dedicated in 1902 as California's first state park. You can wander through the redwood trees on the short half-mile round trip redwood trail. Some of the redwoods date back more than 2,000 years. The drive in (from either the north or the south side) winds through dense forest on a very scenic but narrow road. Old Cadillacs and motor homes are not suggested. Day use is free. The park lies about forty-five minutes from Santa Cruz at 21600 Big Basin Highway in Boulder Creek.

(indoor dining is available). The coastal Italian cuisine features fresh fish, homemade bread, and homemade pasta—the ultimate in exquisite dining at moderate prices. They won't take credit cards or make reservations. 616 Atlantic Avenue, Santa Cruz. 408-426-3736.

- The **Pontiac Grill** offers a 1950s dinerlike atmosphere, complete with a jukebox playing old-time favorites such as Chuck Berry's "Maybelline" and the Drifters' "Please Stay." The grill features hamburgers and more hamburgers, offering a wide range of patties from Firebird Burger, grilled ground turkey, to the Pontiac Burger, a half-pound of charbroiled beef. Moderate. 429 Front Street, Santa Cruz. 408-427-2290.

- For an ocean view and elegant dining right along the boardwalk, go to **Casablanca Restaurant.** This award-winning restaurant boasts a large wine list and cooks continental cuisine with a California twist. Reservations are suggested. Expensive. 101 Main Street, Santa Cruz. 408-426-9063.

- Out on the Municipal Wharf, **Sea Cloud** is a world-renowned gourmet restaurant featuring wild game, meats, fresh fish, and local produce. A wide selection of wines is available. From the dining room you get spectacular views of Monterey Bay. Expensive. Santa Cruz Municipal Wharf. 408-458-9393.

- The **Shadowbrook Restaurant** in Capitola has gained a reputation as the most romantic restaurant in northern California. You ride a cable car to the beautiful forest setting of the restaurant where dancing and outdoor cocktails will romance the most jaded couple. Reservations are suggested. 1750 Wharf Road, Capitola. 408-475-1511.

- **Dharma's Natural Foods Restaurant** claims to be the oldest completely vegetarian restaurant in the U.S. It serves pastas, salads, vegetarian burgers, and Mexican food in large portions. Inexpensive to moderate. 4250 Capitola Road, Capitola. 408-462-1711.

- The **Red Apple Cafe** has the largest breakfast menu in Santa Cruz County and maybe in the whole state. It offers six different eggs benedicts, lunch specials, and homemade soups daily. Inexpensive. 946 Main Street, Watsonville. 408-761-9551.

Lodging

Santa Cruz area lodging ranges from the cozy B&B to the economical Best Western. Many places are conveniently located by the beach or in the mountains, just a quick trip by car to the beach or other sights.

- The **Cliff Crest Bed and Breakfast Inn,** on Beach Hill above the boardwalk, offers a romantic turn-of-the-century atmosphere in a grand 1887 Queen Anne Victorian. It features beautiful gardens and a solarium. Full breakfast and evening wine are included. Moderate to expensive. 407 Cliff Street, Santa Cruz. 408-427-2609.

- The **Darling House** is an elegant oceanside 1910 mansion set among lush gardens and towering palm trees. It offers complimentary gourmet dinners on weekdays off-season. Breakfast is always included. Moderate to expensive in-season, inexpensive to expensive off-season. 314 West Cliff Drive, Santa Cruz. 408-458-1958.

- For up-the-coast accommodations, go to the **New Davenport Bed and Breakfast,** located off State Highway 1 north of Santa Cruz. It serves as a civilized retreat with ocean views, easy access to the beach, whale watching, and elephant seal tours. Inexpensive to expensive in-season, inexpensive to moderate off-season. 31 Davenport Avenue, Davenport. 408-425-1818.

- **Blue Spruce Bed and Breakfast Inn** offers individually decorated rooms in a refurbished home built in 1875. It is located close to local wineries. A country breakfast and afternoon and evening refreshments are included. Moderate to expensive. 2815 South Main Street, Soquel. 408-464-1137.

- The **Mangels House** offers a B&B in a mountain setting. The landmark southern mansion lies among acres of lawn. A full

breakfast, afternoon sherry, and music are provided. 570
Aptos Creek Road, Aptos. 408-688-7982.

• The **Sea and Sand Inn** offers hotel accommodations right in
the beach cliffs overlooking Monterey Bay. You get a
continental breakfast, comfortable rooms, and a view—all
walking distance from the wharf and beach. Expensive
in-season and moderate to expensive off-season. 201 West
Cliff Drive, Santa Cruz. 408-427-3400.

• The **Riverside Garden Inn** is a centrally located
Victorian-style inn. You can walk to the beach or downtown.
It offers complimentary continental breakfast. Inexpensive to
expensive in-season and off-season. 600 Riverside Avenue,
Santa Cruz. 408-458-9660 or 800-527-3833.

• The **Sea Cliff Best Western** is located off State Highway 1
near Aptos and the beach. The restaurant offers continental
cuisine. Moderate to expensive in-season and inexpensive to
expensive off-season. Santa Cruz. 408-688-7300.

• **The Brookdale Lodge** boasts a mountain setting in the heart
of the redwoods. There are many strange but intriguing
aspects of this almost one-hundred-year-old accommodation.
The main banquet room, the Brook Room, has an actual
stream running through it. According to the owner's daughter,
the lodge itself is haunted. She once saw the apparition of the
former owner's daughter (who had drowned in the creek)
walking the halls of the lodge. It must be a friendly ghost as
nothing has ever come of the spirit. Whether or not you
believe in ghosts, you can relax in the outdoor hot tub and
listen for any supernatural activity. Inexpensive to moderate
in- and off-season. 11570 Highway 9, Brookdale.
408-338-6433.

• The **Casablanca Motel** has elegant accommodations with an
ocean view overlooking Monterey Bay and the boardwalk.
Some rooms have fireplaces, private balconies, or shared
terraces. Moderate to expensive in-season and inexpensive to
expensive off-season. 101 Main Street at the corner of Beach
Street, Santa Cruz. 408-423-1570.

Chapter 6
The Monterey Peninsula

Coastal communities seem to be every traveler's favorite. The rocks, the surf, the sands, the smell of the sea, the breezes, the fish, all entrance—hypnotize—visitors of every stripe. The Monterey peninsula has all this and history and culture besides. Note some remarkable contrasts: bustling, commercial Monterey, still with its Spanish colonial and fishing-port patina, alongside quaint, quiet Carmel-by-the-Sea and the funky Victorians of Pacific Grove. No wonder this part of northern California is a favorite getaway destination of northern Californians themselves. A reminder, though, of what locals know but out-of-state visitors sometimes forget. Even when the sun beats down mercilessly inland, the coast may be "under the fog"; the morning shroud may burn off by noon, but ocean breezes can keep the temperatures relatively cool. Bring your shorts and short sleeves if you like, but keep a lightweight jacket and slacks handy.

Monterey

The Monterey peninsula protrudes from the California coastline at the southern edge of Monterey Bay, providing stunning views of the ocean, rich with marine life. Sea otters and seals regularly entertain visitors, frolicking in the surf along the craggy shore or in the Monterey harbor. You can meet the aquatic population at even closer range in the renowned Monterey Aquarium where sharks prowl through fish-filled tanks and schools of sardines dart among a recreated kelp forest. But sea and sea life are only half of the area's attraction. Look into the city itself, one large museum in its own way, full of preserved and restored historic buildings capturing Monterey's important political and commercial past. Visit the place where California statehood officially started: Colton Hall, where delegates met in 1849 to draft the new state's first constitution. Or go shopping in a reconstructed sardine canning plant. You can get the best of Monterey on land, on sea, or under the sea.

Monterey's colonial history dates from 1542 when Don Juan Cabrillo first spotted the Monterey peninsula while cruising California waters in search of territory for Spain. The white sand beaches, the pine forests where Carmel now stands, and the rugged cliffs near what is now Pacific Grove impressed the Spanish explorer, and he claimed the area for the Spanish crown—but from a distance; high seas kept him offshore. Sixty years later, Sebastian Vizcaino, another Spaniard, became the first European to set foot on this piece of land. He called it Monterey after the Conde de Monte Rey, a viceroy of New Spain. Fifty years later, the missionaries and the military arrived. Monterey was successfully colonized.

Monterey quickly emerged as the political center for this section of New Spain. And when Mexico declared its independence from Spain in 1822, Monterey became the first capital of Alta (Higher) California, the Mexican province corresponding roughly to the present state. Then, after twenty-four years of Mexican rule, the peninsula changed flags again. Without firing a shell, U.S. Commodore John Drake Sloat sailed into Monterey harbor in 1846, announced the commencement of the Mexican-American War, and hoisted the Stars and Stripes above the Custom House. Three years later, the constitutional convention met in Colton Hall, and a year after that, in 1850, California was admitted to the Union as the thirty-first state.

The Pacific Ocean brought prosperity to Monterey and shaped its development. The city boomed as a whaling center until the 1880s when the whale population began to diminish. Swapping large sea creatures for small ones, Monterey turned to more profitable sardine fishing. Sardines were pulled from the offshore currents by the ton and hauled to Monterey's canneries for processing. Fish became the nourishing blood that pumped through the heart of Monterey. In the early 1900s, the area bustled with industry. Men and women flocked to the factories to clean, chop, mince and/or can thousands of tons of sardines. The canning industry became infamous for its tough and often unsanitary life. Clouds of rank fishy stench engulfed the factories and burned the inside of the nostrils. John Steinbeck described it graphically and unforgettably in his novel, *Cannery Row*:

"Cannery Row . . . is a poem, a stink, a grating noise, a quality of light, a tone, a habit, a nostalgia, a dream. Cannery Row is the gathered and the scattered, tin and iron and rust and splintered wood, chipped pavement and weedy lots and junk heaps, sardine canneries of corrugated iron, honky tonks and whorehouses, and little crowded groceries and flophouses."

Nonetheless, the area thrived until the 1940s. Then the sardines disappeared.

The reasons for the sardines' departure from the Monterey coastline are not specifically known. Some say they were diverted by a temperature change in the ocean; others claim they were overfished. You can find people who insist it was all a matter of bad karma: the fish simply went where the vibes were better. Regardless of the true reason, fewer and fewer fish turned up in the nets. Monterey moved away from the canning industry and took advantage of its beautiful surroundings as a tourist destination.

The **Monterey Aquarium** is the area's most popular attraction and deservedly so. Indeed, it is undoubtedly one of the top aquariums in the nation and beyond question the tallest: one of its tanks stands three stories high and holds 335,000 gallons of water. Located on Cannery Row, the well-organized aquatic exhibition gives you a diver's-mask close-up of the underwater population from sharks to sea otters.

The Kelp Forest Tank, the largest tank and the keystone exhibit, recreates the seaweed forests under Monterey Bay. Out in the ocean, kelp can grow at an astounding rate of eight inches a day—in the aquarium kelp is carefully pruned to allow sardines, leopard sharks, and their fellows to glide in and out among the long, brown, swaying branches. The Monterey Bay Habitats comprise the second largest exhibit, featuring a myriad of open-ocean fish. Large sharks patrol the four recreated ocean habitats: the deep reefs, the sandy floor, the shale reefs, and the wharf, where salmon, halibut, striped bass, and other fish dart out of the sharks' way.

You may ask why the sharks do not attack the other fish. You can see the answer for yourself: they're well fed. Special feeding shows are given in both exhibits periodically throughout the day. Divers in wet suits wearing SCUBA gear hand-feed the sharks and fish while communicating with the audience by two-way radio. Volunteer guides are also on hand to explain the lunchtime action. Kelp forest shows are scheduled at 11:30 A.M. and 4:00 P.M. The Monterey Bay Habitats feeding shows vary day to day.

For a face-to-face view of the bay's ultimate baby face, visit the popular sea otter tank near the aquarium entrance. Starting from their rocky perch at the top of the aquarium, the playful creatures delight onlookers by sliding, diving, and twirling down their rock slides to splash into the water like a litter of aquatic puppies—or rambunctious kids. Otter feeding shows are three times a day, at 11:00 A.M., 2:00 P.M. and 4:30 P.M.

You can get even closer to the aquarium's marine life at the hands-on exhibits. Here you can pet bat rays, flat diamond-shaped fish that look like shadows gliding along the bottom of the tank, or feel the coarse skin of a starfish. Or visit the "Planet of the Jellies" exhibit and see the elusive, exotic, and plentiful jellyfish as they gently move around their tanks, brought to life with black backgrounds and indirect lighting. The aquarium is open daily 10:00 A.M. to 6:00 P.M. Aquarium admission is $9.75, $7.25 for seniors. Ticket lines are long so it is best to go early in the morning or late in the afternoon.

Cannery Row has vastly changed since Steinbeck's day, and not just because it smells better. Brightly colored factory fronts still line the streets, their names and logos still painted on the front, their connecting bridges still crossing above the street, but the fish processing lines have been replaced by gift shops, ice cream parlors, and restaurants. (Local cynics say that not much has changed; they just process tourists instead of fish.) This is a good place for an afternoon of window-shopping and eating.

The "King of Cannery Row"—the Hovden Cannery, opened in 1916—has been incorporated into the Monterey Aquarium. Parts of the original structure have been refurbished with new exhibit space designed to recreate the open industrial feel of cannery architecture. Farther up Cannery Row, Steinbeck readers should look for the wooden home of the Pacific Biological Laboratory—Doc Rickett's Lab. Doc's lab at 800 Cannery Row is now a men's club and not open to the public.

Cannery Row also caters to the bargain-hunting shopper. The waterfront **American Tin Factory Outlet** stores at 135 Ocean View Boulevard, Pacific Grove, include forty-six factory outlet stores from Aca Joe to Bass Shoe Outlet and boasts discounts up to 60 percent on retail items.

To learn about Monterey's historic past, follow the **Path of History,** a walking tour of more than forty Spanish colonial and early California buildings, many of them incorporated into the Monterey State Historic Park. Here you can walk on a sidewalk made of whalebone, sit in a church built in 1794, stroll the same streets as Robert Louis Stevenson, and recognize why Richard Henry Dana, in *Two Years Before the Mast,* described the Monterey of 1835 as "decidedly the pleasantest and most civilized-looking place in California."

A $4 all-day ticket buys admission to all the buildings open to the public; admission to individual buildings is $2, with the exception of Colton Hall, which is free. Costumed docents are on hand in all buildings. Pick up a free, self-guiding map along with your ticket at Colton Hall or the Custom House, or buy a $2 booklet that gives detailed descriptions of each building.

The Royal Presidio Chapel, Monterey's oldest building, is a good place to begin. The chapel was constructed in 1794 on the site of the original mission, founded in 1770. It has been restored to the look of the colonial period and has been declared a national historic landmark.

The old Monterey Custom House, near Fisherman's Wharf and Custom House Plaza, is the oldest government building on the Pacific Coast. This is the spot where Commodore Sloat took possession of the Mexican territory in the name of the United States government. Begun in 1820 and completed in 1846, the Custom House is officially listed as California Historical Landmark Number One. Exhibits focus on the Mexican period of Monterey history.

Colton Hall, Dutra Street, has been restored to look much as it did in 1849, when forty-eight young men gathered in an upstairs meeting room to draft a constitution for the proposed new state of California. Adjoining is another refurbished building from the 1840s—the city's first jail.

The Stevenson House on Houston Street was the residence of the author of *Treasure Island* for a few months in 1879 during his courtship of Fanny Osbourne. Some of his personal possessions, along with other memorabilia of the time, are on exhibit.

The Larkin House is one of several residences that recall the life of

Monterey's leading citizens in the Mexican and early statehood periods. It was the home of Thomas Larkin, a businessman who was also U.S. consul to Mexican California and played a major role in the transfer of California to U.S. rule.

On Pacific Street California's First Theater dates from 1848, when a group of Army officers began to present theatricals in Jack Swan's saloon. Old-fashioned melodramas are still performed, and the saloon still operates.

Fisherman's Wharf is for strollers, browsers, shoppers, and lovers of good fresh seafood. It is a fascinating mixture of the elegant and the tacky. Candlelit restaurants are interspersed with gift shops, T-shirt vendors, purveyors of walkaway seafood cocktails, and little booths where local artisans display their wares. Fisherman's Wharf history is reflected in the restaurant menus, which feature recipes passed down through the generations of the old fishing families; eating places still vie to see who can produce the best calamari (squid) dishes or cioppino, coastal California's answer to bouillabaisse. From many of the restaurants you can see sea otters and seals swimming in the protected waters, diving for their dinners while you enjoy yours. The best otter viewing is on the south side of the pier.

A WINTER SPORT

Whale watching is a popular winter sport all along the California coast as gray whales migrate south from Alaskan waters to the Mexican Sea of Cortez beginning in November, then start the return trip in March. Excursion boats from Monterey take whale watchers into the ocean for a closer look at the giant migrating mammals. Cruises are aboard fishing boats, last about one and one-half to two hours, and include a narration to explain whale habits. Boats leave from Fisherman's Wharf daily between December and March (January is peak whale-watching season). Reservations are suggested. Cruises run between $12 and $15. For information call Monterey Sport Fishing at 408-372-2203 or Randy's Fishing Trips at 408-372-7440.

A commercial fishing fleet still docks at Wharf #2. Here you can stroll and see the boats unloading their daily catch or enjoy the adjacent beach facilities.

The Custom House Plaza, where Fisherman's Wharf meets land, is the home of the new **Maritime Museum of Monterey,** opened in fall 1992. The museum focuses on Monterey history from the days of its earliest known inhabitants, the Ohlone people, through the arrival of Commodore Sloat to more recent times. Artifacts include finely crafted sextants and compasses used for sea navigation as well as the First Order Fresnel Lens which originally beamed its guiding light from the Point Sur Lighthouse in 1885. The museum also includes exhibits about Cannery Row. Admission is $5.

Pacific Grove

The small community of Pacific Grove, many of its streets lined with colorful old Victorian homes, adjoins Monterey near the tip of the Monterey peninsula. The majority of the brightly painted houses, on hillsides looking out to sea, are found along Lighthouse Avenue and Ocean View Boulevard. Pacific Grove also claims fame as a winter home for the monarch butterfly. Starting in October, hordes of the brilliant orange and black creatures flutter through the skies and cover whole trees. The largest concentration in this area is found in Washington Park, just off the 17-Mile Drive on Melrose Street. Admire but don't touch: injuring butterflies carries a stiff fine.

Pacific Grove boasts a beautiful coastline and some of the area's most scenic outlooks. Drive out onto the sandy Point Lobos, highlighted by the still functional Point Lobos lighthouse, to watch the surf crash into the rocky shoreline like fireworks shooting huge plumes of foam into the air.

Restaurants ————————————————

Seafood is the catchword for Monterey restaurants. Local fishermen supply the restaurants daily with fish from Monterey Bay and the deeper Pacific.

SCENIC DETOUR: 17-MILE DRIVE

For more water fireworks and a spectacular winding drive along the rocky coast, follow the famous 17-Mile Drive connecting Pacific Grove and Carmel. Go at sunset and watch the orange blaze sink into the ocean. From the Pacific Grove gate, the road runs directly to the coast where long sandy beaches and lightly vegetated sand dunes spread along the shore. As you drive south along the ocean, spectacular (and expensive) private homes, varying in architecture and worthy of the name mansion, rise from the dunes or peek out among the wind-gnarled Monterey cypress trees of the Del Monte Forest. Seven of the world's most challenging golf courses are spread through the area, including the famous Pebble Beach, site of the 1992 U.S. Open, the Pebble Beach-AT & T tournament once known as the Bing Crosby Invitational, and other major tournaments. You can stop and enjoy a drink at the Pebble Beach Lodge, whose floor-to-ceiling windows open on a panoramic view of the eighteenth green, said to be one of the most beautiful holes in golf. Ah, the life—golfing along the Pacific Ocean, sitting in the Pebble Beach Lodge, and driving along the 17-Mile Drive home to your thirty-two room summer home set in the pine forests along the water. This life can be yours for an afternoon. Just pay the $6.75 toll for the 17-Mile Drive. Golf is not included in the price, but spectators are welcome.

Along the coastal drive, be sure to stop at Bird Rock and Seal Rock. Splashed by the boiling surf, these two lie just offshore and play home to large numbers of the furred and feathered. Sea lions and harbor seals literally cover the surface area of Seal Rock, lying flipper to flipper and basking in the sun. Bird Rock, beneath a cloud of circling birds looking for a spot to roost, sits in the water next to Seal Rock. Both are visible from a well-marked turnout/parking lot, complete with pay telescopes and explanatory displays. There's also a one-mile self-guided nature walk and a small picnic area.

Toward the end of the drive, note Lone Cypress Point. On a high promontory above the surf, one solitary Monterey cypress stands, shaped and wind blown by the stiff sea breezes. The tree is one of California's most familiar landmarks and the symbol of the Pebble Beach Company. You can hike out onto the point, but the hike is recommended for the sure footed only as the trail is somewhat rocky.

You can exit the drive at State Highway 1 or at the Carmel Gate, a beautiful link between these two very diverse communities.

- The **Sardine Factory** is one of Monterey's most famous restaurants, serving classic continental fare "with a touch of California style." You can dine in two very different but very romantic dining rooms, one with candlelight, surrounded by hardwood paneling with gilded details, and the other a glass-domed courtyard centered on a white stone fountain. Expensive. Reservations are suggested. 701 Wave Street. 408-373-3775.

- For fine Italian dining on the old Fisherman's Wharf, try **Cafe Fina.** The pasta dishes are complemented by the harbor view; sea otters and seals swim in the calm water. Moderate. 47 Fisherman's Wharf. 408-372-5200.

WINE, CALAMARI, AND SONG

The Monterey peninsula yearly calendar teems with special events, but probably the most renowned center around music. The Monterey Jazz Festival, held each September, is the oldest jazz festival in the U.S. and attracts the world's top jazz musicians and vocalists, plus jazz lovers from all over the world. For information call 408-373-3366. Bach has his day (or month) in July, during the Bach Festival at Carmel; call 408-624-1521. Another summertime event is the week-long round of chamber music, lectures, and symphony performances known as Encore California International Musicfest. In March, Dixie-land Monterey brings the saints marching into cabarets and small clubs across downtown Monterey.

For those who would rather eat or sip than listen and tap their feet, the Great Monterey Squid Festival, held at the Monterey Fair-grounds each May, offers two days of calamari cuisine, plus cooking demonstrations and displays. The Monterey Wine Festival, sponsored by the National Restaurant Association, brings wine masters and chefs together to share knowledge about fine wines and cuisine. More than 100 wineries participate. For information about any of these events, call the Monterey Visitor and Convention Bureau at 408-649-1770.

- The historic standard for Monterey Bay seafood is the **Old Fisherman's Grotto,** also located on Fisherman's Wharf. Locals claim that the Grotto's clam chowder is the best on the West Coast, if not in the world. Check the specials for the freshest, just-off-the-boat fish. Moderate. 408-375-4604.

- Kalisa's **La Ida Cafe** not only offers reasonably priced dining (huge sandwiches ranging from a sardine sandwich with marinated artichokes to a standard hamburger) but also claims fame as the scene of John Steinbeck's reference to Eddie, the part-time bartender, who routinely drained the night's leftover drinks into a jug beneath the counter for Mac and the boys at the Palace Flophouse. The La Ida Cafe was originally a boardinghouse that turned into one of Cannery Row's three major "institutions of commercial love" in 1936. Today, only the cafe remains, but owner Kalisa Moore has preserved the ambience of its notorious past even to the point of an occasional belly dancer. Moderate. 851 Cannery Row. 408-372-8512.

- A hearty breakfast before an afternoon of bargain shopping can be had at **First Watch** in the American Tin Cannery (the outlet store center). Inexpensive. 125 Ocean View Boulevard. 408-372-1125.

Lodging ————————————————————

Beautiful and classic bed and breakfasts abound on the Monterey peninsula, many of them in Pacific Grove where quaint Victorians offer a quiet retreat from the busy streets of Monterey. Other more moderate and centrally located lodging is available in all price ranges. Make reservations a month in advance for summer weekends; two weeks for weekdays (less time required for hotels).

- The **Del Monte Beach Inn** offers the classic B&B atmosphere at moderate prices. The inn was built early in the twentieth century and has changed very little. The house is furnished in oak antiques and has a homey atmosphere complete with quilts and comforters. It is located across the street from the beach and half a mile from Fisherman's Wharf. Breakfast is continental plus, including granola, fruit and "picnic" eggs (hard-boiled). Reservations for August and special events should be made thirty days in advance, ten days at other times. Inexpensive to moderate. 1110 Del Monte Boulevard, Monterey. 408-649-4410.

- The **Old Monterey Inn** has won a host of awards for its decor and hospitality and is renowned for its romantic and calming atmosphere. Televisions and phones have been banished from the rooms, most of which feature fireplaces. The building is of English Tudor Country House architecture and rises three stories. There is no elevator. Expensive. 500 Martin Street, Monterey. 408-375-8284.

- **Green Gables Inn** is an old Victorian B&B located across the street from the beach and a fifteen minute walk from the Monterey Aquarium. Its interior decor features an old carousel horse, high ceilings, and colorful antique wallpaper. Green Gables serves a full breakfast, and offers wine and hors d'oeuvres in the evenings and cookies and sherry at night (cookies are out all night). Expensive. 104 5th Street, Pacific Grove. 408-375-2095.

- **Seven Gables Inn** has fourteen rooms, all with ocean views. The B&B boasts a full sit-down family style breakfast and high tea in its salon full of antiques. There is a two-day minimum stay on weekends. Moderate to expensive. 555 Ocean View Boulevard, Monterey. 408-372-4341.

- For a historic hotel, make a reservation at the **Monterey Hotel,** just a five-minute walk from Fisherman's Wharf. Erected in 1904, the hotel has been declared a national historical landmark in recognition of its late Victorian-style architecture. A continental breakfast is served. Expensive. 406 Alvarado Street, Monterey. 408-375-3184.

- The **Spindrift Inn** lies in the center of the action. Located on Cannery Row, this inn serves a full breakfast in its old-world atmosphere. Expensive. 652 Cannery Row, Monterey. 408-646-8900.

- **Andril Fireplace Cottages** offers reasonably priced hotel accommodations in a beautiful residential neighborhood of Pacific Grove. 569 Asilomar Street, Pacific Grove. 408-375-0994.

- The **Best Western DeAnza Inn** offers economical lodging (as economical as Monterey gets) near the junction of State Highways 68 and 1, three or four minutes from downtown Monterey. Moderate. 2141 Fremont Street, Monterey. 408-646-8300.

Chapter 7

Carmel-by-the-Sea

Although the two communities grew up as neighbors on the Monterey peninsula, the industries of Monterey never infiltrated the pleasant, undeveloped white sand beach in Carmel, which was protected from them by law. The artists and writers who discovered Carmel pushed through a 1929 city ordinance declaring that business development shall forever be subordinate to the residential character of the community. The citizens of Carmel—or Carmelites, as they call themselves—have fiercely upheld the spirit of the law, determined to guard the small-town atmosphere. Here, the bars are pubs, the city is called a village, for a time the streets were unpaved, there is still no mail delivery, the homes are "cottages" and carry names, not specific street numbers—they are designated east and west of Ocean Avenue. Art galleries—twenty-eight of them, not counting antique galleries, restaurants, pubs and boutique-y shops—fill the tree-shaded blocks, but there's nary a McDonald's, chain hotel, or convention center. The few shopping complexes are surprisingly well concealed; the shops are tasteful and understated (and frequently pricey). What Carmel has most of all is mood and atmosphere, which it surprisingly retains even on the busiest tourist Saturdays. It's ideal for a pleasant afternoon of window-shopping, investigating the half-hidden courtyards where the most interesting shops wait, art appraisal, or just relaxing on the beach. The quiet, easy pace has attracted many film stars and other celebrities who live here. Ironically, Clint Eastwood, in his film roles the very epitome of action, once served as mayor of this slow-moving town.

The one not so relaxing feature of Carmel is parking. Parking places in the center of the village all have strictly enforced time limits. The majority allow one-hour parking although some two-hour parking is available. For easy access to the town center, use the parking garage at Sunset Center, Eighth and San Carlos streets. Parking charge is $1 per half hour with a fourteen-hour maximum. If you do not mind a bit of a walk (nothing in Carmel is very far from anything), park in the free lot on Third Street just off Junipero Serra Avenue.

Carmel Beach is truly a well-protected gem thanks to that far-sighted bit of 1929 legislation. White sand, blue water, and smashing surf spread out along the shore. The beach is a short downhill walk from the village center. Sit and enjoy the joggers, the surfers, and the view over the Pacific.

The Carmel Mission is located at the southern edge of the village and is officially titled The Basilica of Mission San Carlos Borromeo del Rio Carmelo. Father Junipero Serra, the Spanish missionary who came to California to spread the gospel of Christianity by converting the Native Americans, founded a chain of missions in California, each a day's travel apart (by horse) from the next. Carmel's mission, established in 1770, was the second one founded and is Father Serra's burial place. It's also one of the best preserved—its whitewashed stucco walls, carved pews and kneelers, and gilt-trimmed altar have been painstakingly restored and appear little changed since Father Serra's day. You can walk through the courtyard and church, wander through the parish hall, pay respects at Father Serra's grave, and learn about the mission's early history in its small museum whose exhibit rooms include a colonial-era kitchen and Father Serra's sleeping quarters where he died. In 1960, Pope John XXIII raised the Carmel Mission's status to Minor Basilica, one of only two in the western United States. The mission is still very much a place of worship; there is no admission charge, but a $1 donation is suggested.

Shops and Galleries

• The **Miner's Gallery Americana, Inc.,** one of the largest galleries in Carmel, exhibits the works of more than sixty gifted painters and sculptors. The art is displayed in eight

SCENIC DETOUR

South of Monterey and Carmel lies some of the the most spectacular coastline in California. For twenty-six miles between Carmel and Big Sur, State Highway 1 hugs the rugged shoreline and winds around the edges of sheer cliffs that may drop as much as 1,000 feet to the ocean below. You get a bird's-eye view as the waves roll in, swell, and crash against the tan cliff faces, spewing white water in every direction. Take advantage of the many roadside turnouts where you can see off into the horizon and look for fishing boats, giant freighters, or sailboats.

Point Lobos State Reserve, called "the greatest meeting of land and water in the world," lies off State Highway 1, just south of Carmel. Its breathtaking ocean views have inspired many visitors, including Robert Louis Stevenson, who used this point as a model for Spyglass Hill in *Treasure Island.*

The Big Sur Land Trust is dedicated to the preservation of the Big Sur area's rich natural beauty which has attracted authors, poets, and artists to settle in the region. Novelist Henry Miller, poet Emil White, and composer Harry Partch all made their homes here. Go to the Henry Miller Memorial Library to see a record of their lives and an extensive collection of their works, including old photographs and a portrait of Henry Miller. The library is located thirty miles south of Carmel on State Highway 1. Call 408-667-2574.

different, yet elegant rooms with knowledgeable staff members available for questions. Sixth Avenue and Lincoln Street on the northeast corner. 408-625-5071.

• The **Galerie Blue Dog, Ltd.,** offers a different and whimsical series of paintings by George Rodrigue, who has achieved an international reputation for the blue dog that turns up in most of his work. Rodrigue modeled the blue dog from the memory of his late pet, Tiffany, who died several years ago. Although rarely painted while she was alive, Tiffany now enters most of his scenes, always in full face with wide, staring eyes and with her rear right leg protruding at an awkward angle and set in the most unlikely situations: among a crowd of Renaissance nudes or at the feet of a man dressed in polyester pants and buckle boots. Sixth Avenue between Lincoln and Dolores streets. 408-626-4444.

- Thomas Kinkade has been recognized as one of the foremost living painters of light. His unique studio, **Thomas Kinkade Garden Gallery of Carmel,** displays his works in a studio garden at the end of a cobblestone lane. On the ocean between Lincoln and Dolores streets in Der Ling Lane. 408-626-1927.
- The **Hanson Gallery** exhibits a wide range of contemporary art, featuring such artists as Peter Max and Mark Kostabi. Ocean Avenue between San Carlos and Dolores streets. 408-625-3111.
- **Masterpiece Gallery** specializes in works of the California School, some of them dating from the 1860s. Dolores Street near Sixth Avenue. 408-624-2163.
- **Michael Moran Studios** is a sculpture gallery, much of it in bronze. Mission Patio, Mission Street between Fifth and Sixth avenues. 408-626-3300.

Pubs

It is said, "It's hard to describe Carmel without talking about pubs." In Carmel, English-style pubs looking like they might have been transplanted from Beaconsfield or Brompton replace the bars or cocktail lounges found in most American communities, adding a cozy, homey atmosphere to Carmel nightlife. Subdued lighting, dart boards, televisions, and wooden stools and tables adorn the pubs, which usually serve an upscale and expanded version of traditional pub fare.

- The **Hog's Breath Inn,** Clint Eastwood's pub, takes pub fare to new extremes. You can drink beer or sip wine on a large outdoor patio while choosing among such dishes as the "Dirty Harry Dinner" (ground chuck with sauteed mushrooms) or "For a Few Dollars More" (sixteen-ounce New York steak) or simply fresh red snapper. Strategically located fireplaces warm the outdoor diners in the cool Carmel nights. The Hog's Breath lunch menu also succeeds in name-dropping from Eastwood films: You can order the "Sudden Impact" (broiled Polish sausage, jack cheese, and jalapeño peppers on a French roll) or "Mysterious Misty," a more obscure reference to Eastwood's thriller *Play Misty for Me* (Maggie's special tuna sandwich served hot with tomato and melted cheddar) or a simple ham and cheese omelette, hold the Eastwood marquées. Moderate. No reservations are needed except for parties of eight or more. San Carlos Street between Fifth and Sixth avenues. 408-625-1044.

- **Bud's Pub** is one of Carmel's favorites, combining English, Irish, and American flavors. The lengthy menu features steak and kidney pie, bangers and mash, and Bud's famous miniburgers. Moderate. Dolores Street and Sixth Avenue in the Su Vecino Court. 408-625-6765.

Restaurants —————————————————————

- The **Mission Ranch** (which formerly was part of the Carmel Mission) along the Carmel River has been converted into a hotel and restaurant, also owned by Clint Eastwood. It's just outside Carmel's boundaries, and therefore free from some of the strict Carmel legislation, including an ordinance that prohibits live music. The restaurant boasts the only piano bar in the region as well as good continental cooking. Expensive. 25720 Dolores Street. 408-625-9040.

- The **Fabulous Toots Lagoon** is a local favorite specializing in ribs, pasta, seafood, and steaks. Dolores Street between Ocean and Seventh avenues. Moderate. 408-625-1915.

- **Village Corner** is a basic breakfast and lunch place specializing in egg dishes and sandwiches and Greek/Mediterranean dishes at lunch. Pitas, Greek salads, and homemade pies. Inexpensive. Dolores Street and Sixth Avenue. 408-624-3588.

- **Anton and Michel** is elegant, with candlelight and a patio centered around a fountain. International dishes (rack of lamb, chateaubriand) and local seafood are specialties. Expensive. In the Court of the Fountains, Mission Street between Ocean and Seventh avenues. 408-624-2406.

- **Ristorante Piatti** specializes in homemade pasta, often served with a nouvelle cuisine touch. Grilled and roasted chicken and beef dishes are also served. Sixth and Junipero Serra avenues. Moderate. 408-625-1766.

- The **General Store**, near the free parking lot on Junipero Serra Avenue, is another long-time local favorite offering a truly international menu featuring quiche, calamari, pasta, and tacos. Brunch is served on Saturday and Sunday. There is a patio with outdoor fireplaces. Moderate. Fifth and Junipero Serra avenues. 408-624-2233.

Lodging

There are forty-one members of the Carmel Innkeepers Association, which does not count B&Bs or many lodging places outside the village. Write P.O. Box 1362, Carmel, California 93921, for a full list and map. Reservations for summer weekends should be made a month in advance, two weeks in advance for weekdays. Reservations are advised at other times of year, too. Because of Carmel's restrictive legislation, no commercial ventures are allowed on the beach, but some inns and B&Bs have ocean views and are within walking distance of the water.

- **Highlands Inn** is luxury with a capital L. Rooms have separate living and sleeping areas, decks, fireplaces, and ocean views. The inn features an award-winning restaurant. Very expensive. State Highway 1, four miles south of Carmel. 408-624-3801.

- **Green Lantern Inn,** four B&B cottages set in a quiet garden, is in the heart of the village and a short walk to the beach.

Moderate. Seventh Avenue and Casanova Street. 408-624-4392.

• **Sandpiper Inn at the Beach** is a small antique-decorated B&B with rooms and cottages, a short walk from the beach. Moderate to expensive. Bay View Avenue at Martine Way. 408-624-6435.

• **Cypress Inn,** in the heart of town, is an older, small hotel with a quiet, relaxed ambience. Moderate to expensive. Lincoln Street and Seventh Avenue. 408-624-3871.

• **Spinning Wheel Inn** specializes in personal service with breakfast and a newspaper brought to your room and flowers in the room changed daily. It is a short walk to town or to the beach. Moderate. Ocean Avenue and Monte Verde Street. 408-624-2429.

• **Carmel Studio Lodge** is a more standard motel with pool, television sets, and in-room coffeemakers. It is near shops. Moderate. Fifth and Junipero Serra avenues. 408-625-8515.

Salinas and Environs

Information about things to see and do in the Salinas area is available from the Salinas Chamber of Commerce: 408-424-7611.

Steinbeck was the chronicler of Doc, the girls, and the smells along Cannery Row, but his birthplace and home territory are in Salinas, over the hills from Monterey, the slightly disguised locale of *East of Eden* and the novelette *The Long Valley.*

The **Steinbeck House,** the author's birthplace, is operated by the Valley Guild as a lunch-only restaurant. The Victorian frame house contains some of the author's boyhood possessions from his early years. The house is located at 132 Central Avenue, Salinas. Call 408-424-2735.

The **Steinbeck Library,** renamed for the author, includes photographs, first editions of Steinbeck works, letters, original manuscripts, and tapes of interviews he conducted here in doing research for *East of*

Eden. The library is located at 110 West San Luis, Salinas. Call 408-758-7311.

Jose Eusebio Boronda Adobe is said to be the only Mexican-period adobe dwelling in Monterey County that is still open to the public. The house is furnished with period furnishings and other artifacts. It is open Saturday and Sunday, 10:00 A.M. to 2:00 P.M. Admission is free. Located in Salinas. Call 408-757-8085.

San Juan Bautista State Historic Park, twenty miles north of Salinas on U.S. 101, preserves a nearly unaltered example of an early mission village. The village is built around a large plaza, containing a blacksmith shop, pioneer cabin, and jail. The mission itself, still in use, was founded in 1797 and occupies one side of the plaza. The side streets of the village, which later became an important stage stop, are lined with antique shops and art galleries. Mission open daily, 9:00 A.M. to 5:00 P.M.; winter, 9:00 A.M. to 4:00 P.M. Donations. 408-623-4528.

Pinnacles National Monument, off U.S. 101 near Soledad, consists of 16,000 acres of weird pinnacles, spires, cliffs and other rock formations along a central ridge of mountains. It's primarily a hiking and walking park although some of the most dramatic formations can be seen by car. It is hot in summer; spring is the best time to visit. The narrow roads are not recommended for campers or trailers. Admission is $3 per car. Call 408-389-4485.

Chapter 8

Across the Golden Gate: Marin County

Californians from outside the area regard Marin County as a wealthy community full of mansions. While this is an exaggeration, large homes do dot the landscape, some tastefully set into the hillside and others pretentiously looming on the ridge crests. Although these showpieces are not concentrated in one specific locale, look out for them on Mount Tamalpais or in the foothills around San Rafael. You are bound to spot one or two, especially higher up.

To the locals, Marin County is a haven from the San Francisco traffic and fog. But this area has much more to offer than suburban settings and full days of sunshine. While the hills rising to the east and extending down to the Golden Gate Bridge block the gray mist creeping in from the ocean, they also provide a vast playground full of scenic trails, tall redwoods, and, down the western slope, beautiful coastline. You can investigate the San Francisco Bay and Delta Model, a one-and-one-half-acre scale replication of the bay used to study the currents and the human impact on this body of water or examine the innovative architecture of Frank Lloyd Wright's Marin County Civic Center. Just a trip across the Golden Gate Bridge from San Francisco, and you can escape the fog and entertain yourself for a long afternoon or a couple of days.

As you cross the Golden Gate, you will get a quick reintroduction to the Golden Gate National Recreation Area as it continues in Marin County along the coast. Just look to the north off the west side of the bridge into the green mountains that drop into the Pacific, and you will see the headlands and hillsides that continue north for another twenty miles.

The city of **Sausalito,** the first notable town you hit after crossing the bridge, huddles around the edge of Richardson Bay (an inlet of San Francisco Bay)—so close, in fact, that some of the residences actually extend out on the water. A community of houseboats, docked along the Sausalito shore, has become the permanent home for a number of locals. You can walk the wooden pier sidewalks through this floating suburbia and examine the often elaborate houseboats, some of which rival the dwellings of the landlocked. Or admire the sailboats and seagoing motorboats in one of the nine harbors and three marinas berthed along the shore. Just park the car in downtown Sausalito and follow the masts.

Sausalito itself resembles one of those quaint Mediterranean fishing villages, albeit a bit—a big bit—tonier and upscale. Pastel-hued buildings spill down the steep hillside to the waterfront; some of the narrow streets are little more than cobbled stairways. Restaurants built on piers jut into the water, with decks where guests sit in directors chairs and sip chardonnay. Bridgeway, which winds along the water, is a line of boutiques, craft studios, capuccino dispensaries and designer clothing outlets. The town actually was a fishing village in an earlier day, then became an artists' colony, then a haven for commuters shuttling to San Francisco by ferry. Now it is a mecca for browsers and shoppers, especially on weekends.

The community not only rests by the water, it also studies it. The U.S. Army Corps of Engineers built the **San Francisco Bay and Delta Model** in Sausalito as a working water-filled re-creation of the bay and the Sacramento and the San Joaquin deltas that feed into it. The designers recognized the vital importance of the bay and the significance of any large-scale and unpredicted change in this environment. Some six million people live in the San Francisco Bay Area, many of them dependent on the water resources for fishing and freight shipping. The rest need to worry about changes in the water levels and shoreline as the bay gradually evolves.

In the late 1940s John Reber offered a solution to some of California's water problems. He proposed setting concrete dividers in the water to section off fresh water reservoirs in the bay. The problem was that nobody knew how the sectioning would affect the rest of the environment. Thus the Corps of Engineers developed the bay part of the Bay and Delta Model, completed in 1958, to test the plan. While they learned that the divisions would have a dramatic impact on the level and salinity of the bay and that much of the drinking water gained would evaporate away, the engineers gained recognition for the potential usefulness of the model. The delta part was added in 1966–1969 to study the impact of the deepening of navigation channels.

Today, they are still using this working replication of the bay to gain new information about this vital body of water. And you can learn about it, too. The model is open to the public, and you can walk around its edges and pick out landmarks, islands, and cities like Berkeley and Alcatraz, marked by flags rather than by miniature buildings. The bay model offers a free forty-five-minute audio tour (given on a personal stereo with headphones) that explains the characteristics of the different areas. Or you can just go it on your own and occasionally listen in at one of the informative phone centers, eavesdropping on recorded descriptions, repeated at regular intervals. These are strategically located at each of the different sections of the bay. For instance, the South Bay phone talks about the poor flushing action of the water around the Dumbarton Bridge (that you can see extending across the bay in the model) because of the shallow water and high levels of silt.

Catch the multimedia presentation in the theater (located after the bay evolution and history displays). It provides much background history of the model and the bay in a fact-packed nine minutes. Admission, the audio tour, and the theater presentation are free. The model is open in the winter, Tuesday to Saturday, 9:00 A.M. to 4:00 P.M., and in the summer, Tuesday to Friday, 9:00 A.M. to 4:00 P.M. It is located at 2100 Bridgeway Street, Sausalito. Call 415-332-3871.

The Golden Gate National Recreation Area (GGNRA) starts at the edge of the low mountains just west of U.S. 101 and continues to the coast. Locals use the rugged landscape with its carefully protected wildlife and fauna as a backdrop for outdoor activities. Many jog or take bike rides, others prefer a scenic drive, and some take frequent escapes into its green and untouched interior that extends from the upper lip of the Golden Gate all the way north to Point Reyes. Appreciate the nature by whatever method you choose but also visit two interesting man-made installations in the GGNRA, the coast artillery bunkers and the Marine Mammal Center.

The U.S. military installed the coast artillery batteries at various periods over the past 100 years to protect against potential invaders entering the bay. The first battery was built in 1895 and the latest, a Nike missile base, was erected in the 1970s. Today the artillery has long since been removed and only the concrete pillboxes remain, along with some large buildings and other smaller fortifications scattered across the hillside. Although you cannot enter the fortifications, you can look across the mouth of the bay and focus your camera as soldiers in decades past leveled their guns on the water with the Golden Gate Bridge and San Francisco skyline as background. Professional photographers usually snap the bridge from this angle. Three batteries lie right on Conzeiman Road that branches off U.S. 101 just after the Golden Gate Bridge and before the Waldo Grade Tunnel. At the end of Conzeiman Road go south on Field Road to see three others. Each one has interpretive panels that explain the structures.

The **Marine Mammal Center** lies on the Pacific Coast past the artillery bunkers in the Marin Headlands of the GGNRA. The center acts as an aquatic mammal hospital, saving seals, sea lions, whales, dolphins, porpoises, and sea otters that have been injured by anything from spilt oil to shark attacks. You can watch volunteers teach seals and otters how to hunt for food and live off the ocean in anticipation of their release. Visitor hours are 10:00 A.M. to 4:00 P.M. every day of the year. Admission is free.

The **Point Bonita Lighthouse,** the oldest working lighthouse on the West Coast, marks the northern tip of the Golden Gate. It has operated since 1855, shining its light across the water for over 130 years. You can take a half-mile hike that takes you across a bridge and through a tunnel out to the lighthouse for more tremendous views. From here you can see through the Golden Gate and down the peninsula, or turning north, you can see all the way to Point Reyes on a clear day. You can also enter the lighthouse base and check out the small bookstore and escape the cool breeze. The lighthouse trail is only open on weekends. Sunset walks are available. The lighthouse is located at the end of Field Road on Point Bonita. Call 415-331-1540.

Towering redwoods with thin rays of sunlight streaking through the dense branches fill the visitor with appreciation for nature in **Muir Woods National Monument,** nestled into the slopes of Mount Tamalpais. Hiking trails for all levels of athleticism thread through the giant trees, from a quick one-mile hike that winds you through the ancient groves on a wide-paved path (wheelchair accessible) to a long 5.2-mile hike that takes you up 800 feet for a view of the Pacific. The oldest trees date back 1,000 years while most have lived 500 to 800 years. The size of the trees in Muir Woods will impress you, the tallest being about 252 feet and the widest 14 feet across. Check the Cathedral and Bohemian groves for these evergreen monsters. Admission is free and the park is open daily 8:00 A.M. to 7:00 P.M. No picnics or dogs are allowed. Take Highway 1 north off U.S. 101 and then follow the signs.

From breathtaking trees back to breathtaking views, **Mount Tamalpais** offers an end-to-end vista of the Bay Area from the mouth of the Golden Gate all the way down the Peninsula (on a clear day). To scale the mountain by car, take Ridgecrest Boulevard off the Panoramic Highway (that leads to Tamalpais State Park), and you will climb and wind to the east peak of the mountain. Pack a picnic and enjoy the panorama from one of the benches that line the parking lot. You can also follow a steep trail up to the very tip of the mountain to get the "I'm-on-the-top-of-the-world" feeling. Parking lot and trails cost $5 per car (to be deposited in a drop box).

"Tamalpais" means "sleeping woman" to local Native Americans who worshipped the mountain and thought it to have mystic powers because its curves look like that of a woman on her side. You can make out the woman's figure best from the north looking south. While the outlook from the top impresses, the novelty of finding the woman entertains.

The village of **Tiburon** sits on the end of a finger of land that extends into the top inside edge of the bay, forming its own inlet, Richardson Bay. From here you get a free shot at the San Francisco skyline, yet another outpost for picture snapping. Here you can escape the fog and enjoy a pleasant afternoon of dipping in and out of boutiques or waltzing along the red-bricked promenade along the water.

Just a mile offshore, the 780 feet of Mount Livermore jut out of the bay in **Angel Island State Park.** Bring your walking shoes because all the attractions sit on the east side of the island and are only accessible by foot. The island has been used for many different purposes throughout its history. It was first established as a fortress during the Civil War. Then it served as the "Ellis Island of the West," a holding area for new immigrants. Its other capacities have included a quarantine center, a World War II prison camp, and a missile station as recently as 1962. You can wander around the old buildings where placards explain their various purposes. Docent-led tours take you through them from spring to summer. Angel Island makes a good day trip, popular for family outings. You can reach Angel Island by public ferry from Tiburon ($5) or San Francisco ($8). Call 415-435-2131.

The **National Audubon Society/Richardson Bay Audubon Center** holds eleven acres of varying habitats: grasslands, coastal brush, and freshwater pond. It also includes a bird sanctuary located in Tiburon at the northernmost end of Richardson Bay. You can take the self-guided nature trail through the wetlands and gaze at the San Francisco skyline while looking for a snowy egret, a great blue heron, or a black-crowned night heron, all of whom live in the sanctuary year-round. The wetlands hold the largest concentration of birds during the colder months when migrating waterfowl take their winter residence in the Bay Area. From November to March you can spot cormorants, ruddy ducks, surf scooters, the western grebe, and the rarer Clark grebe (graceful long-necked fishing birds with black-and-white plumage). Land birds tend to continue south seeking drier winter homes. In late fall and early spring many varieties of sparrows—white, golden crown, and fox—join yellow warblers and flycatchers swooping over the tall grass.

Leave it to the birds, that's what Dr. and Mrs. Benjamin Lyford did with their home, built in 1876. After a visit to the Centennial Exposition in Philadelphia in 1876, they designed their dairy farm in the Victorian country mode, one of the first Victorians in the area. This landmark, known as the **Lyford House,** was barged from Strawberry Point to the sanctuary in 1957 to be preserved as a historic landmark. You can take a docent-led tour of the house which is open October through April, Sunday 1:00 P.M. to 4:00 P.M. The sanctuary is open Wednesday to Sunday 9:00 A.M. to 5:00 P.M. The house is located at 376 Greenwood Beach Road, Tiburon. Call 415-388-2524.

The **Marin County Civic Center** differs from your average town municipal building. Its metallic exterior lined with circles and semi-circles molds perfectly with the hillside just as it should. Frank Lloyd Wright designed the structure, which was finished in 1969. You will see architectural students examining the elliptical skylight that runs the length of the building or studying the plans displayed in the lobby. You can walk through this one-of-a-kind building on your own during business hours, but for explanations of the revolutionary design concepts used, take a free guided tour, Monday to Friday 9:00 A.M. to 3:00 P.M. The center is located at 30 Sir Francis Drake Boulevard, San Rafael. Take the North San Pedro Road exit off U.S. 101 and go east. The civic center will be one block on your left. Call 415-499-6104.

The **Mission San Rafael Archangel,** the twentieth of twenty-one California missions, was founded in 1817 as a recuperation center for the infirm. Apparently, the Christian-converted Native Americans in San Francisco were not acclimated to the cold, foggy weather. Pneumonia spread rapidly so the missionaries sent them over to sunny San Rafael to recuperate. The small mission lies right in downtown and is open daily 11:00 A.M. to 4:00 P.M. Admission is free. Call 415-456-3016.

You can see the early Chinese influence north of San Francisco in the **China Camp,** a historic Chinese village containing some relics from their fishing past. Rangers lead tours during the summer season every Saturday and Sunday at 1:00 P.M. and explain the antique equipment used to catch shrimp. Tours at other times may be arranged upon request. The camp is located on North San Pedro Road, San Rafael. Call 415-459-9877.

OFF-THE-WALL TOURS

Marin County offers two diverse tours that veer from the normal sightseeing agenda yet represent prominent aspects of our society— fast food and jail.

While most people do not consider McDonald's a sightseeing stop on a vacation, the **Marin County McDonald's restaurants** say think again. Believe it or not, you can see behind the scenes of America's most successful fast-food chain. A knowledgeable guide will lead you through the kitchen where you can see McDonald's regular orders through all stages of evolution, from ground beef to Big Mac and from mayonnaise and pickles to special sauce. Tours last about thirty minutes and can be arranged at any one of the five McDonald's in the area, Monday to Friday 9:00 A.M. to 11:00 A.M. and 2:00 P.M. to 4:00 P.M. Call Tom Mathews at 415-897-3477.

The easily disturbed beware. The medium security San Quentin State Prison, California's largest and oldest, is in the tourist business. You get the unprecedented experience of entering the prison grounds when you visit the **San Quentin State Prison Museum** that reveals 140 years of prison history, including exhibits and displays. In terms of age, the prison outdoes just about anything in the area except the San Rafael mission. Its prisoners have actively participated in a number of social enterprises including highway construction and assembling war supplies. You can see old photographs of the structure which was built by convicts who were originally held on a ship offshore in 1852.

Restaurants ————————————————————

Marin holds a wide range of restaurants scattered around the county but specifically has an excellent choice of fine-dining establishments. Dine in style in an old brick factory or with the renowned chef, Bradley Ogden. Many of the restaurants are in Marin County towns not previously mentioned but within ten to fifteen minutes of most locations in the county.

The prison houses 3,000 convicts (California plans to expand the facilities to hold 6,000), and some of them work on the grounds around the museum (but not *in* the museum). Although this should not be a problem, the guards enforce strict rules of conduct for visitors so no hanky-panky goes on in either direction. Cameras, prescription drugs (unless OK'ed by the guards), knives and, obviously, guns are not allowed inside. The prisoners wear jeans and denim shirts. Thus, no jeans may be worn by visitors so that guards can immediately distinguish visitors and residents. Conversing with convicts is not allowed.

Outside the prison you can see the end results of the vocational programs created to teach skills that the prisoners can use after their release. Inmates design and construct furniture and arts and crafts, some of which are sold in private retail shops outside the prison. You can purchase the prisoners' works at the **San Quentin State Prison Gift Shop,** located just outside the prison walls. The store sells clocks, leather crafts, belt buckles, jewelry, and other trinkets. The prison museum and store are loosely scheduled to be open Monday 1:00 P.M. to 5:00 P.M., Tuesday to Thursday 8:30 A.M. to 4:30 P.M., Friday to Sunday 8:30 A.M. to 3:00 P.M., and at other times according to staff availability. The suggested donation is $2 for adults, $1 for seniors. To get there follow I-580 west from U.S. 101 (toward the Richmond-San Rafael Bridge). Take the San Quentin (last Marin County) exit, right to San Quentin village. Call ahead to visit the museum, 415-454-8808.

- The **Lark Creek Inn** serves classic American cuisine as prepared by Bradley Ogden, listed as one of the Great American Chefs and author of several cookbooks. Jackets are required for dinner and reservations should be made three to four weeks in advance. Expensive. 234 Magnolia Avenue, Larkspur. 415-924-7766.

- **Remillard's** offers classical French cuisine in a nontraditional setting. You actually eat in the chimneys of an old brick factory. Dinners are dressy. Reservations are suggested a week in advance. Expensive. 125 East Sir Francis Drake Boulevard, Larkspur Landing. Call 415-461-3700.

- **Savannah Grill** boasts an upper-class setting and cajun food for a little spice. Expensive. 55 Tamal Vista Boulevard, Corte Madera. 415-924-6774.

- For a medium-priced Italian meal try **Marin Joe's,** a local favorite. 1585 Casa Buena Drive, Corte Madera. 415-924-2081.

- **Le Chalet Basque** offers an out-of-the-way location for an out-of-the-way cuisine. Basque food comes from the mountainous regions in northern Spain. Basque sheepherders brought their cuisine to California when they immigrated in the late 1800s. This restaurant, a local favorite, has been open for over forty years. Reservations are necessary. Moderate to expensive. 405 North San Pedro Road, San Rafael. 415-479-1070.

Lodging

Many visitors stay in the thick of San Francisco wishing that they could relax in sunny suburbia (where the rates are a little bit lower). Relief is just across the Golden Gate in Marin County (although rush hour commutes across the Golden Gate are not recommended).

Many B&Bs exist in Marin County, but they do not advertise in the eastern part of the county. For B&B information, call Inns by Design at 415-382-1462.

Sausalito holds two luxury hotels, both with a bay view:

- **Alta Mira Hotel** has twenty-nine rooms in its Victorian-era building. Cottages are available. The restaurant serves continental fare and includes a deck where you can enjoy your meal while looking across the bay. Reservations are suggested (request one of the six rooms with a view). Expensive. 125 Bulkey Street, Sausalito. 415-332-1350.

- **Casa Madrona** boasts thirty-four individually decorated rooms (no two are alike), most of which have views. The hotel is divided between two buildings, one part built in 1983 in contemporary style and the other built in 1885, the oldest Victorian in Sausalito. Expensive. 801 Bridgeway Street, Sausalito. 415-332-0502.

- **Holiday Inn** and **Embassy Suites** in San Rafael offer comfortable lodging with pools and restaurants (the Embassy Suites have an exercise room to boot). Both moderate. Holiday Inn, 1010 Northgate Drive, San Rafael. 800-HOLIDAY or 415-479-8800. Embassy Suites, 101 McInnis Parkway, San Rafael. 800-EMBASSY or 415-499-9222.

Chapter 9

Up the
Marin-Sonoma Coast

Sir Francis Drake was here first. In 1579 Queen Eliza-
beth I's favorite explorer/circumnavigator/scourge of the Spanish Ar-
mada sailed into what is now called Drake's Bay in the present Point
Reyes National Seashore and liked the surroundings so well that he
stayed five weeks. He claimed the area in the name of Her Majesty back
home, dubbing it New Albion or New England because its craggy prom-
ontories reminded him of the white cliffs of Dover. Drake has been followed by seamen, sheepherders, loggers, sightseers, vacationers, geologists, and escapists. Yet much of the area, although only a stone's throw
from San Francisco, remains wild, empty, and engaging. One of Drake's
crewmen described it as "a goodly country, and fruitfull soyle, stored
with many blessings fit for the use of man." That description still holds
today.

State Highway 1, in this section known as the Shoreline Highway,
is the coast's main artery threading along the shore from Muir Woods to
points north. It's a drive with great views, small towns, and picturesque
farmlands.

Point Reyes

Point Reyes is a geological special. The rocks of the rugged peninsula exactly match those of the Tehachapi Mountains, 300 miles to the
south. The explanation is the gradual creep of the earth's tectonic plates.
The Pacific plate, including Point Reyes, is edging northwestward about

three inches a year. The rest of the continent is moving westward. Where the two plates meet is a network of jagged rifts and faults that grind against each other and build up tremendous pressure until they suddenly shift with a jolt. One of them, the infamous San Andreas Fault, bisects the Point Reyes peninsula. When it cut loose in 1906, the result was the devastating San Francisco earthquake which thrust the Point Reyes peninsula twenty miles northwestward. You can still see evidence of the fault—streams, for instance, with abrupt bends in their course. Even the weather is said to vary on either side of the fault. East of the Inverness Ridge can be warm and sunny, west can be foggy and chilly.

Point Reyes National Seashore is the centerpiece of the coastal area. It incorporates Point Reyes itself, a spit of land jutting into the Pacific Ocean at an acute angle, plus some 65,000 acres of open and forested country, sandy beaches, steep coastal bluffs, and estuaries. The area teems with wildlife of both land and water varieties. You can watch seals lazing on the offshore rocks, turn your head 180 degrees and see deer browsing in the woodsy underbrush. Some 361 species of birds, from pelicans to wrens, have been spotted here over the years. According to one estimate, some twenty species of whales, dolphins, and porpoises inhabit the National Marine Sanctuary offshore. The park appeals to nature lovers and hikers, but also to sunbathers and picnickers.

Enter the park at the primary gateway, the Bear Valley Entrance, at State Highway 1 at Olema. The visitor center here sits almost athwart the San Andreas Fault; you cross the fault, entering what the geologists call "the island in time," as you turn off State Highway 1. The visitor center provides an excellent introduction to the park, explaining the whys and whatevers of its geological heritage as well as providing exhibits and displays about its wide range of wildlife; the exhibit area includes more than 100 plant and animal specimens. Artifacts from the days when Point Reyes was known as the "graveyard of ships" also are on display. A special exhibit describes the migration of the gray whales. Kule Loklo, a replica of a Miwok Indian village with crude huts and demonstrations of basket weaving and other crafts, adjoins the center.

Just beyond the visitor center, Limantour Road leads to **Limantour Beach** and estuary. The beach is sheltered and the waters are calm (but quite chilly), fine for swimming and picnicking. The estuary is a favorite place for birdwatching that is noted for its wide variety of waterfowl. Harbor seals and their pups often are seen nearby.

Another route into the park is through the towns of Inverness Park and Inverness along the Sir Francis Drake Highway. This road leads through rolling, chaparral-covered country to the park's major beaches. **Point Reyes Beach North** and **Point Reyes Beach South,** collectively known as The Great Beach and separated by a headland, are windswept beaches, excellent for picnicking and beachcombing but under no circumstances for bathing. Even more than most of the northern California coast, Point Reyes beaches are unsafe for swimmers. Thanks to the coastal Japanese current, the waters are cold, and the surf is fierce with hazardous riptides and treacherous undertows. However, the sands are soft and the weather, especially in spring and fall, can be warm and pleasant.

Drake's Beach, on the opposite side of the point, is more protected. Here you can wade in Drake's Bay, or sunbathe, or snack at the small beachfront cafe. (Like much of the coastal area, it specializes in barbecued oysters.) The Kenneth C. Patrick Visitor Center tells the story of Drake's visit, pointing out that his vessel the *Golden Hinde* had a crew of only eighty and was about the length of two modest-size city buses. A stone cross and a plaque commemorate Drake's visit. A full-size skeleton of a minke whale is on display, and a saltwater aquarium introduces you to the local marine life. There are also exhibits dealing with the early Indian settlements on the peninsula and with beef and dairy cattle ranching, which continues in the part of the seashore known as the pastoral zone. A highlight of the Drake's Beach year is the annual sand castle contest, in which innovative builders from all parts of California and beyond collect to create masterpieces of turrets and parapets, some of which outdo Versailles—in miniature.

Point Reyes Light stands at the very tip of the point on the Drake Highway beyond the beach. It's a ten-minute walk from the parking area to the lighthouse, after which it's 300 steps up to the old Fresnel light itself. If you make it to the top, however, the view up and down the coast can be exhilarating. The area around the point was a seaman's nightmare, often shrouded in fog with stiff winds and rocky ledges at the base of the point; following the coastal currents, shipping hugged the shore and the light was a stern "Keep Off!" warning. The nearby seas are said still to hide the wreckage of many doomed ships, some of them (legend says) Spanish galleons laden with gold and precious stones. A small visitor center is devoted to lighthouse history and rescues and to the gray whale migration. The lighthouse is considered one of the best spots on the coast to watch the gray whales in their annual journeys. The light, installed in 1877, was turned off for good in 1975 and is now maintained by a private nonprofit group. The lighthouse and visitor center are open Thursday to Monday.

Johnson's Drake's Bay Oyster Farm, inside the seashore, pioneered the cultivation of oysters in the waters around Point Reyes. (Other oyster farms have grown up on Tomales Bay, on the opposite side of the peninsula.) Owner Charlie Johnson and his wife Makiko, along with Japanese marine biologists, transplanted the Japanese method of cultivating oysters on strings hung from platforms out of range of their enemies on the sea bottom. The Johnson family is delighted to welcome visitors and explain their methods, in addition to selling oyster cocktails, oysters on the half shell, and pint and quart jars (the extra-small oysters are tastiest and tenderest) in their somewhat spartan and nondescript frame headquarters. A free pamphlet includes the farm's history and a selection of recipes. You'll find the farm off Drake Highway, along an unimproved road "paved" with oyster shells. Call 415-669-1149.

The Tule Elk Range on Pierce Point Road off Drake Highway, is home to a herd of the great animals, who once were numbered in the thousands, and now have been successfully reintroduced after an absence of nearly a century. They often can be seen browsing near the roadside.

Tomales Bay State Park features waters that are at least ten degrees warmer than the ocean, surf-free, and therefore preferable for swimming. And, when the oceanside is foggy, it's often sunny at Tomales Bay's Heart's Desire Beach. The beach is equipped with barbecue grills and picnic tables—perfect for an afternoon outing. Call 415-669-1140.

Inverness and **Inverness Park** are small resort and second-home communities along Tomales Bay. Many San Franciscans vacation here in homes and cottages by the bayside or tucked into the wooded ravines of Inverness Ridge, often with spectacular views across the water. Artists and craftspeople have congregated around Inverness, too, and there are a number of intriguing small craft and gift shops, including some producing Shaker-type furniture.

Point Reyes Station, on State Highway 1, is the very model of an old western town with broad streets, canopied sidewalks, and old red-brick buildings. It's an old railroad town; once upon a time the entire three-block downtown was a railroad yard. Now it prides itself on being "the busiest burg in West Marin" and a "commercial center," but with only 700 people, that may be an overstatement. It's also, of course, the jumping-off place for the National Seashore. A few small art galleries and craft shops and two bookstores attract visitors. It is a good place to stop and poke around on an idle afternoon.

Along the Coast

Reading from south to north, the coast is strung out with beach communities, nature and wildlife preserves, and old-timey towns and fishing ports. (The inland Golden Gate National Recreation Area and Muir Woods are described in Chapter 8; attractions north of the Russian River are in Chapter 11.)

Stinson Beach is the beach resort closest to San Francisco and the suburban residential areas of Marin, a popular destination for weekend day-trippers. Part of it is within the Golden Gate National Recreation Area; the remainder is a county park. Popular with both board surfers and bodysurfers, the mile-long beach also allows plenty of space for picnicking, beachcombing, sunbathing, and volleyball. Across State Highway 1 from the beach park, the village of Stinson Beach is a line of art galleries, gift shops, small restaurants, and drinking oases.

The Audubon Canyon Ranch, three miles north of Stinson on Bolinas Lagoon, is the nesting place for the great blue heron and great egret. You can view the giant wading birds up close and extremely personal during the mating season from a rookery overlook at Picher Canyon. The private, nonprofit organization also conducts nature programs and docent-led tours. The overlook is open during the mating season, mid-March through mid-July, 10:00 A.M. to 4:00 P.M. on weekends. There is also a small museum and hiking trails. Call 415-868-9244.

Agate Beach, part of the Duxbury Reef State Marine Reserve, farther north on State Highway 1 at Bolinas, is famed for tidepools rich with marine life. More than two miles of shoreline are exposed at low tide, allowing fascinating study of crabs, anemones, and other creatures trapped in the pools by the outgoing tide. Although the beach is rich in shells, shell collecting is discouraged. The beach is located off Elm Road, Bolinas. Call 415-499-6387.

Ever see birds banded? Your opportunity to observe this technique, used to trace migrations, is at the **Point Reyes Bird Observatory's Palomarin Field Station,** off Mesa Road in Bolinas. Birds are retrieved for banding from mist nets that are put up at dawn and taken down by 1:00 P.M. Most banding is done in the early morning, before 10:00 A.M., after which the birds are released. A detailed tour of the facility is included. The station is located at 4990 Shoreline Highway, Stinson Beach. Call 415-868-0655.

Bodega Bay is a fishing village and one-time whaling port that has grown into an arts-and-crafts colony and a weekend getaway spot but still retains its fishing-village atmosphere (except on busy, tourist-crowded weekends). More than 300 commercial and sportfishing charter boats still homeport here, and a favorite weekday pastime is to go down to the docks and watch the fishermen unload their catch, especially when the salmon are running. Although most of the fish wind up in markets or on local restaurant plates, fishermen still sell them directly off the boats. Sheltered beaches both north and south of the town attract swimmers and shell collectors; Schoolhouse Beach is a particular favorite for beachcombing because summer storms deposit large amounts of shells and driftwood. The area is also popular with birdwatchers, who can spot killdeers, plovers, curlews, and several varieties of gulls. Galleries and craft shops are strung along State Highway 1 along with shops specializing in alder-smoked salmon.

Bodega Head, a rugged promontory jabbed into the sea, shelters the harbor and is a favorite and not very difficult hike, offering sweeping views down the coastline and out to sea. Luxury resorts both north and south of the town enjoy commanding views of the ocean.

A Little Inland

Petaluma is Sonoma County's second-largest city, and—although it seems far inland—a once-busy and still active river port: it gives visitors quite a jolt to drive up U.S. 101 and see a vast flotilla of pleasure boats in the midst of what seems a sea of agricultural land. The Petaluma

River and deep-water canal plus a major railroad hub explain this part of Petaluma's history, which centered around shipping of fruits and other produce from the rich farmlands of the county as well as redwood logs from the mountainside. As one result of those flush times, Petaluma boasts literally hundreds of well-maintained Victorian office buildings, storefronts, and residential mansions, including some of the finest examples of iron-front architecture in the U.S. (At one time, it was believed that iron-front buildings were fireproof; unlucky owners found out the hard way that the idea was fallacious.) A brochure outlining a self-guided walking tour of Petaluma's Victorian architecture is available from the Chamber of Commerce, 215 Howard Street, Petaluma 94952. Call 707-762-2785.

California's oldest adobe structure, built in the 1830s as the ranch home of General Mariano Vallejo, the last military commander of Alta California before the Bear Flag revolt launched the California Republic, is the centerpiece of **Petaluma Adobe State Historic Park**. The collection includes clothing, tools, and other artifacts from the Mexican period; there is a self-guided tour. The park is open daily 10:00 A.M. to 5:00 P.M. Admission, including the house, is $1. The park is located at 3325 Adobe Road. Call 707-778-0150.

Samuel P. Taylor State Park is a 2600-acre, little-known forest of towering redwoods strung along Papermill Creek. In the deep shade under the redwoods are lush growths of ferns. There are also groves of oak and madrone, browsing deer, and hawks soaring overhead. You can even skinny-dip in the Old Swimming Hole at the Swimming Hole Bridge. There are hiking trails and picnic tables. You'll find the park on Sir Francis Drake Boulevard, West Marin. Call 415-488-9897.

The **Marin French Cheese Company** has been making Brie, Camembert, and two specialty cheeses called schloss and breakfast cheese since 1865. The fifth generation of cheese makers now operates the place, producing wheels of Brie for the "Rouge et Noir" label, in cellars that were dug by hand more than a hundred years ago. A guided tour of the small factory provides a primer on cheese making, explaining not only the origins of Camembert and Brie and the differences between the two (basically, Brie is made in larger wheels) but also how to determine the proper ripeness for eating. You also receive a free pamphlet with cheese recipes. The factory is surrounded by five acres of grounds with picnic tables and a duck pond. A gift shop sells cheese and wine, as well as cookbooks and souvenirs. The cheese company is located on Petaluma-Point Reyes Road. Call 707-762-6001.

Restaurants

- **Vladimir's** specializes in hearty Czech food, a legacy from a Czech colony that settled here in the early 1900s. On a terrace with a view of Tomales Bay (and also the Sir Francis Drake Highway), costumed waitpersons serve chicken paprikash and baked garlic rabbit. The price is fixed for both lunch and dinner. Reserve on weekends. Moderate to expensive. Sir Francis Drake Highway, Inverness. 415-669-1021.

- **Manka's,** also Czech, sits on a dramatic Inverness hilltop with views across Tomales Bay. Dinner is served in a wood-paneled dining room with a cheerful fireplace. It is open Friday to Sunday for dinner. Expensive. 30 Calendar Way, Inverness. 415-669-1034.

- **Chez Madeleine,** Point Reyes Station, with candlelight is cozy, comfortable and French influenced. Try the boeuf bourguignon. There is music in the evenings. Moderate to expensive. State Highway 1, Point Reyes. 415-663-9177.

- **Tides Wharf Restaurant** overlooks Bodega Bay Harbor and the fishing fleet. Not surprisingly, the specialty is local seafood. Try the Bodega Bay chowder and ask about the catch of the day. Moderate to expensive. 707-875-2777.

- **Rancho Nicasio** is a fifty-year-old community gathering place on the small town square in the farming hamlet of Nicasio, off the Point Reyes-Petaluma Road. It is decorated like the old-fashioned hunting lodge it once was. There is live music and dancing on Friday and Saturday nights. The menu includes local oysters, local chicken, and local sausage. Moderate. 415-662-2219.

- **Sand Dollar** is Stinson Beach's favorite for hamburgers and other lunchtime fare. The sundeck overlooking the ocean is a popular dining spot. Moderate. State Highway 1 at Stinson Beach. 415-868-0434.

- **Dempsey's Ale House** is the home of the Sonoma Brewing Company's microbrewery, dispensing its own product. The patio overlooks the Petaluma River. The restaurant offers standard pub fare with blues music on Saturday nights. Moderate. 50 E. Washington Street, Petaluma. 707-765-9694.

Lodging

Seven small B&Bs and inns of the Point Reyes area have banded together in Inns of Point Reyes to provide a one-call referral service. P.O. Box 145, Inverness, California 94937. 415-663-1420. Seashore Bed and Breakfasts of Marin offers a similar service for six other B&Bs. P.O. Box 1239, Point Reyes Station, California 94956. 415-663-9373.

- **Golden Hinde** is on the beach at Tomales Bay, Inverness. Many rooms have fireplaces and some have kitchens. Boat rental is available. Reserve well in advance for weekends. Moderate. 800-339-9398.

- **Blackthorne Inn** was dubbed a "carpenter's fantasy" by *Sunset* magazine and so it is—a bizarre furbelowed and gingerbready structure with five quixotic rooms designed around a water tank. Moderate to expensive rates include a country breakfast. There are special winter prices. 266 Vallejo Avenue, Inverness Park. 415-663-8621.

- **Inn at the Tides** is a luxury resort overlooking the harbor at Bodega Bay. All sixty-eight rooms have bay views; many have woodburning fireplaces. They offer complimentary breakfast and a Sunday brunch (not complimentary). Expensive. State Highway 1. 707-876-3182.

- **Petaluma Inn** is a Best Western close to old town Petaluma and to the riverfront. There are seventy-five rooms with an adjoining restaurant. Moderate. 200 S. McDowell Boulevard, Petaluma. 707-763-0994.

• **Point Reyes Hostel** has dormitory accommodations with a kitchen available, at Limantour Beach in the Point Reyes National Seashore. Reservations are a must. $9 per person per night. Limantour Road, Point Reyes National Seashore. 415-663-8811.

Chapter 10
The Wine Country:
Napa Valley

Sunshine, cool afternoon breezes, and wine, wine, wine. The Napa Valley has it all and more. Consisting of the communities of Napa, Yountville, Oakville, Rutherford, Saint Helena and Calistoga, and all the vineyards between, the Napa Valley is known primarily for its more than 175 wineries that annually produce many thousands of gallons of chardonnay, pinot noir, zinfandel, merlot, and other wines, red, white and blush. The Napa Valley is the premier grape-growing and wine-producing region in America, rivaling the best in France. You can see the process that makes these wines great. Most of the wineries offer guided tours, many of them give free tastings (others charge minimally), and all of them sell bottles and cases of their best— often you can get special vintages exclusively available at the winery store. You don't have to be a wine enthusiast or even drink wine to enjoy the tours, however. In a quickly passing forty-five minutes to an hour, the tour guides pass out a plethora of food suggestions, wine trivia, and serving advice while walking you through the steps involved in turning grapes into wine.

Napa Valley's reputation for wine overshadows its many other attractions. The area around Calistoga, for instance, is a hotbed of geothermal activity with its own Old Faithful geyser, a number of natural hot springs surrounded by resorts, and a petrified forest. The energy generated by the boiling and bubbling underground even helps to light the lamps of San Francisco. And, to stay away from the seismic activity and still enjoy nature, you can ride a horse to the top of the foothills for a panoramic bird's-eye view of the entire region. The Napa Valley offers plenty of diversions to complement the winery tours or simply entertain you on their own.

History

The pioneers who came into the valley rightfully saw it as a land of promise and adopted the name given it by Native Americans; in the Miwok language, Napa means "plenty." George Yount, a trapper and explorer, recognized the area's potential early and established the first homestead in the valley over 150 years ago, in the area that was to be named Yountville after his death. In the mid-1800s, vintners discovered that the Napa Valley climate was perfect for growing grapes, with its hot mornings and cooling afternoon breeze off the ocean. A collection of wineries sprung up around Yountville and beyond—by the late 1860s fifty vintners were producing wines in the fertile valley. The next decade saw two of the valley's renowned wineries developed, Inglenook and Beringer, two big wineries that survived Prohibition and still operate today. Prohibition combined with *phylloxera,* a plant louse that destroys the vine roots, acted as a double whammy virtually knocking out the young wine industry in the 1920s. However, the repeal of Prohibition in 1933 sparked a resurgence in wine production that has lasted to the present day.

The modern age of wine making has seen unrivaled cooperation among the Napa Valley wineries. Sharing techniques and new technologies, this region has collectively boosted itself to become one of the most prestigious wine regions in the world. In the process, Napa has become one of the most popular tourist destinations in northern California.

Wineries

Winery tours guide you through the behind-the-scenes world of wine making from viticulture (grape growing), to the initial fermentations, to the storage and aging of the wines. If you are lucky enough to be in Napa during harvest (usually in late August), you not only see the process from crush to bottle but also inhale the multitude of aromas involved in wine making from the fresh smell of newly crushed grapes to the butterscotch aroma of the barrels. At this time of the year, tour guides will often let you sample the sweet, flavorful grapes used to make the wine. At all times of the year you can taste the final liquid product. Wine tasting usually includes four or more different wines ranging from a light crisp chardonnay to a heavy cabernet sauvignon to a sweet dessert gewürztraminer.

The wineries described present some of the most interesting and descriptive winery tours which offer slightly different perspectives and lots of information. However, no matter what the tour guides tell you, a wine barrel is a wine barrel, so when the winery tours start repeating themselves, check out sparkling wine production or brandy distillation—or start with one of them.

As you drive up the Napa Valley on State Highway 29, the valley's main stem, the first enterprise of note that you see actually makes sparkling wine. The French-owned **Domaine Chandon,** located just north of the town of Napa on State Highway 29, prides itself on producing its sparkling wine by the traditional *champenoise* method developed in France. The tour guide will carefully point out that only sparkling wine made in the Champagne region of France can be designated champagne under European law. Although these laws are not applicable in the U.S., French-owned Domaine Chandon reserves the champagne label for its upscale French product, instead producing in California a very drinkable (and very popular) sparkling wine.

The production of sparkling wine differs considerably from that of still wines. On Domaine Chandon's complimentary tour you get to see many of the intricate extra steps unique to the production of bubbly. You walk by rows of racked bottles in the process of mechanical riddling, where a machine slowly shakes the upside-down bottles to drive the sediment toward the bottle's neck, behind the special bottle cap used in production. Then you watch the disgorging, when the neck of the bottle is soaked in a very cold brine solution that freezes the wine and yeast collected in the neck. The bottle cap is removed, the frozen plug shoots out, and the remaining wine is corked, retaining most of its bubbles. The Domaine Chandon tour lasts forty-five minutes to an hour and ends in the tasting room, where you can purchase sparkling wine by the glass for $3 to $5 or take a few bottles home for your next New Year's Eve party. Tours are conducted May to October, daily on the hour, 11:00

A.M. to 6:00 P.M.; April to November, Wednesday to Sunday 11:00 A.M. to 6:00 P.M. Take the Yountville Veterans Home exit off State Highway 29 and proceed west across the railroad tracks to the winery. You can spot the Domaine Chandon sign just off State Highway 29 coming south. Call 707-944-8844.

Domaine Chandon also boasts a much-acclaimed restaurant, featuring French dishes from the Champagne region prepared with a California twist. The chef prides himself on taking advantage of fresh regional produce as well as creating dishes that complement the Domaine Chandon sparkling wines. (A broad range of still wines is available for those who care to save the bubbly for special occasions or aperitifs.) The restaurant is open daily for lunch 11:30 A.M. to 2:30 P.M. (Closed on Monday and Tuesday in November through April.) Dinner is served Wednesday to Sunday at 6:00 P.M. For reservations call 707-944-2892.

Continuing north on State Highway 29, you next reach the **Robert Mondavi Winery** on the left, acclaimed for its wine as well as its cutting-edge methods of viticulture. In the age of environmentalism, the wine industry has looked to organic methods of pest control and has developed new techniques to avoid using herbicides. Robert Mondavi, a pioneer, emphasizes that divergence from the old ways isn't a matter of being politically correct but rather stems from his desire to guarantee the soil's fertility for generations to come. To learn about these new tech-

THE OAKVILLE GROCERY

There are few better combinations than fine wine and gourmet food. The Napa Valley offers an abundance of fine wine that you can take home to enjoy in your hotel, but if you want food to match, go to the Oakville Grocery. You can choose from a large variety of cheeses, sausages, mustards, breads, and, of course, wine. It's the perfect place to outfit yourself for a diligent afternoon of picnicking. This humble general store sells all the amenities for properly extravagant sandwich making. It is located right on the east side of the Saint Helena Highway (State Highway 29) in Oakville.

WINE TERMINOLOGY

Glancing through a gourmet magazine, you may have come across a wine critique and found yourself drowning in a wine ocean of strange and seemingly inappropriate vocabulary. Napa Valley wine lovers and grape growers revel in this vocabulary, dropping arcane terms with every upraised glass. Although tour guides make a concerted effort to define each vocabulary term, often stopping at every other sentence to explain, for example, the anatomy of a wine (nose, leg, or body), a few words always slip through the dictionary net. Here are some of the most commonly used, bizarre, or esoteric terms. Insert any of them into the most innocent question and you will sound like a true connoisseur.

Balance: all the different tastes in the wine. Acidity, sugar, tannin (acidic, tart flavor that comes from the grape skins and seeds), fruit combine to produce a pleasant flavor in which one taste does not dominate the others.

Body: the strong taste in the wine, opposite of watery.

Bouquet: smell. The bouquet is a very important aspect of wine since the nose is far more discerning of flavor than the tongue.

Brut: very dry, usually applied to Champagne or sparkling wine.

Character: how the different wine flavors combine, forming the individual and distinctive taste of the wine.

Chewy: used to describe the body of a good red wine. A chewy wine gives the taster a sensation of tiny solid particles on the tongue.

---

niques and more, take the free winery tour which has a well-earned reputation for a wealth of information and organized presentation. Enjoy free tasting at the end of the tour. Reservations are necessary. Tours are given daily on the hour 9:00 A.M. to 5:00 P.M. You'll find the winery on the west side of Saint Helena Highway (State Highway 29), Oakville. Call 707-963-9611.

St. Supery, located almost directly across the highway from Robert Mondavi, developed award-winning wines from the beginning. Al-

Complex: a wide range of different tastes. Good wines boast a large number of identifiable tastes, all well balanced.

Earthy: the taste from the soil in which the grapes were grown. Considered good in small doses.

Foxy: the taste of wild or uncultured grapes. (A bad word in the Napa Valley.)

Legs: the tiny drops of wine that run down inside the bowl of a glass after the wine has been swirled around inside it. It suggests good quality glycerin (syrupy alcohol content sometimes referred to as residual sugars). Low quality glycerin comes down the glass in sheets.

Nose: strong bouquet (see above).

Varietal: refers to wines made from predominantly one grape variety such as chardonnay or cabernet sauvignon.

Often adjectives such as assertive, aggressive, robust, mellow, and smooth are used to describe the way in which the wine spreads its flavor in the mouth. These words and many others will come to mind if you pay special attention when sampling. Note the way the wine first tastes in your mouth, then record the sensations it delivers to the tongue and how long the taste lasts after you have swallowed. Good wines should not strike the palate but instead slowly saturate the tongue and then linger in the mouth with a lasting gusto.

The moral of the wine slang: avoid off-balance, foxy, legless wines with too much earthiness and a weak nose. Drink full body, chewy reds with complex tastes and assertive rather than aggressive flavors.

though one of the youngest wineries in the valley, it has already earned a remarkable reputation not only for the quality of its wine but also for the character of its tour. The guided tour starts in the Atkinson House, a refurbished Victorian decorated with historic photographs and paintings that capture the feel of yesterday's Napa. It then takes you through the fermentation process and ends with a wine tasting. During the tour you will be introduced to Smella Vision, better known as the "Sniffer," a machine with tubes protruding from the base that isolates and identifies the different aromas typically found in the wine bouquet (see Wine Terminology, pages 122–123).

You can also visit St. Supery via a self-guided tour, following informative placards that explain each step in the process. St. Supery's gallery of modern art features painting exhibitions changing every three months. Wine tasting costs $2.50. It is open daily 9:30 A.M. to 4:30 P.M. It is located at 8440 Saint Helena Highway (State Highway 29), Rutherford. Call 707-963-4507.

The **Inglenook Winery,** one of the few major labels to survive Prohibition, was started by a Finnish sea captain, Gustave Niebaum, whose goal was to produce "the finest wines, to equal and excel the most famous vintages in Europe." It seems that the whole Napa Valley has collectively realized Niebaum's dream with Inglenook in the vanguard. The Inglenook-Napa Valley 1941 cabernet sauvignon made the winery famous worldwide and has been called one of the best cabernets ever produced in the valley.

Nestled into tall trees and covered by ivy, the winery takes its name from the Scottish term "nook" meaning a warm and cozy corner. The tour leads you through the estate and the winery, describing the history as well as the wines. A complimentary tasting follows the tour. Tours are given daily 10:30 A.M. to 4:30 P.M. The winery is located at 1991 Saint Helena Highway (State Highway 29), Rutherford. Call 707-967-3352.

Beringer Vineyard, established in 1876, is another Prohibition survivor (due to production and sales of sacramental wines, they contend with a smile). Today, Beringer's experience and heritage combine in its fermentation and blending process, producing award-winning wines that consistently compete with the best in France.

The Beringer tour differs from many of the other tours. While guides do not show the actual wine-making plant, they do take you through the barrel-aging area, caves that were dug by hand over 100 years ago and are still used today. The tour ends in the Rhine House, a large mansion full of sparkling stained glass where you sample (for free) the special Rhine House cabernet sauvignon (sold only at the winery), among others. This tour provides the visitor with an exceptional amount of information about wines: storing, serving and drinking, including food suggestions—all presented in a well-organized and entertaining manner. Also, in the Rhine House Founders Room, you can sample the top-of-the-line reserve wines for a nominal fee. Reservations are suggested. Open daily for tours and tastings 9:30 A.M. to 5:00 P.M. It is located on Highway 29, Saint Helena. Watch for the sign on the west side of the highway. Call 707-963-7115.

The **Sterling Winery** epitomizes the wine industry's reputation for luxury and elegance—but with a modern façade. Contrasting with the traditional ivy-covered stone and brick wineries, the Sterling Winery building takes its architecture from the Mediterranean, a white stucco structure built into the hillside that stands majestically atop a 300-foot knoll. While the building is impressive, the trip to the winery building highlights the entire visit. From the parking lot, located just off State Highway 29 on Dunaweal Lane, you swoop high above the vineyards aboard a sky tram, a ski gondola-type transport lifting you through stunning panoramic views to the winery complex. Enjoy the vista from one of the strategically located picnic areas. In the winery, follow the informative self-guided tour. Detailed placards explain the Sterling winemaking process. Finish up in the tasting room where you can relax in chairs for a civilized sit-down glass of wine. Both the winery and the tasting room are open year-round daily 10:30 A.M. to 4:30 P.M. The visitor's fee is $6 and includes the sky tram ride, tasting, and a $2 discount toward a bottle of Sterling wine. The winery is located at 1111 Dunaweal Lane, Calistoga. Call 707-942-5151.

The Silverado Trail (actually a road) offers an alternate return route south from Calistoga and through the wineries on the eastern side of the Napa Valley.

Rutherford Hill Winery sits in the low mountains, a half mile off the trail, where, from its perch on the hillside, you can see far across the valley. Rutherford picnic areas offer yet another comfortable locale to enjoy both the wines and the view. The Rutherford Hill tour takes you through primary stages of wine production and includes information about viticulture and wine-making techniques, but the most interesting part of the tour is . . . spelunking. Rutherford Hill boasts the most extensive cave system in the U.S. excavated for wine storage. The tour ends, of course, in the tasting room where current vintages are available for sampling. Wine tasting costs $3. Tours are free, beginning every hour on the half hour. Daily tasting hours are 10:30 A.M. to 4:00 P.M. The winery is located at 200 Rutherford Hill Road, Saint Helena, just off the Silverado Trail. Call 707-963-7194.

Although most of the Napa Valley wineries grew up along State

Highway 29 on the twenty-eight-mile stretch of road between Napa and Calistoga, you will find some diverse offshoots of the wine industry just to the south of the valley, toward San Francisco.

The **Carneros Alambic Brandy Distillery,** just off State Highway 121, distills rare alambic brandy out of lightly fermented grapes from the Napa Valley—the first facility of its kind in the United States. The distillery, built in 1982, resembles those found in the brandy region of France. Guided tours point out the techniques and machinery that differentiate alambic brandy from conventional brandy. You will see the exotic Still House where the copper alambic stills, shaped like the onion domes of Russian Orthodox churches, vaporize and then condense the alcohol. In the Barrel House that holds the largest stock of aging alambic in the country, the strong vanilla smell will clear your sinuses. The tour ends in the sniffing room where you can smell the various blends and stages of brandy that make up the alambic final product. (No tasting is available.) The distillery is open in spring and summer daily 10:00 A.M. to 5:00 P.M., in the fall and winter, Thursday to Monday 10:30 A.M. to 4:30 P.M. It is located at 1250 Cuttings Wharf Road, Napa. Call 707-253-9055.

The **Hakusan Sake Gardens,** also located just south of the Napa Valley, represents the most modern sake production facility in the world. No guided tours are available but you can take the short self-guided walking tour along the plant building. Placards explain the machines visible through the window and their role in the conversion of rice into sake. Make the tasting room your last stop on the self-guided tour where you can admire the well-pruned Japanese garden while sampling some complimentary sake. The tasting room is open daily 9:00 A.M. to 6:00 P.M. The gardens are at One Executive Way, Napa, located at the corner of state highways 29 and 12; the entrance is one block east of the intersection, at Kelley Road. Call 707-258-6160.

Other Attractions

The best of Napa Valley's nonwine related attractions lie in the northern part of the valley.

Calistoga's **Old Faithful Geyser** is one of three geysers in the world granted the title because of their clockwork performance. As with its more famous namesake in Yellowstone National Park, the appearance of the geyser area can be deceiving. From the seemingly innocent flat patch of earth, uprising steam and boiling water begin to seep through the surface, growing in intensity just before the eruption of the geyser. Then, with a hiss and a boom, Old Faithful shoots thousands of gallons of boiling water and steam sixty feet into the air. The show lasts about four minutes, after which Old Faithful goes back to sleep for another forty minutes before cutting loose again. The regular forty-minute intervals continue night and day. However, on occasion, the geyser is late or actually skips a show, and some scientists have linked these delays to major earthquakes. Seismological records seem to show that the geyser changes schedule two to fourteen days before an earthquake, although scientists have yet to ascertain whether the geyser can reliably predict a coming tremor. Entry to Old Faithful costs $4.

Some say that the northern Napa Valley has the largest geothermal area in the world. This monster of natural energy has been tapped in the **Geyserville** area, bordering Calistoga. The heat and water rising from the earth are converted into electric power via a series of turbines and feeds into the power supply of the Pacific Gas and Electric Company (PG and E), the northern California public utility. The geothermal field produces enough energy for a city of 100,000 people. Sorry, no tours are available because it is a high-security area.

The area's natural hot springs, however, can be enjoyed by all visitors. The surrounding resorts offer many services that complement a sit in the hot springs. A mud bath and/or a massage before a soak in the warm water rids the most tense traveler of any leftover office stress.

A large number of resorts have grown up around these springs, but none are more famous than **White Sulfur Springs,** a 330-acre resort that offers beautiful hikes, massages, and natural hot tubs. The family-owned operation is said to be California's oldest resort, rivaling the famed Saratoga Springs in New York state. White Sulfur has all the amenities for a relaxing escape—from its location, hidden in a secluded canyon, to no telephones or televisions, to 86-degree (on average) hot springs. The resort's advertising proclaims, "If you like the country, enjoy a year-round babbling brook, and like the simple life, White Sulfur Springs is just the place for you." If you do not want to stay overnight, you can purchase a day pass (provided that a special group has not reserved the whole place) that gives you access to the challenging hiking trails, where you wander through the foothills at the east edge of the valley, then lets you recuperate in the relaxing hot springs afterward. Day passes cost $6 Sunday to Thursday and $12 Friday and Saturday. Room rates are $75 on weekends for a room with full bath to $125 for a kitchenette, full bath, and wood stove. Reservations should be made at least a week in advance. The springs are located at 3100 White Sulfur Springs Road, Saint Helena. Call 707-224-0727.

The **Petrified Forest,** five miles west of Calistoga, is more evidence of the area's seismic activity. Some six million years ago, Mount Saint Helena erupted, spewing volcanic ash across a forest of gigantic redwoods. The eruption uprooted and toppled the trees, which were then infiltrated with silica and minerals, in effect turning them to stone while preserving their texture—the process called petrification. It is open in summer daily 9:00 A.M. to 6:00 P.M., in winter 9:00 A.M. to 5:00 P.M. Admission is $3. The forest is located at 4100 Petrified Forest Road. Call 707-942-6667.

Wild Horse Valley Ranch, located just east of the city of Napa, is one of the best-known equestrian centers on the West Coast. In fact, the U.S. Olympic equestrian teams of the 1970s trained here. Nestled deep in the hills of southeastern Napa County, the ranch offers horseback rides for people of all ages, levels, and experience. The ranch encompasses 4,000 acres of land; you can ride through open meadows, around the cross-country course, near reservoirs, and up hills for big-sky views of the valley. Take the two-hour trail ride to enjoy all this open land. Rides cost $25. Skilled instructors give private, semiprivate, and group lessons that range from $35 for a one-hour private lesson to $18 per person in a group. Lessons, trail rides, and cross-country schooling are available Wednesday to Monday 8:00 A.M. to 5:00 P.M. Wild Horse Valley Ranch is located just southeast of Napa. Call for directions and information: 707-224-0727.

A number of resorts have grown up around Calistoga's hot springs with a wide variety of soothing body treatments from basic massage to a seaweed bath and wrap. **Dr. Wilkinson's Hot Springs** is one of the best-known names for body therapy. Far from fictional, Dr. John Wilkinson started as a chiropractor in Calistoga and later developed this spa. You can get a massage and then recline in a warm mud bath that gently suspends you, allowing your muscles total relaxation. Dr. Wilkinson asserts, "Natural, simple relaxation—that's what we're all about." Appointments are required and lodging is available from $49 to

$94. The springs are located at 1507 Lincoln Avenue, Calistoga. Call 707-942-4102.

The **International Spa** repertoire includes a large number of different body therapies with facilities for two people to share. Here you can get an acupressure massage, a seaweed bath and wrap, and a mud bath for two. Appointments are required. The spa is located on First Street in Calistoga, one block east of Washington Street, which runs north off State Highway 29. Call 707-942-6122.

Candles add that extra touch to a fine dinner and good wine. Stop by the **Hurd Beeswax Candle Factory** in the Freemark Abbey Winery complex to find the right candle to bring a new glow to your dinner. Wax workers, busy as bees, produce the candles right in the shop. You can watch as they roll the beeswax, cut out shapes, and form them into flowers or embed dried real flowers directly into the wax. The candle factory also displays some bees at work. You watch, from behind a glass door, as the little workers construct their hive. The shop is open daily 10:00 A.M. to 5:30 P.M., but candles are made weekdays only. Call 707-963-7211. The adjoining Freemark Abbey Winery offers tours daily at 2:00 P.M. Tasting costs $5. You'll find the complex at 3020 Saint Helena Highway (State Highway 29), North Saint Helena, on the corner of Lodi Lane. Call 707-963-9696.

The **Hess Collection Winery** boasts a notable collection of contemporary art in its historic stone building that dates back to the turn of the century. The winery offers self-guided tours through the gallery that end in the tasting room. Tasting costs $2.50. The winery is open daily 10:00 A.M. to 4:00 P.M. It is located at 4411 Redwood Road, Napa. Call 707-255-1144.

Restaurants ————————————————

The restaurants in the Napa Valley cater to the middle-upper-class wine drinker. While the atmosphere ranges from the ultimate in elegance to candlelight casual, restaurants generally serve a continental or California cuisine, based on fresh local produce, and often incorporating local wines in the preparation. Many also take advantage of Napa's bright sunshine and pleasant temperatures and have patio seating in the daytime as well as in the evening.

WINE ON THE RAILS AND UP IN THE AIR

What better way to enjoy Napa Valley fine wines than while eating a gourmet meal and watching the scenery pass in front of you? The Napa Valley offers unusually appetizing meals on a train ride or a hot-air balloon flight.

The **Napa Valley Wine Train** takes you on a three-hour excursion from Napa to Saint Helena and back in the luxury of a restored Orient-Express-style train. In the elegance of the old-fashioned dining car with its spotless linens, polished crystal, and gleaming silverware, energetic waiters and waitresses serve fine continental cuisine. Tender and lovingly prepared meats combine with the freshest local produce to rival the best restaurants in the valley. Of course, the wine list includes a large number of the best Napa Valley wines to enjoy with your meal. Take the train for dinner in high summer for the four-course meal that pauses with a sorbet to cleanse the palate before the main course—what luxury! But when the days get shorter so that you miss the scenery on the dinner train, take advantage of the brunch or lunch train where you can wine, dine, and see the rows of vines pass as the train slowly rolls to your culinary satisfaction.

Meals are served during two seatings, one on the way to Saint Helena and one on the way back. When you are not eating, you can be tasting. You can select from the wine list and buy wine by the glass, or just sink into the plush lounge chairs with a satisfied stomach and a warm cup of coffee. On weekends and holidays brunch trains depart at 9:00 A.M. The lunch train leaves Monday to Friday at 11:30 A.M.

• **Brown Street Brewery and Restaurant** serves California cuisine accompanied by—would you believe, in the Napa Valley—West Coast microbrewed beer on tap. A long list of dinner specials changes nightly. Dress is casual. Moderate. 1300 Brown Street, Napa. 707-255-6395.

• **Chanterelle Restaurant** offers continental cuisine, specializing in seafood. Try the poached salmon made with a special champagne sauce. It serves lunch and dinner. Moderate. 804 First Street, Napa. 707-253-7300.

and on weekends and holidays at 12:30 P.M. The dinner train (no rides on Monday) departs Tuesday to Friday at 6:30 P.M. and on weekends and holidays at 6:00 P.M. Boarding starts a half hour before departure, and all trips last about three hours. Tariffs for the train only cost about $30 per person. You pay for the gourmet meals on the train, ranging from $22 to $25 for lunch and under $50 for dinner (not including wine; tipping is not necessary). You can ride the train without eating just to enjoy the wine and countryside, but the meal is recommended—the food is terrific and the countryside beautiful. Reservations are suggested. The train boards at 1295 McKinstry Street, Napa. Call 707-253-2111.

Another Napa Valley attraction that combines many of the best aspects of the region and reserves time for the rest is **hot-air ballooning**. Balloons lift off around 6:30 in the morning, giving the aerial traveler the best views of the lush vine-covered valley in the best possible, early morning light. And a champagne brunch tops off the whole expedition. Enjoy romance, intrigue, glorious photo opportunities, and, after landing, great food. The brunch flight ends at around 10:00 A.M. with plenty of time to visit a good number of wineries or take a massage and soak in one of the many spa resorts. Rides leave from all parts of the valley depending on which balloonist you choose. Reservations required. Rides cost around $165 per person. Napa's Great Balloon Escape (707-253-0860) takes off from Calistoga. Napa Valley Balloons, Inc. (707-253-2224) leaves from Yountville, and Bonaventure Balloon Company (707-944-2822) leaves from Rutherford.

- For casual Italian food with a continental flair, eat at **River City**. Enjoy the rack of lamb with a mustard sauce on the mahogany deck overlooking the Napa River. Moderate. 505 Lincoln Avenue, Napa. 707-253-1111.

- The **Penguins Restaurant** specializes in Mediterranean cuisine in an old-fashioned dining room with candlelight. Try the bouillabaisse. Moderate. 1533 Trancas Street, Napa. 707-252-4343.

- **California Cafe Bar and Grill** serves California and Mediterranean cuisines. Check out the apricot-stuffed pork loin. Lunch and dinner are served. Moderate to expensive. 6795 Washington Street (State Highway 29 and Madison Street), Yountville. 707-944-2330.

- **Anestis Grill** boasts upscale casual dining that combines Greek with California fare. The leg of lamb on a French rotisserie offers a rich, satisfying meal. Lunch and dinner are served. Moderate. 6518 Washington Street, Yountville. 707-944-1500.

- **Garden Grill Restaurant** cooks up Costa Rican food. Only breakfast and lunch are served. Moderate. 1140 Rutherford Road at Rancho Caymus Inn, Rutherford. 707-963-1777.

- **Valeriano's Italian Restaurant** makes all its food from scratch, including bread, pasta, and dessert. The ambience is casual. Only dinner is served. The connected trattoria, **Johnny's on the Sidewalk,** by the same owners, serves lunch and dinner. Johnny's is inexpensive; Valeriano's moderate. 1457 Lincoln Avenue, Calistoga. 707-942-0606.

Lodging ——————————————————————

The best lodging is in the town of Napa unless you are looking for one of the spa resorts, primarily located in the northern part of the valley around Calistoga. Napa has a wide range of bed and breakfasts as well as more moderate lodging, although all accommodations in the valley have inflated prices.

- The **Beazley House** is a traditional B&B, built in 1902. Rooms are available with a fireplace and/or spa. Moderate. 1910 First Street, Napa. 707-257-1649.

- The **Churchill Manor** offers B&B accommodations in its old Victorian built in 1889. It also offers fireplaces and spas. Moderate. 485 Brown Street, Napa. 707-253-7733.

- **La Belle Epoque** B&B holds wine tasting in its elegantly decorated lounge. Moderate. 1386 Calistoga Avenue, Napa. 707-257-2161.

- **Auberge Du Soleil** is the ultimate in luxury resort hotels. Its grounds include a pool, a spa, tennis courts, a gourmet restaurant, and a masseuse. Expensive. 180 Rutherford Hill Road, Rutherford. 707-963-1211.

- The **Vintage Inn** also caters to the resort oriented with a pool, spa, and tennis courts. Expensive. 6541 Washington Street, Yountville. 707-944-1112.

- **Chablis Lodge** offers more economical lodging, still in the Napa Valley. Moderate. 3360 Solano Avenue, Napa. 707-257-1944.

- **Wine Valley Lodge** is another economical alternative to the pricy B&Bs and resort hotels. Moderate. 200 South Coombs Street, Napa. 707-224-7911.

Chapter 11
The Wine Country: Sonoma

Sonoma County has an Avis complex. People seem to think that this rich producer of vintage is Number 2 among California wine-growing regions, behind its better-publicized neighbor to the east, spelled N-A-P-A. Consequently, Sonoma wine makers say they must try harder. In fact many of California's premium wines originate in Sonoma County, and local boosters will tell you proudly (and aggrievedly) that Sonoma wines consistently win more medals for excellence, even though Napa has twice as many wineries. (Napa replies that it depends on who's counting.) The test, of course, is in the tasting. Seventy-five wineries, many of them small, picturesque family operations, invite you to come and find out for yourself.

Sonoma is also awash in history—political, religious, botanical, and literary. The town plaza in Sonoma was the scene of the comic-opera "Bear Flag Revolt," in which a raggle-taggle bunch of revolutionaries ran a newly minted flag up the flagpole and declared California a republic. The republic lasted twenty-two days until the United States, with its cry of "manifest destiny," annexed California as a territory. As for botany, the "plant wizard" Luther Burbank fell in love with the area's rich soil and felicitous climate, developed or improved hundreds of plant species, and turned its valleys into great gardens. And the rough-hewn author Jack London, home from his gripping tales of the frozen north and the stormy seas, settled in what he called "The Valley of the Moon" and left behind a lavish literary heritage.

The settlements of Sonoma are strung along two long valleys, following State Highway 12 on the east and U.S. 101 on the west, joining at the county seat (and largest city) of Santa Rosa. The Russian River here turns west, cutting through the redwood-timbered Coast Range to the sea. One way to enjoy the area to the fullest is to head north on State Highway 12 from Sonoma through the vineyards and orchards to Santa Rosa, continue north on U.S. 101 to the wineries and pleasant communities of Healdsburg, Geyserville, and Cloverdale, then reverse direction and follow the Russian River Valley westward before returning to U.S. 101 and points south.

Sonoma

The city of Sonoma was the first European touchdown point in the area and is by far the most historic. The northernmost and last of the string of missions established by the Franciscan order (and the only one after the Mexican takeover) was founded here in 1823. The **Mission de San Francisco Solano de Sonoma** is no longer used for religious services and is now a museum. But it remains the centerpiece of the historic town plaza, the largest such plaza in California and the heart of the old town. A number of lovingly preserved adobe structures, each of which played a role in early California history, encircle the plaza. This is the scene of the ill-starred "Bear Flag Revolt"; a flagpole (still carrying the Bear Flag) and a plaque in the plaza mark the auspicious (or inauspicious) early-morning events of June 10, 1846, that made California a short-lived republic.

The mission alternately fell into ruins and was rebuilt after the revolutionary Mexican government and then the United States took over the mission buildings and lands. For a time, indeed, it was used to stable horses and store hay. Restoration began in 1909 and has been carried out in phases since. The small chapel has been redecorated in the style of the early design. The mission is a classic example of colonial period architecture with thick adobe walls, small windows, and an interior courtyard. Museum exhibits describe the life of the Native American tribes before the missionaries' arrival. An excellent archaeological exhibit explains the methods of constructing with adobe, using mud and straw.

Flanking the mission and overlooking the plaza is the **Sonoma Barracks,** where the thirty-three Bear Flag followers surprised the sleeping Mexican troops, taking eighteen prisoners and capturing nine brass cannon. The commandante, General Vallejo, also was aroused from bed and surrendered politely. At first he was jailed at Sutter's Fort, but later he took a role in drafting California's state constitution, went on to be elected state senator and then Sonoma's mayor, and became one of its leading citizens.

The partially restored barracks, like the mission, is constructed of whitewashed adobe with heavy timbered doors and balconies and designed around a central courtyard used as a drill field. On the second floor a typical barracks dormitory includes rows of narrow straw-ticking mattresses on which the soldiers slept, their rifles stacked nearby. Exhibits on the first floor describe the "golden age of the Californios," the settlers who took over the lands after secularization and raised cattle for hides and tallow, spending their days dancing, gambling, horseracing, and in "splendid idleness." They also had a disdain for business, making them easy prey for sharp Yankee traders. Some of them, not surprisingly, never forgave "Los Osos," the Bear Flag band, for interrupting their idyll.

Three other buildings along the square should not be missed. Directly across from the mission is the **Blue Wing Inn,** a long, low, adobe structure originally built to house soldiers and during the gold rush converted into an inn, saloon, and gambling house. The **Toscano Hotel,** next to the barracks, has been a hotel since the 1850s. Its lobby-reception room-card room has been furnished with period antiques and is open for docent-conducted tours on weekends, as is the separate kitchen. Nearby, the two-story servants' quarters are all that remain of the original Vallejo home, **La Casa Grande.** It was in this imposing home that Vallejo, his brother, and brother-in-law were captured on the day of the Bear Flag revolt.

Vallejo's later home, **Lachryma Montis** (Tears of the Mountain), is a half mile from the plaza, a long walk or a short drive on Spain Street. The gracious residence is more Victorian than adobe in design, with a gingerbread roofline. Surrounded by gardens and with an entry lined with trees, the house is furnished with many of the Vallejo family's possessions and gives a feeling of being lived in by a family of culture and refinement. Vallejo eventually lost most of his wealth and landholdings, but remained unembittered, spending his last years reading and writing a five-volume history of the Mexican period, which he donated to the University of California's Bancroft Library.

Most of the historic buildings and the plaza are incorporated in the

Sonoma State Historic Park. Brochures and self-guided walking-tour maps are available in the Sonoma Valley Visitors Center on the plaza. Buildings in the historic park, including the mansion, are open daily 10:00 A.M. to 5:00 P.M. A single $1 admission covers entrance to all. Several other original buildings around the plaza retain their Mexican-period appearance and are planned for eventual incorporation into the park, but are now in private hands.

The **Sonoma City Hall** occupies the center of the plaza and is something of an architectural oddity: its four façades are identical so that none of the merchants whose enterprises face the plaza looks at the city hall's back side. (The city hall appeared as the Tuscany County Court House in the TV series "Falcon Crest.") Several shops and boutiques around the plaza are devoted to Sonoma County's two most notable commodities—wine and food. The **French Bakery** is known for its sourdough bread; there is also a sausage maker and a cheese factory where you can watch Sonoma Jack produced via a self-guided tour and picture windows.

The **Buena Vista Winery,** about a mile east of the plaza, is the birthplace of California premium wines and a good beginning for a Sonoma wine-tasting tour. In 1857, the Hungarian Count Agoston Haraszthy established the area's first commercial winery with vines from Europe, following in the footsteps of the missionaries who had been making sacramental wines since 1824. Caves were dug out of the limestone and cut into blocks for the winery building. A long eucalyptus-lined avenue leads through the park to the handsome winery, a state historic landmark. Be sure to visit the dark, cool, aromatic caves where the wine is stored and aged in oak barrels. The winery is very much of the present as well as the past, however. Buena Vista sauvignon blanc, cabernet, and merlot have won many awards. The winery is open daily 10:00 A.M. to 5:00 P.M. It is located at 18000 Old Winery Road. Call 800-926-1266.

Glen Ellen

Glen Ellen is a small and cozy-looking bend-in-the-road village off State Highway 12 as you head north from Sonoma. The two-block main street has a scattering of shops and restaurants but is best known for a popular winery and as the gateway to **Jack London State Historic Park.**

The author of *Call of the Wild, The Sea Wolf, White Fang,* and *Martin Eden* loved what he called "The Valley of the Moon," a title he gave to one of his novels. London, a radical political figure, a lecturer, a world traveler and adventurer, an experimental farmer, and a war correspondent as well as a novelist, lived at his Beauty Ranch in the hills above Glen Ellen for eleven years before his sudden death of kidney failure in 1916 at age forty. The 800-acre park includes the ranch, woods, meadows, and his grave marked by a large lava boulder. Three years after his death, Charmian London built the **House of Happy Walls** as a museum to commemorate her husband. London's restored study includes his typewriter, desk, original illustrations from his books, the campaign hat he wore during the Vera Cruz expedition of 1914, and the ship's bell and chronograph from the schooner *Snark,* which he and Charmian sailed in the South Seas. Also on display are first editions of the fifty-three books he wrote (three published after his death) and some of the 600 rejection slips he collected before his first writing was accepted. London kept a meticulous record of each rejection.

The most striking feature of the park, however, are the ghostly ruins of **Wolf House,** a 15,000-square-foot mansion designed by London himself, which burned to the ground a few days before he was to move in. The fire was never explained. London's dream home was to be spectacular, indeed. Made of unbarked redwood logs, volcanic rock, and concrete, it had twenty-six rooms, a monster library, a sleeping tower, nine stone fireplaces, and a reflecting pool. London, who became a millionaire from his prolific writings, spared no expense. You can still get a feel for the immensity and grandeur of the place just by walking about its overgrown remains. A short hiking trail leads to the ruins of the house.

Beauty Cottage, set among vineyards on a hilltop, is where the Londons lived and where London did his writing, sometimes working for nineteen hours at a stretch. It is also where he died. The newly restored white frame house opens in 1993. A longer-range plan is to restore the farm and farm buildings where London tried his experimental methods of hog raising and timber cultivation. The park is open daily 10:00 A.M. to 5:00 P.M. Admission and parking is $5, for seniors, $4. Call 707-938-5216.

Sonoma Valley Wineries

At last count, Sonoma County boasted 130 wineries, of which seventy-five were open for tastings (some by appointment only). The same figures show that there are 32,000 acres of vineyards within the county, producing some 14 million cases of wine annually. There are eleven viticulture districts in the county: 85 percent of the grapes pressed in a wine must originate in that district for the wine to receive an official appellation of the district. Wines of every variety are produced somewhere within the valley, and the suggested visits by no means cover the complete range. Indeed, half the fun of exploring the wine country is to seek out and select pet wineries for yourself.

A few words about tastings: Limit the number of wineries you visit in one day; more than three or at most four leaves you with a dull palate. Don't count on paying less than retail price by buying at the winery. However, there are often end-of-vintage bargains, specials, and case and half-case discounts. Also, some limited-production wines are available only at the winery, and smaller wineries may sell only at the winery itself. Brush up on your wine terminology—see Chapter 10.

Sebastiani Winery, a few blocks from the Sonoma plaza, is a large, long-established winery primarily known for its table wines. There is an excellent and informative guided tour, one of the best explanations of how wine goes from grape to barrel to bottle. The winery is at 389 East Fourth Street, Sonoma. Call 707-938-5532.

The **Glen Ellen Winery,** in the hills adjoining the Jack London State Historic Park, should be a first-tasting stop as you head north from Sonoma. Surrounded by flowers, with a gleaming pond and a redwood-shaded picnic grove, the winery's setting is spectacular; there is an excellent guided tour. Glen Ellen pioneered the production of inexpensive chardonnays and cabernet sauvignons that even wine connoisseurs acknowledge are eminently drinkable. But it also produces premium wines under the Benziger label. Tasting are offered daily 10:00 A.M. to 4:30 P.M. The winery is at 1883 London Ranch Road, Glen Ellen. Call 707-935-3000.

B.R. Cohn Winery typifies the small, specialized winery blossoming in the Sonoma Valley. It concentrates on chardonnay, cabernet sauvignon, and merlot, producing only a limited quantity of each. The winery is operated by a local boy who went off to manage the

Doobie Brothers rock group, then returned to establish the business. The winery is open daily 10:00 A.M. to 5:00 P.M. It is located at 15140 Sonoma Highway (State Highway 12), Glen Ellen. Call 707-938-4064.

Chateau St. Jean actually is housed in a chateau, a French-style mansion constructed in the 1920s as a winter home for a wealthy Michigan couple. The tasting room is the former living room of the old estate. A self-guided tour includes a visit to the winery's landmark tower, from which you have a sweeping view of the valley's vineyards and of Sugarloaf Ridge, the mountain backdrop for the winery. Chateau St. Jean is known for dry white wines—chardonnay and fumé blanc, and late-harvest riesling and gewürztraminer. A separate winery, at Graton in western Sonoma County, produces sparkling wines. Tours are conducted daily 10:30 A.M. to 4:00 P.M., tasting 10:00 A.M. to 4:30 P.M. The chateau is located at 8555 Sonoma Highway, Kenwood. Call 707-833-4134.

Kenwood Vineyards specializes in premium reds, including cabernet sauvignon and pinot noir. With exclusive rights to the vineyards at the old Jack London farm, Kenwood also produces a special Jack London wine. Senior discounts of 15 percent are offered on purchases of one to five bottles. Open daily 10:00 A.M. to 5:00 P.M., the vineyards are located at 9592 State Highway 12, Kenwood. Call 707-833-5891.

Smothers Brothers Wines capitalizes on the fame of the television comedians and on one of their running gags. You can buy "Mother Liked Me Best" T-shirts, sweatshirts, and aprons, Smothers Brothers audio tapes, and posters. Oh, yes, you can also taste "Mother's Favorite" white and "Mother's Favorite" red, at 25¢ a taste. Good for laughs. The winery is open daily 10:00 A.M. to 4:30 P.M. It is located at 9575 State Highway 12, Kenwood. Call 707-833-1010.

Landmark Vineyards, abutting Kenwood Vineyards, produces premium chardonnays. A dramatic mural is the backdrop for its new tasting room. The vineyards are open daily 10:00 A.M. to 5:00 P.M. Tours are by appointment only. The vineyards are located at 101 Adobe Canyon Road, Kenwood. Call 707-833-1144.

Healdsburg and the Russian River Wine Road

Healdsburg, a neat, pleasant community just off U.S. 101, is the starting point for the designated Russian River Wine Road, which includes fifty-three wineries in the northern part of Sonoma County. Five tasting rooms are in Healdsburg where the immaculate, leafy town square and array of antique shops attract many buyers on weekends. A complete list of wineries, with map, may be obtained from Russian River Wine Road, P.O. Box 46, Healdsburg, California 95448. 707-433-6782.

Kendall-Jackson tasting room faces the plaza in Healdsburg, although its principal winery is at Lakeport in adjoining Lake County, and many of its grapes come from Mendocino and Santa Barbara. Its chardonnays have won many prizes, including the title of World's Best Chardonnay in the International Wine and Spirits Competition. Its white wines are widely marketed, but several premium wines are available only at the tasting room. The winery is open daily 10:00 A.M. to 5:00 P.M. It is at 337 Healdsburg Avenue, Healdsburg. Call 707-433-7102.

Clos du Bois's large winery, located a few blocks from downtown Healdsburg, is particularly known for its chardonnays and cabernet sauvignons; some of its reserve chardonnays cost $150 a bottle. It has a cheerful and hospitable tasting room. It is located at 5 Fitch Street, Healdsburg. Call 707-433-5576.

Dry Creek Vineyard is one of the largest producers in California, with a full range of varietal wines. Tastings are offered daily 10:30 A.M. to 4:30 P.M.; tours are by appointment. The winery is at 3770 Lambert Bridge Road, Healdsburg. Call 707-433-1000.

Windsor Vineyards' tasting room lies just off the plaza; its winery is at the nearby community of Windsor. Windsor is said to have won more awards than any other winery. You'll find the tasting room at 239A Center Street, Healdsburg. Call 707-433-2822.

Simi Winery is one of the oldest in California. Its stone cellars date back more than a century. Tastings are offered daily 10:00 A.M. to 4:30 P.M.; guided tours are at 11:00 A.M., 1:00 P.M., and 3:00 P.M. The winery is at 16275 Healdsburg Avenue, Healdsburg. Call 707-433-6981.

J. Pedroncelli Winery is a family-style winery tucked into the hills off U. S. 101. Tastings are offered 10:00 A.M. to 5:00 P.M. daily, tours are by appointment. It is located at 1220 Canyon Road, Geyersville. Call 707-857-3531.

Korbel Champagne Cellars lies along the River Road, which follows the Russian River after it turns west toward the ocean. It is noted for its champagnes—which it labels "champagne" even though purists maintain that designation must be limited to the wines from Champagne in France. There is an excellent guided tour of the champagne cellars.

Tastings are offered daily. The cellars are located at 13250 River Road, Guerneville. Call 707-887-2294.

Santa Rosa

Santa Rosa likes to call itself "The City Designed for Living"—a clean, comfortable, and modest-size city of 115,000 with leafy neighborhoods that are a pleasure to walk through, a network of parks and gardens, and a thriving downtown. Well-preserved Victorian mansions are found throughout the city, especially on **McDonald Avenue.** Mableton at 1015 McDonald Avenue was used as the setting for the Walt Disney movie *Pollyanna*. Santa Rosa has provided the backdrop for many TV series.

Luther Burbank certainly loved the place. The man who transformed America's farms and gardens is still mentioned with reverence; his touch and his name are found everywhere. Burbank came to Santa Rosa from New England in 1875 and pronounced it "a chosen spot." Over the next fifty years, the botanical wizard introduced or improved more than 800 varieties of plants—including over 200 varieties of fruits, many vegetables, nuts and grains, and hundreds of ornamental flowers. "I shall be content if because of me there shall be better fruits and fairer flowers," Burbank said, and he certainly succeeded. He is responsible for the russet potato, the Santa Rosa plum, the Burbank cherry, and the Shasta daisy, a showy white flower that required seventeen years of patient grafting to perfect. During his lifetime of work, Sonoma County advanced to the eighth richest agricultural county in America.

Anyone with a green thumb or even so much as a houseplant or window box will want to spend two or three hours at the **Luther Burbank Home and Gardens,** strolling through what Burbank called his "magic garden." Although most of his experiments were carried out at a larger experimental farm at Sebastopol, this was the place he loved most. The acre and a half brims over with flowers and specimens the master developed, such as a monster spineless cactus, his effort to develop fodder for cattle in arid countries. A paradox walnut, which provides a fast-growing supply of ornamental wood, towers over the Shasta

YOU PICK 'EM

Luther Burbank described Sonoma County as "the chosen spot of all this earth as far as nature is concerned." As you drive through the rich farmlands and orchards on the back roads, observing its productive bounty, you realize that the great horticulturalist may not have been exaggerating—and you have plenty of opportunity to obtain convincing, first-hand evidence.

Perhaps more than any other area of California, Sonoma County's agricultural districts are lined with roadside produce stands selling Santa Rosa plums right off the trees, table grapes right off the vines, berries fresh from the bushes. In this day of industrialized agriculture, the family farm still thrives in Sonoma County, and many of the small towns and cities have regular farmers' markets where the growers themselves retail their produce. A fun day is to drive around the county and make up a picnic as you go, buying fruit from the stands, bread from the small bakeries, cheese from the factories, sausage from the butchers, oysters from the seaside oyster farms, or salmon from the smokehouses, all washed down with wine from the local vineyards, much of which can only be purchased at the wineries themselves.

"Farm Trails of Sonoma County" lists the local family farms and produce stands that sell directly to consumers, including a map that shows each location. The folder is even cross-indexed by type of produce, allowing you to locate the nearest plum orchard in your vicinity. Some of the farms are "you pick" places where you can pluck your own Gravenstein apples off the tree. Many of them also sell preserves, chutneys, dried fruit—and yes, Christmas trees. You can find those rare varieties of apples you recall from your childhood, like Jonathans and Arkansas Blacks, that are now seldom sold in supermarkets.

The pamphlet may be obtained free by writing Sonoma County Farm Trails, P.O. Box 6032, Santa Rosa, California 95406, or phoning 707-586-3276.

daisy beds. Burbank himself was buried in this garden under his favorite Cedar of Lebanon tree (which had to be destroyed in 1989 because of a root disease). The home is decorated with photographs of notables like Thomas A. Edison and Henry Ford who came to visit Burbank and with furniture made from the paradox walnut. The tour includes a visit to his surprisingly small greenhouse, scarcely larger than a two-car garage. Gardens are open daily 9:00 A.M. to 6:00 P.M. Admission is free. House tours are April to October, 10:00 A.M. to 4:00 P.M. Admission is $1. The house and gardens are at Sonoma and Santa Rosa avenues, Sonoma. Call 707-524-5445.

Another household name—at least to travelers over fifty—is enshrined at the **Church of One Tree Ripley Museum.** Built from a single redwood tree, the museum is devoted to the late Robert L. Ripley of "Believe It or Not" fame, a Santa Rosa native son. The museum is laden with drawings and examples of oddities discovered and breathlessly described by Ripley in his newspaper feature: "Cow With Its Heart in Its Neck—Normal Otherwise." Also on display are the battered suitcase he carried in his travels in search of oddities and photographs of Ripley with celebrities of the times like Ed Sullivan, Shirley Temple, and Lou Gehrig. The museum is open March 1 to October 23, Wednesday to Sunday, 11:00 A.M. to 4:00 P.M. Admission is $1.50; 75¢ for seniors. It is located at 492 Sonoma Avenue, Santa Rosa. 707-524-5233.

More recent household names, **Charlie Brown** and **Snoopy,** have their shrine and museum adjoining the Redwood Empire Ice Arena. The creator of "Peanuts" and all its round-headed little characters, Charles Schulz, is a Santa Rosan (and amateur hockey player who works out at the arena). The museum is filled with cartoons and the cartoonist's memorabilia plus what is undoubtedly the largest selection of Snoopy merchandise in the world. There is, of course, a gift shop. The museum is located at 1667 W. Steele Lane, Santa Rosa. Call 707-546-3385.

Historic Santa Rosa and environs are on display in the **Sonoma County Museum,** converted from the old city post office, a stone turn-of-the-century structure. It is open Wednesday to Sunday 11:00 A.M. to 4:00 P.M. The museum is located at 425 Seventh Street, Santa Rosa.

Railroad Square, a redeveloped historic area near the old depot, is noted for antique emporiums, clothing boutiques, bookstores, and small restaurants. It is located between Third and Fifth streets, off U.S. 101 downtown Santa Rosa exit. Call 707-578-8478.

The Russian River

Meandering among redwoods, the Russian River flows down a fertile valley to the sea. Once upon a time, this area was heavily logged to supply lumber for the homes of San Francisco; later the railroads ran excursion trains to this woodsy playground just beyond the coastal fog belt. Both the timber and the resort atmosphere still attract summer visitors. Aptly named River Road, following the waterway, is now the traveler's route into the area.

Armstrong Woods State Reserve is a 750-acre stand of virgin redwoods, saved from the sawmills by the conservation movement in the early 1900s. Many hiking trails wander among the towering trees, quite a few of them easy going for casual visitors who simply want to admire the forest giants. Steeper trails lead into the backcountry of the adjacent Austin Creek State Recreation Area, which also features primitive campsites and fishing in a man-made lake.

Guerneville, an old logging town, is the visitor headquarters. From here and the nearby hamlets of Forestville and Rio Nido, visitors swim, sunbathe, canoe, or laze down the river in inner tubes or rafts. Craft shops and a few galleries cluster along the main street. The town is also the scene of the Russian River Jazz Festival each September, a smaller-scale weekend of music that attracts some big-name players.

Duncans Mills, farther down river, is an old Victorian hamlet completely restored to the look of the 1890s when it was first a logging center and then a destination for railroad excursions. The last train came to town in 1935, after which Duncans Mills slid into sleepy obsolescence. It was revived in the 1970s and 1980s. The old railroad depot became a museum; other buildings along the main street were restored as shops, restaurants, and galleries. The Duncans Mills general store provides an authentic glimpse of the merchandising of the past.

Restaurants ————————————————————————

- The **Union Hotel** and **Negri's** are Occidental's Italian-dinner specialists, on opposite sides of the Bohemian Highway, Occidental's Main Street. Their standard family-style dinner

SCENIC (AND DINNER) DETOUR

From Duncans Mills turn south on Moscow Road through riverside resort cottages to the Bohemian Highway; turn right. This two-lane road winds through wooded hills and some pasturelands to the hilltop, one-street hamlet of **Occidental,** deep in the redwoods. The charm of the town is a well-kept secret, but not among the hungry. Family-style Italian restaurants strive to outdo each other in gargantuan Sunday dinners. Seated at long tables, the diners share the pasta and the wine and make friends. (See Restaurants.)

After patting your waistline with satisfaction, continue south on the Bohemian Highway, pass through the sleepy village of **Freestone,** then turn west on the Bodega Highway to the hamlet of **Bodega** (not Bodega Bay). Another step back in time, the few buildings appear much as they did in Bodega's heyday in the 1890s, when it supported seven sawmills. Stop at the old schoolhouse, built in 1871, and see if you can recall where you've seen it before. It was featured in the Alfred Hitchcock thriller, *The Birds,* and is now a bed and breakfast.

Reverse direction on the Bodega Highway, through the open country to **Sebastopol,** the apple center of California, at the junction of state highways 116 and 12. This is rich agricultural country, lined with roadside stands selling Gravensteins and cider (and jams and apple pies). The highlight of the year is the Gravenstein Apple Fair in August, but Sebastopol's art studios and small shops make it a pleasant visit at any time of year. From here, follow State Highway 12 back to U.S. 101 at Santa Rosa, or State Highway 116 to U.S. 101 at Rohnert Park.

includes (deep breath) homemade minestrone, antipasto, ravioli, zucchini fritters, and a main course of your choice. Chicken cacciatore is the favorite, and don't forget dessert—all served, of course, with local wines. All this at budget prices—four courses and cacciatore is $10.95. Union Hotel, 707-874-3555. Negri's, 707-874-3623.

- The **Feed Store,** on the plaza in Sonoma, was just that once—the menu included hay and grain for your sheep and cattle. Converted into a budget restaurant, it's a charming and inexpensive place for breakfast or lunchtime sandwiches while touring Sonoma's historic area. 529 W. First Street, Sonoma. 707-938-2122.

- **Mixx,** in Railroad Square in Santa Rosa, specializes in a cuisine made with fresh local produce. Moderate. 135 Fourth Street, Santa Rosa. 707-573-1344.

- **Jacob Horner,** on the plaza in Healdsburg, insists that none of the vegetables in its California cuisine grows more than two miles from the restaurant. Lamb, duck, and chicken dishes are specialties. 106 Matheson Street, Healdsburg. 707-433-3939.

- **Omelette Express** is the place for a filling breakfast and a quick lunch. 112 Fourth Street, Santa Rosa. 707-525-1690.

- **Marioni's,** on the Sonoma plaza, specializes in seafood and steaks. Lunch and dinner are served on a pleasant patio. 8 West Spain Street, Sonoma. 707-996-6866.

Lodging

A central lodging service is provided by Bed and Breakfast Inns of Sonoma Valley, 800-284-6675.

- **Sonoma Mission Inn** is the luxury spot of the Sonoma Valley, a sprawling pink-adobe complex centered on a spa. "Retreat, relax, and restore," says the brochure, meaning beauty treatments, body treatments, massage, and oh, yes, lavish and comfortable rooms. Golf is nearby. The inn is a favorite with Bay Area residents wishing to get away from it all. State Highway 12, in the town of Boyes Hot Springs. Expensive to very expensive. Lower rates in winter. 707-938-9000

- **El Dorado Hotel** is a small adobe hotel, beautifully refurbished, on the plaza in Sonoma. All rooms have balconies overlooking the plaza, the mountains, or the hotel's inner courtyard. Complimentary continental breakfast is offered on the patio. Moderate to expensive. Higher rates on weekends; reduced rates in winter. 405 First Street West, Sonoma. 707-996-3030.

- **Thistle Dew Inn,** a six-room B&B near the Sonoma plaza, is decorated in 1900s antiques. Serves a full gourmet breakfast on the deck in summers. For the energetic, the inn offers complimentary bicycles to pedal around town. Moderate to expensive. 171 West Spain Street, Sonoma. 707-938-2909.

- **Jack London Lodge** is a comfortable, newly redecorated motel near the entrance to the Jack London State Historic Park and to the Glen Ellen wineries. Moderate. 13740 Arnold Drive, Glen Ellen. 707-938-8510.

- **Sonoma Chalet** is a Swiss-architecture B&B in a farmland setting, on the edge of Sonoma. Several of the rooms have fireplaces. Moderate to expensive. 18935 West Fifth Street, Sonoma. 707-938-3129.

- **Los Robles Lodge** is a large and conveniently located motel near the center of Santa Rosa. Moderate. 925 Edwards Avenue, Santa Rosa. 707-545-6330.

Chapter 12
The North Coast:
Jenner to Rockport

Bring a car with rack-and-pinion steering, a pair of stout walking shoes, an eye for bargains, and a healthy appetite. You might want binoculars, too. California State Highway 1 clings to the precipitous northern California coast for 116 miles from Jenner to Rockport, offering sweeping blue-water and white-water views, majestic headlands, secluded coves, seas of lupine and golden poppy, cozy inns, small villages forgotten by time, artisans and craftspeople turning out everything from patchwork quilts to totem poles, creative chefs cooking up dishes like—are you ready?—wild boar stuffed with dates and walnuts. And over all there's the fog, which can cast an eerie, outward-bound quality to the whole landscape.

This part of the rugged Pacific shoreline is not as well publicized as the southerly Big Sur stretch, possibly because it's less accessible. But it's every bit as breathtaking, as television and film producers have discovered. As you drive along, you'll recognize backdrops from "Murder, She Wrote" (masquerading as Cabot's Cove, Maine), *Same Time, Next Year,* and a dozen other memorable and forgettable productions. The great gray whales have discovered it, too. The northward migration of the giant seagoing mammals, headed from their winter quarters in the Sea of Cortez to Alaskan waters, brings whale watchers to the shores in February and March.

Head north along the Shoreline Highway, and here's what you'll encounter.

Jenner is a small hillside community that spills down to the mouth of the Russian River and the ocean where seals can often be seen sunning themselves on the rocks. Downtown Jenner straggles around a curve on State Highway 1 and consists of a few craft studios and small restaurants. But it is the gateway to some of the most dazzling coastside scenery—to be enjoyed more by passengers than the driver, who must give full attention to the wheel. (Connoisseurs say the best views are actually from the southbound lane, but the lack of a guardrail between you and a 200-foot plunge into the drink can be a trifle distracting.) The highway winds along the edge of sheer cliffs, into creek canyons and out again, past small beaches and in the lee of steep mountains. The road is plentifully provided with scenic overlooks to enjoy these views.

Fort Ross, sixteen miles north of Jenner on Highway 1, recaptures a little-known chapter of American history—when a Russian colony thrived on the California shore. The Russian-American Trading Company, owned by the Czar and friends, established the settlement to serve as a hunting station for the valuable sea otter pelts, to raise provisions for the Russians' outposts in Alaska, and to trade with the Spanish colonists farther south. The settlement flourished for a few years until the otters had been depleted, then it was sold to John Sutter of gold rush fame. The Russians retreated to Alaska, remaining there until Alaska was sold to the United States in 1867.

Only the commandant's house remains from the original Russian colony. For its time, it was a splendiferous place where one could find, a French visitor wrote, "a choice library, a piano, and a score of Mozart." Some traces of the paneling and decor remain, along with the wide-board flooring, but the furnishings have disappeared. The other buildings within Fort Ross's reconstructed stockade include the officers' barracks fitted with tools, furniture, and kitchen utensils of the period; the manager's house, armory, and storage area; and an onion-domed church, the first Russian Orthodox church in North America. The original church was shaken down in the 1906 earthquake but rebuilt using some of the original timbers; the chapel bell was recast from the metal that remained after the original melted in a disastrous fire in 1970. A walking-tour map available at the visitor center explains the fort's history; interpretive talks are given twice daily on weekends. Incidentally, Fort Ross was never a fort, and "Ross" is not a person's name but a corruption of "Russia." The fort is open daily. Admission is $5 per car, $4 for seniors. Call 707-847-3286.

Kruse Rhododendron Preserve, north of the village of Fort

Ross, should be visited in April to May when the showy flowers are in bloom. A winding, unpaved road snakes uphill through the preserve where rhododendron of many varieties and shades of pink and white and purple thrive under the shelter of giant redwoods. The state preserve has no headquarters or visitor center, but turnouts and hiking trails threading through the preserve allow visitors to enjoy the display.

Sea Ranch once was a working sheep ranch continuing for ten miles on both sides of State Highway 1. Today it is an environmentally conscious and award-winning development of second homes tucked unobtrusively into the oceanside meadows and amid the redwoods on the hillsides. Coastal access ways spaced intermittently allow visitors to tramp to the beaches, study the seals on the rocks, and inspect the myriad life forms in the tidal pools. The Lodge at Sea Ranch, center of the community, perches on a cliffside with dramatic views of land and water. Call 707-785-2426.

Gualala (pronounced Wa-la-la by the locals) is an old and rambunctious logging town rapidly transforming itself into a colony of artists, craftspeople, and retirees. The funky old Gualala Hotel, favorite of the loggers, still reeks of rough-and-ready Wild West atmosphere. The novelist Jack London supposedly considered the hotel's long bar his favorite drinking spot.

Point Arena Lighthouse, at 115 feet the tallest on the Pacific Coast, is no longer a working lighthouse now that coastwise shipping has become virtually extinct. It's been taken over and lovingly preserved by a nonprofit group, Point Arena Lighthouse Keepers. But you can still climb up and examine the two-ton light and enjoy views up and down the coast; it is also a favorite place to watch the migrating whales in winter. A museum, located in the old Fog Signal Building, displays photographs and maritime artifacts from the lighthouse's heyday. Three small houses, once occupied by lighthouse personnel, are available for rental; proceeds go to maintain the lighthouse. The lighthouse is open daily 11:00 A.M. to 2:30 P.M., on summer weekends 10:00 A.M. to 3:30 P.M. Admission is $2. For information write Point Arena Lighthouse Keepers, Box 11, Point Arena, California 95468. Or call 707-882-2777.

Garcia River Flats, north of Point Arena, is also the wintering ground for whistling swans. The giant birds arrive from the Arctic and the Soviet Union about Thanksgiving and can be seen through March when they leave for a return trip.

The **Pygmy Forest at Van Damme State Park,** a mile south of Mendocino, looks like a natural bonsai display—hundred-year-old trees, only a few feet high, are twisted into grotesque shapes. The explanation for this oddity is that highly compact, lava-like soil over a hard clay base is depleted of nutrients during the annual spring runoff. The dwarf trees thus must constantly fight for life. The park is open year-round, daily. Park admission is $5 per car.

Mendocino

Mendocino is the jewel of the coast. Approaching from the south on Highway 1, you see its gingerbread rooftops and spires clustering on the precipice of a bold headland, Pacific surf splashing at its feet. The town was founded by displaced New Englanders in the late 1800s as a logging port and still has a Downeast quality about it. The loggers moved elsewhere in the 1920s and 1930s, leaving the community lazing in the sun until hippies and artists, attracted by the atmosphere and cheap living, discovered it simultaneously in the 1950s. Since then Mendocino has become ever more boutique-y and pricey but retains much of its old time charm, thanks to visionary townsfolk who rammed through draconian legislation preserving its original look. The town has also officially been declared a historical district.

Mendocino is a town for walking. Don those stout shoes and stroll its wooden sidewalks, admiring the tidy and well-preserved Victorian homes and old saltboxes with their carefully tended gardens. Peer into shop windows displaying handcrafted gold jewelry, ceramics, and intricately carved toys and poke into art galleries and bookshops, many of them displaying the works of local authors. (Mendocino, to its credit, has relegated the T-shirt shops to locations largely out of sight.) Main Street runs along the brow of the headland, its century-old buildings limited to the inland side so that window-shoppers and browsers have an unobstructed view of cliffs and surf. Lansing Street is a line of slightly askew wooden structures housing shops and galleries and nestling against Mendocino's most famous landmark, the Masonic Hall, with a carved redwood figure of Father Time majestically perched on top. Mendocino architecture is designed around the rooftop cylindrical cistern, an obvious necessity in a town where rain comes seldom and never after April 1.

Mendocino prides itself on its flowers, and a highly recommended tour is the antique rose-garden walk. Obtain a map from the Fort Bragg-Mendocino Coast Chamber of Commerce (707-961-6300) which will guide you to dozens of small gardens where rose varieties of every hue, developed before 1900, flourish in the Mendocino climate of sun, fog, and TLC. Sniff and admire to your horticulturist's content; plucking or invading the gardens is taboo.

Summer weekends (not the best time to go; try April and May weekdays, when the blooms are at their height, days are balmy, and weekend tourists are bent over their desks at home) draw large crowds, attracted by special events like the Mendocino Arts Festival. For information, call the Chamber of Commerce, 707-961-6300. The Mendocino Music Festival (707-967-2044), whose orchestra mixes musical locals with off-duty performers from the San Francisco Symphony, offers a week of concerts in a cliffside tent where the beating of the surf provides a percussion background. The Mendocino Art Center (707-937-5818) displays the works of local sculptors and painters.

Two museums devote themselves to the coast's history. The **Ford House Museum and Visitor Center,** at Mendocino Headlands State Park, is housed in a 120-year-old mansion built by the owner of the Mendocino Lumber Company. The museum features an exhibit on the history of redwood logging, Pomo Indian artifacts, and the area's natural history, along with a scale model, Mendocino in miniature as of 1890. Open 10:00 A.M. to 5:00 P.M. daily. For more information call 707-937-5397. **Kelley House,** built in 1861, is the town's historical museum, operated by Mendocino Historical Research. It sits amid gardens of wildflowers and camellias, located around a small pond, and is a prime example of "balloon construction," in which the sawn redwood vertical studs run from floor to roof. Its water tower is fitted with a wooden-bladed windmill. In the garden you'll come upon an old wooden bench engraved "Behold the Sea," which once stood in front of Kelley's Main Street store facing the water, and an antique cannon, salvaged in 1967 from the wreckage of a China trader that hit the rocks and sank off Mendocino in 1850. Guided walking tours of the town are offered. The museum is open Friday to Monday, 1:00 P.M. to 4:00 P.M. Admission is $1. Call 707-937-5791.

Mendocino Headlands State Park, the spot to picnic and enjoy the view of rocks, ocean spray, and dive-bombing pelicans, is a good walk from the center of the village or a few minutes by car. From this vantage point you can see far up and down the coast where the waves roll in powerful succession to splash upon the rocks and carve wave tunnels, some of them 100 feet deep. According to legend, ships have been driven into the tunnels by the sea and never seen again. For information call 707-937-5397, daytime only.

Fort Bragg

Fort Bragg, fifteen miles north of Mendocino on Highway 1, is the metropolis of the coast with a population of 5,000. Originally founded as a military outpost in 1857 to keep an eye on the Mendocino Indians, it was named for Captain Braxton Bragg, a Mexican War hero who later became one of the Confederacy's leading generals. The fort was closed in 1864 and gave way to a booming timber town and port; logging is still the town's main industry. The heart of the downtown—bounded by Main, Laurel, Redwood, and Franklin streets—is classic, pastel Victorian structures built after the 1906 earthquake shook the town to rubble. They house antique dealers, craft shops, small restaurants, and clothing boutiques. Only one building—the ex-military commissary adjoining the refurbished, gingerbread City Hall on Franklin Street—remains from the original fort. An excellent walking-tour map is available from the Chamber of Commerce, 332 N. Main Street. Call 707-961-6300. (Mailing address: P.O. Box 1141, Fort Bragg, California 95437.)

The **Skunk Railroad** is Fort Bragg's most popular tourist attraction and a favorite with old-time railway buffs. Originally a logging carrier bringing the felled redwoods to the sea, it now carries passengers forty curvy and challenging miles (the longest straight stretch is less than a mile) through the densely wooded Coast Range to Willits, crossing thirty bridges and trestles en route. Rolling stock includes old-fashioned coaches with upright leather seats and one open observation car for photographers and sightseers. Trains are drawn by a diesel engine and during summers and on special occasions by "Ole 45," an 1890s steam locomotive. The official name of the road is California &

Western; it got the "Skunk" nickname from the powerful fumes of the original locomotive—"You can smell it before you can see it," old-timers said. Full-day round trips between Fort Bragg and Willits are $23; half-day trips to the midway station at Northspur are $18.50. The railroad is open daily in summer and weekends only in winter. The station is located at the foot of Laurel Street, Fort Bragg. Call 707-964-6371.

Georgia-Pacific Lumber, lineal descendant of the original logging company, offers summers-only tours three times a week of its oceanside mill, one of the world's largest. You can see not only how high-pressure water strips the bark from the giant logs and high-speed saws reduce the logs to planks and beams, but also how, in this high-tech age, laser beams are used to indicate the most productive cut. The indoor tour of the working mill is followed by a visit to the mill's nursery where more than three million seedlings of many varieties are grown for replanting on forested lands all over the U.S. Visitors are given a seedling to take home; you can also order them in quantity for shipment. Wear flat shoes (no high heels). Located at 90 West Redwood Avenue, Fort Bragg, California 95437. (To order seedlings, include "Georgia-Pacific Nursery" in the address.) Call 707-964-5651.

A section of the largest-known redwood tree ever cut in Mendocino County stands at the mill entrance. It required sixty man-hours to fell the tree, which stood 334 feet high and measured 21 feet in diameter when it came down in 1943. Biologists have calculated that the giant specimen began life as a seedling in A.D. 190, about the time the Roman Empire was at its height.

The **Guest House Museum** is the original home of the logging firm's founder, C. R. Johnson, and after his death was used for guests of the mill. It's completely built of redwood, right down to the stairway spindles and lustrous paneling. The museum is open March to October, Wednesday to Saturday, and weekends only in winter; admission is $1. The rear garden includes rolling stock from the pre-1900s Skunk, including specially built cars for hauling giant logs and a steam locomotive with conical stack shipped around Cape Horn in the 1880s.

Noyo Harbor, on the southern edge of Fort Bragg, is a working fishing harbor, one of the few remaining on the north coast. These days, the quarry is often sea urchins, those spiny creatures considered a delicacy in the Japanese market. Party boats also put out for salmon and bottom fish.

SCENIC DETOUR

State Highway 128 branches off from State Highway 1 near the hamlet of Elk and heads inland to a junction with the main north-south highway, U.S. 101, at Cloverdale. Southbound, the road follows the course of the Navarro River through thick forests of towering redwoods, most of them protected in state parks. Then it bursts into the lush and isolated Anderson Valley. Orchards and roadside fruit-and-vegetable stands selling apples and peaches of old-fashioned varieties you no longer find in supermarkets alternate with vineyards and small wineries with an informal, "nice-of-you-to-drop-in" atmosphere—the tasting room is likely to be manned by the wine maker himself. Boonville, largest of the valley's three small towns, is said to have developed its own language, Boontling, so that residents could converse without outsiders understanding them; "bahl gorms" is Boonville's way of saying "good food," "pike" is to walk, and "harp" is to talk. Beyond the secluded valley, the highway winds over grassy hills to another cluster of wineries around Cloverdale.

Restaurants

Restaurants along the north coast are both plain and fancy, inexpensive and pricey. A selected list of those between Gualala and Westport is furnished by the Fort Bragg-Mendocino Coast Chamber of Commerce: 707-961-6300. Here are some recommendations.

- **Cap'n Flint's** stands on the waterfront at Noyo with fine views of the busy harbor. Not surprisingly, it concentrates on fresh seafood. A specialty is fish and chips featuring the local red snapper. Inexpensive. 32250 North Harper Drive, Fort Bragg. 707-964-9447.

- **St. Orre's,** a mile north of Gualala on Highway 1, serves wild boar—not to mention rabbit, venison, pheasant, and other game dishes done with a new-cuisine touch. The price-fixed meal includes three courses and dessert. Expensive. 707-884-3303.

- The **Bay View Cafe** advertises itself as Mendocino's only ocean-view restaurant. The deck overlooks Main Street and the headlands. Moderate. 45040 Main Street, Mendocino. 707-937-4197.

- The **Mendocino Bakery** features sandwiches, soup, pizza, and pastries and is a favorite with locals. Great for a quick lunch during a walking tour. Inexpensive. 10483 Lansing Street. 707-937-0836.

- The **Grey Whale** features seafood and local specialties in a relaxed atmosphere. Moderate. 615 North Main Street, Fort Bragg. 707-964-0640.

Lodging

Every bend in State Highway 1 seems to reveal another small inn, B&B, or an occasional, upscale get-away-from-it-all resort. Many are comfortable and intimate remodeled farmhouses, some more than 100 years old, offering only three or four rooms with the bath down the hall; some are larger; none are Hiltons or Sheratons. A full listing of lodging places between Gualala and Westport is available from the Fort Bragg-Mendocino Coast Chamber of Commerce (707-961-6300). Mendocino Coast Accommodations (707-937-1913) centralizes reservations for about thirty lodging places in that community. Meanwhile, here are a few recommendations.

- **Heritage House,** three miles south of Mendocino at Little River, is the romantic place where Alan Alda and Ellen Burstyn rendezvoused annually in the film *Same Time, Next Year*. The seaside cottages they presumably occupied are now named, respectively, "Same Time" and "Next Year." Arrayed around ornamental gardens that are a tourist attraction in themselves, the inn's fireplace-equipped cottages are scattered over a thirty-seven-acre hillside bowl with magnificent coastal views including offshore seastacks and a natural arch sculpted by the waves. Modified American Plan (full breakfast, dinner for two). Expensive. Located in Little River. 707-937-5885.

- The **Grey Whale** is a comfortable, unpretentious but refurbished hotel in the heart of Fort Bragg, overlooking the sea (and, of course, in season, the whale migration.) Its penthouse is the highest point in Fort Bragg. Moderate. Main Street, Fort Bragg. 707-964-0640.

- The **Surf Motel** is a no-nonsense motel with views of the surf. Moderate. State Highway 1, Gualala. 707-964-5361.

- **Little River Inn and Resort** is for golfers, tennis players, hikers, beachcombers, and relaxers. The rambling structure perches on 225 hillside acres with good ocean views. Expensive. Little River. 707-937-5942.

- The **Mendocino Hotel** is the town's oldest, built in 1868. It maintains its Victorian-era atmosphere with antiques and reproductions, but it has been completely modernized. Many of the rooms are decorated with old photographs of early residents. It is in the heart of the shopping belt, looking out toward the headlands. Moderate to expensive. Main Street. 707-937-0511.

- **Sea Ranch** rents fully furnished homes and condominiums for two nights or more, with up to four bedrooms. Two-night rentals for ocean-view properties start at $250; for those tucked into the trees, rates begin at $190. State Highway 1. 707-785-2426.

- **Timber Cove,** between Jenner and Fort Ross on one of the loneliest (and loveliest) stretches of the coast, is a redwood architectural gem of the Japanese style, set in a wildlife preserve overlooking the ocean. There is a two-night minimum. It is enjoyed primarily for escape. Expensive. 707-847-2321.

- **Campgrounds,** most of them with trailer hookups, speckle the coast. A list of locations and facilities can be obtained from the Fort Bragg-Mendocino Chamber of Commerce, P.O. Box 1141, Fort Bragg, California 95437; 707-961-6300.

Chapter 13

The Redwood Empire

Contrary to what you may have heard, when you've seen one tree, you *haven't* seen 'em all. In fact, you ain't seen nuthin' until you've visited the two northwesternmost counties of California, where any tree shorter than a ten-story building is dismissed as a mere sapling. This is the land of the giants, redwoods 300-plus feet tall—grove after silent grove of them where the sunlight softly seeps through the boughs, and awed visitors speak in hushed tones as if they were in a cathedral.

It is also a land of controversy. Many of the majestic monsters have been protected in state and national parks, but argument still rages about how many more should be sheltered from the woodsman's axe. Conservationists argue that even the present park groves are threatened by logging practices that foster downstream erosion. Loggers counter that trees have a limited lifespan anyway and should be selectively thinned to make way for younger, hardier specimens.

In a backhanded way, logging has contributed to another aspect of the north coast's visitor appeal. When the timber industry boomed in the late nineteenth and early twentieth century, lumber barons built increasingly massive and ornate homes. Victorian mansions and buildings are now among the area's leading tourist attractions.

So is the sea. The rocky, fogbound coast, some of it accessible only by the most heroic hiking, is a world of small fishing villages, old timber ports, secluded coves and beaches, lonely lighthouses, and picture-postcard views. Which is not to put down the rest of the landscape. Some of the most peaceful, restful pastoral land in California—and some of the loveliest back-roads drives—are found in Humboldt and

159

Del Norte counties. And so are some of the state's densest forests and most rugged mountains.

A number of unwelcome visitors came to the Redwood Empire in May 1992. As the place where three tectonic plates come together, the California-Oregon coast is one of the most seismically active areas on earth. Sharp earthquakes caused severe damage to several of the small towns and ignited a fire in the central district of Scotia, a lumber-company town on U.S. 101. Rebuilding began within a few weeks, and residents say cheerfully that everything was back to normal early in 1993. They claim the quakes gave them something to talk about besides the weather. With forty inches of rainfall a year and a winter that can seem like one long drizzle, the Redwood Empire is the wettest spot in Calfornia. However, that's what makes the trees grow.

The Redwoods

Start with the trees. In fact, it is almost impossible *not* to start with the trees, for redwoods are found all along U.S. 101, a.k.a. "The Redwood Highway." At a number of places along the route, four-lane expressway has been built to bypass the protected groves—a boon to both visitors and trees. Where possible, follow old Route 101, which threads right among the trees, allowing you to appreciate their mammoth size and beauty up close. But don't simply drive through. Get out of your car at the frequent turnouts and walk among the towering giants. Although cousins of the *Sequoia gigantea* of the Sierra Nevada, the *Sequoia sempervirens* of the coastal mountains are mere spring chickens by comparison. The Sierra Nevada "big trees" may live 3,000 years or more; the maximum lifespan of coastal redwoods is closer to 2,000 years. Although smaller in girth, redwoods are taller and they grow faster. Branches begin much higher on the trunk. You may look up 100 feet before the first limbs branch out. The redwoods provide clear, straight lumber.

Richardson Grove State Park, just south of Benbow, is the first stand of the mighty trees you meet as you head north on U.S. 101. They are not the largest, though, but merely a sample of the magnificent forests yet to come.

Now follow the signs to the **Avenue of the Giants,** the former

U.S. 101 designated as a state scenic route. (There are eight marked entrances between Redway, north of Garberville, and Pepperwood, thirty miles north.) Along this two-lane highway the trees are literally so close you can stick your head out of the passenger's side window and almost touch them. As the trees reach upward, the sun disappears into their lofty boughs, and soft light dapples intricate patterns on the forest floor like sunshine filtering through a stained-glass window. Moss, compacted rust-colored needles, and shade-loving flowers carpet the forest floor and soak up the sounds. Here is where the feeling of being in a Gothic cathedral begins. All that appears to be missing are the Gregorian chants and the votive candles.

The Avenue of the Giants leads through **Humboldt Redwoods State Park,** part of which follows the sparkling South Fork of the Eel River. Get out of your car here and walk along the riverbanks in the cool shade for fine vistas of the trees. Many of the trees within a few feet of the road tower above 300 feet, the vertical equivalent of a football field. The avenue encompasses a few of the tourist gimmicks left over from the Redwood Highway's earlier days. At Myers Flat, you can actually drive through a living tree or onto a fallen monster log. The One Log House, also at Myer's Flat, is a forty-ton log house carved out of a tree 2,000 years old. The Eternal Tree House, at Redcrest, is a twenty-foot room carved out of a 2,000-year-old living tree. For more information write Avenue of the Giants Association, Miranda, California 95553, or call 707-923-2555.

The biggest trees of all in Humboldt Park are found in the **Rockefeller Forest** where the Dyersville Giant was measured at 350 feet. The park visitor center, open in spring and summer, furnishes information on the park and on the trees. It has an excellent explanation of the redwood forest ecosystem. The visitor center is on U.S. 101, near Weott. Call 707-946-2311.

Redwood National Park still stirs controversy. Environmentalists and the logging industry fought over it for decades. The park was finally established in 1968, partly through the influence of Lady Bird Johnson. It stretches for forty miles along the coasts of Humboldt and Del Norte counties and incorporates three older state parks, Prairie Creek Redwoods, Del Norte Coast Redwoods, and Jebediah Smith Redwoods state parks, which contain the most majestic trees and continue to be separately administered. The conflict centered around environmentalists' concerns that the consequences of heavy logging threatened

SCENIC DETOUR

Turn west off U.S. 101 at the town of Fernbridge toward **Ferndale**. (Watch for signs.) A five-mile drive through redwoods and pastures takes you to this charming community, a small town of beautifully preserved and/or restored Victorian homes and storefronts. Many of them are occupied by weavers, painters, woodworkers, and ceramicists. The homes and gardens have been so immaculately kept that the entire village has been declared a state historic landmark. The designation has been reinforced by local insistence on tasteful standards for both shops and their merchandise.

Ferndale was one of the major victims of the May 1992 earthquakes, in which the damage caused by the initial shock was compounded by an aftershock felt as far away as San Francisco. Some of Ferndale's finest examples of Victorian architecture were knocked off their foundations. The town has come back "better than ever," the locals say. You may still encounter evidences of repair, however.

The stately homes are a legacy from Ferndale's halcyon days as a dairy-farming and lumbering center. A few have been converted into B&Bs and craft and gift shops; the outstanding example is the Gingerbread Mansion, built in 1895 as a doctor's office, home, and hospital and now a B&B (see Lodging, following). The majority of restored homes are not open to the public. However, Fern Cottage, built in 1866 for a family of Scandinavian dairy farmers and restored with painstaking authenticity, is open by appointment. The cottage is at 212 Centerville Road, Ferndale. Call 707-786-4735. You can also obtain a self-guided walking-tour map of the town, which identifies the buildings and describes their history, from the Ferndale Chamber of Commerce, 451 Main Street. Call 707-786-4477.

The **Ferndale Museum** contains a fine small exhibit of an-

the virgin forests already under protection—that topsoil washed down from the logged-over areas clogged the streams and interfered with the root systems of the trees in the parks, especially one creekside grove containing what are believed to be the tallest trees in the world. Amid heated dispute, the park was greatly enlarged in 1978. The debate continues with environmentalists insisting that the park boundaries be ex-

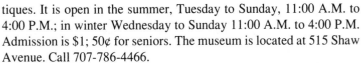

tiques. It is open in the summer, Tuesday to Sunday, 11:00 A.M. to 4:00 P.M.; in winter Wednesday to Sunday 11:00 A.M. to 4:00 P.M. Admission is $1; 50¢ for seniors. The museum is located at 515 Shaw Avenue. Call 707-786-4466.

Beyond Ferndale, continue on Mattole Road over Rainbow Ridge, headed for what is known as "The Lost Coast." It is not a drive for the fainthearted. The two-lane road has more than its share of twists and squiggles, and those prone to motion sickness would be advised to turn back at Ferndale. For others, however, the drive through the redwood groves and secluded valleys can be a rewarding voyage through some of the most spectacular backcountry California has to offer. The road reaches the coast at Cape Mendocino and its still-vigilant lighthouse. Off these rocky headlands, many a coastal vessel went to its tragic end. You get a poignant reminder at Centerville, five miles west of Ferndale, where the Centerville Cross, overlooking Centerville Beach, memorializes thirty-eight passengers who died when the steamer *Northern* sank in 1860.

Below Cape Mendocino, the road turns back inland. The remote roadless area to the south is the true lost coast, so challenging and surf-smashed that highway engineers totally bypassed it. Ribbons of hiking trails run through the area for those with experience and determination. Mattole Road, meanwhile, swings through forests and dairying country, leapfrogging across the rushing Mattole River to picturesque **Petrolia,** site of the first oil strike in California, a bonanza that quickly played out. Petrolia was another victim of the May 1992 quakes still in the process of pulling itself together. The road then leads through scenic backcountry to the minuscule, old-timey town of **Honeydew,** finally passing through parts of Humboldt Redwoods State Park before rejoining U.S. 101 at South Fork. The drive requires three hours minimum. A full day is better.

tended farther for additional protection. That would further enhance the park's reputation as the most expensive national park ever. The 1978 addition not only bought out private lands but gave cash settlements and retraining allowances to the loggers who lost their jobs when the old-growth forests were placed off limits.

All this fuss seems far away when you are surrounded by the trees.

The national park visitor center at Orick, dramatically located almost directly on the Pacific, has excellent educational displays about the redwoods and the area's early history. A shuttle bus ($2 in spring and summer) from the center takes you to a trail from which you can see the world's three largest known redwoods, topping even the 356-foot specimen in Humboldt Redwoods State Park. The Howard Libbey Tree, which most people simply call the "tall tree," is the giant of them all, reaching up 367.8 feet. Mighty as they are, ironically, they do not truly stand out because so many of their neighbors are giants, too. The visitor center, with its beachfront location, is also a fine vantage point for watching the annual gray whale migration and for sighting waterbirds in adjacent Freshwater Lagoon. For information call 707-488-3461.

Prairie Creek Redwoods State Park, probably the most spectacular of the state parks, is home to another species of mammoth mammal—the Roosevelt elk. (They look tame and gentle from a distance, but are by no means Bambis, especially in the rutting season.) A special parking area along old U.S. 101 allows you to watch a prime herd of elk browsing across the meadow. Many of the bull elk weigh more than 700 pounds and sport racks of antlers greater than six feet. This area also has its own visitor center.

Much of the national park can be reached only by hiking trails. A short drive, however, takes you to Lady Bird Johnson Grove, dedicated to the First Lady who was such an inspirational force in establishing the national park. A circular self-guided trail leads you through the trees and explains the history of the trees and park. There are campgrounds and spaces for recreational vehicles throughout the state parks. Campground reservations are usually necessary. For information write Redwood National Park, 1111 Second Street, Crescent City, California 95531, or call 707-946-2409.

Eureka

Eureka, the largest community in the Redwood Empire, has been a mining center, a logging center, and most recently, a tourist destination (while remaining the area's commercial hub). Evidence of its past prosperity can be seen in the dazzling number of well-preserved Victorian homes built in the 1880s and 1890s when the lumber barons were striving to outdo each other in opulent display. More than 100 homes and commercial buildings dating from lumbering's Golden Age are sprinkled around the town. A brochure outlining a drive-by tour is available from the Eureka Chamber of Commerce, 2112 Broadway Street. Call 707-442-3738.

You must have seen pictures of the **Carson Mansion,** whose carved towers and arches and fretwork balconies may very well make it the most photographed Victorian in America. In reality, the light-gray and slate-colored showplace is every bit as imposing and eye-catching as it is in its portraits. Built in the mid-1880s for the lumber magnate William Carson and his family, the Carson home is the premier work of the Newsom brothers, architects responsible for the most extravagant of the Eureka mansions. Nearby is another of their productions, affectionately known as the Pink Lady. Both buildings are in private hands and not open for visitors. The Carson Mansion is a private club. It is located at Second and M streets.

Old Town Eureka, with its gas lamps and brick streets, is one of the best examples of yesterday's preserved/restored business districts. Many of the storefronts feature the pillars, arches, and stained glass of the Victorian age. Buildings in the waterfront complex trace back to the 1850s when first the miners and then the loggers made the district hum with business. Even the more recent additions date from the early 1900s. The landmark buildings house antique and gift shops, with a mix of professional offices thrown in.

Clarke Memorial Museum formerly was the Victorian-age Bank of Eureka. Now it houses a fine exhibit of turn-of-the-century antiques and coastal Indian basketry. A donation is suggested. The museum is open Tuesday to Saturday 12:00 P.M. to 4:00 P.M. It is located at 240 E Street. Call 707-443-1947.

That eminent warrior, Ulysses S. Grant, served at **Fort Humboldt** in 1854, protecting the settlers against the presumably hostile Indians and writing about his days at the nation's northernmost and loneliest military outpost in his memoirs. "Sam" Grant was a captain then, and after his service he went back to Illinois to become a storekeeper until the Civil War broke out and rocketed him to victory and fame. The fort now crowns the **Fort Humboldt State Historic Park.** The former hospital is now a museum with artifacts from Grant's day as well as donkey engines and locomotives from the pioneer logging period. They fire up the boilers the third Saturday of each month during summer. The fort is

SCENIC DETOUR

State Highway 299 east of Arcata opens a vast country of dense forests and sparkling, fish-filled mountain streams, laden with parks, resorts, and campsites, and laced with hiking trails for hikers of all abilities. Like most roads leading into the wilderness of the California mountains, the route features steep grades and switchbacks and probably should not be attempted in winter. Stop first at **Blue Lake,** five easy miles east of U.S. 101 along the Mad River. This is a small town of old homes and pleasant gardens nourished by the wet winters. Stop for a picnic and visit at the **Mad River Fish Hatchery,** two miles south of town on Hatchery Road, open daily during daylight hours. Steelhead and salmon are raised here. In town, the old depot of the Arcata and Mad River Railroad has been converted into a fascinating small museum.

Continue on State Highway 299 over the Coast Range to **Willow Creek,** at the junction of State Highways 299 and 96. Since some of the nearby peaks reach 5,000 feet, this is a more challenging drive. Willow Creek nestles in the heart of a vast virgin stand of Douglas firs and is completely surrounded by the Six Rivers National Forest, one million acres of backcountry open to fishermen, hunters, campers, backpackers, kayakers, and white-water rafters. The blue-green Trinity River sparkles through the dense woods. Willow Creek itself is primarily a jumping-off place and supply point for the outdoors community. Skootenberg Press publishes a list of resorts and recreational opportunities, available free at most local businesses.

open daily during daylight. Admission is $3. The fort is located at 3431 Fort Avenue, off Broadway and Highland streets. Call 707-445-6567.

To pamper your sweet tooth, visit **Sjaak's La Chocolaterie,** which offers tours (and samples) by prearrangement. You'll find it at Second and F streets. Call 707-445-0236.

Antique sawmill machinery, dating from the 1890s, is used at the **Blue Ox Millworks** to fashion gingerbread reproductions of the fretwork that adorned Victorian houses. There's a one-hour self-guided tour. The millworks is at the foot of X Street. Call 707-444-3437.

Samoa Cookhouse is the last of the old-time cookhouses once

Turn north at Willow Creek on State Highway 96. This two-lane highway follows the course of the Klamath River, one of the famous spawning grounds for the Northwest's king salmon. Threading its way through the deep canyon and heavy forests, the highway takes you to **Hoopa Valley Indian Reservation,** twelve miles north of Willow Creek on the flank of the Salmon Mountains. The **Hoopa Tribal Museum** here is definitely worth a visit. The collections trace the culture and history of the tribe and several related tribes of the Northwest, with displays of basketry, ceremonial regalia, redwood dugout canoes, and tools and implements used by the tribes. Tours can be arranged to the ceremonial grounds and to the ruins of 1851-vintage Fort Gaston, where a dwelling is said to have been once occupied by U.S. Grant. Open daily, it is located on State Highway 96 at the Hoopa Shopping Center. Call 916-625-4110.

Twenty-eight miles beyond Hoopa, the small former mining community of **Orleans** slumbers in the sun. Once a headquarters for active placer mining, it retains an old hotel and other buildings from its mining-camp heyday. The small, recently-opened **Orleans Mining Company Museum** exhibits artifacts from both the mining and logging periods. It's on State Highway 96. Call 916-627-3213.

From Orleans, the intrepid may venture farther on State Highway 96 over the 100-mile course of the Klamath through the Klamath Mountains to I-5 north of Yreka. Others may wish to retrace their route at this point back to U.S. 101.

found in all the north coast logging communities. It still serves lumber-jack-size meals (see Restaurants, following). A museum displays kitchen utensils from the lumber-camp era. The cookhouse is across Humboldt Bay via Samoa Bridge. Call 707-442-1659.

Loleta is a charming small dairying community just off U.S. 101 north of Eureka. You can watch cheese making via a viewing window at the Loleta Cheese Factory, 252 Loleta Drive. Call 707-733-5470. The **Humboldt Creamery** offers tours by appointment of its milk bottling and butter production. Take the Fernbridge exit off U.S. 101. Call 707-725-6814.

Trinidad probably enjoys the most magnificent setting on the entire coast. This small fishing village overlooks a secluded cove where seastacks and the massif of Trinidad Head shelter it from the sea. The Trinidad Head Walk, not too strenuous, opens stunning vistas of shore and sea along its entire length. Trinidad is still an active dock for salmon and sport fishermen. Catch is sold right off the boats and featured in local fish-and-chips emporia.

Arcata, a college town built around a leafy central plaza, is known for the murals that decorate its walls—among other assets. The murals depict the area's history, including its founding as a mining center that grew into a logging port and then the home of Humboldt State University. A brochure describing and interpreting the murals can be obtained from the Chamber of Commerce, 1062 G Street. Call 707-822-3619.

The **Arcata Railroad Museum** displays photographs, artifacts, and memorabilia from the heyday of the Arcata and Mad River Railroad, a short line that brought timber to the coast and connected the interior villages. The museum is on the third floor of Jacoby's Storehouse. A wildlife sanctuary at **Arcata Marsh** conducts guided walks year-round for birdwatchers and photographers. Walks and tours are conducted each Saturday at 8:30 A.M. The sanctuary is at the foot of I Street.

Restaurants

- **Abruzzi** delivers great pasta dishes from the Abruzzi region of central Italy, a district along the Adriatic coast. Both the pasta and the sauces are homemade. Moderate. 791 Eighth Street, Arcata. 707-826-2345.

- **Benbow Valley** specializes in barbecued beef; people come from all over the north coast for its barbecued beef sandwiches and ribs, served with a homemade sauce. Fish and chips is another specialty. Inexpensive to moderate. 6840 Benbow Drive, Garberville. 707-923-2790.

- **Hotel Carter** is an outpost of California cuisine, with emphasis on fresh produce. Expensive. 301 L Street, Eureka. 707-444-8062.

- **Lazio's** started as a small seafood restaurant attached to a fish processing plant on the Eureka waterfront. The restaurant outgrew the plant and recently was moved to Eureka's Old Town. Moderate. 327 Second Street, Eureka. 707-443-9717.

- **Lost Coast Brewery** makes its own suds. Recommended is the fish and chips accompanied by the house amber ale. Inexpensive. 617 Fourth Street, Eureka. 707-445-4480.

- **Oh's Townhouse** is best known for its steaks: you choose your own from a showcase and they cook it to your liking. Moderate to expensive. 206 West Sixth Street, Eureka. 707-443-4652.

- **Samoa Cookhouse** lets you eat the way lumberjacks used to eat—seated at long tables, putting away mountains of beef, mashed potatoes, vegetables, French toast, sausage, scrambled eggs, and other dishes that stick to the ribs. This last of the old-time lumber-camp cookhouses serves breakfast, lunch, and dinner, usually with a limited menu. The attached museum displays cooking utensils from the old camp kitchens. Moderate. Cookhouse Road, Eureka. 707-442-1659.

- The **Seascape** sits on the pier in Trinidad and overlooks the pleasant cove. Not surprisingly, seafood is the specialty of the house. Moderate. Trinidad Bay. 707-677-3762.

- **Rolf's Park Cafe** is the place to go for great game dishes—boar, elk, and buffalo, for example. They serve fresh seafood, too. Both the restaurant and the chef have won awards. In pleasant weather, dine on the patio shaded by towering redwoods. Moderate to expensive. 123664 U.S. 101, Orick. 707-488-3841.

Lodging —————————————————————————

The Eureka B&B Association provides a free centralized reservation service for nine B&Bs, along with a free brochure. P.O. Box 207, Eureka, California 95502. 707-441-1215. The Eureka/Humboldt County Convention and Visitors Bureau also publishes a listing of hotels, motels, inns, and B&Bs within the county. 1034 Second Street, Eureka, California 95501. 800-346-3482.

- The **Benbow Inn** is the showplace of the north country—an elegant, English Tudor edifice surrounded by gardens, with a history dating back into the 1920s. The spacious rooms have recently been renovated (including the bathrooms) and decorated with antiques. Many of the rooms have fireplaces, private entrances, and private patios. There is a first-class dining room with a noted Sunday brunch. Expensive. 445 Lake Benbow Drive, Garberville. 707-923-2124.

- **Carson House Inn,** across the street from the Carson Mansion, is a large and comfortable motor inn that has just increased its capacity with the addition of a new wing. Moderate to expensive. 1209 Fourth Street, Eureka. 707-443-1601.

- **Carter House Inn** is a reconstructed seven-room Victorian with open parlors, marble fireplaces, and antique furnishings. Some of the rooms share a bath. Expensive. 1033 Third Street, Eureka. 707-445-1390.

- **Hotel Carter** is a small, European-style *auberge* with an emphasis on hospitality and service. Expensive. 301 L Street, Eureka. 707-444-8062.

- **Iris Inn** is a small B&B that serves a gourmet breakfast and pampers guests with books, newspapers, and personal service. Housed in a 100-year-old Queen Anne Victorian. Moderate. 638 West Sonoma Street, Eureka. 707-444-3410.

- **Seafarer** is a modern motor inn, convenient to downtown Eureka and to the Old Town district. Inexpensive to moderate. 270 Fifth Street, Eureka. 707-443-2206.

- **Hotel Arcata** is the town's seventy-five-year-old hotel overlooking the town plaza. Rooms have recently been refurbished. Moderate. 708 Ninth Street, Arcata. 707-828-0217.

- **Lost Whale B&B** is right on the water at Trinidad, with its own private beach. All six rooms have beautiful views. Country breakfasts are served. Moderate to expensive. 3452 Patrick Point Drive, Trinidad. 707-677-3425.

• **Trinidad B&B** also overlooks Trinidad Bay, with coastal views from almost every room. Hiking trails lead into the redwoods. Moderate to expensive. 560 Edwards Street, Trinidad. 707-677-0840.

• **Gingerbread Mansion B&B** survived the Ferndale earthquakes, Victorian architecture and all, and has resumed its place as one of the most photographed buildings in northern California. It is surrounded by a handsome English garden. Expensive. 400 Berding Street, Ferndale. 707-786-4000.

Chapter 14
Sacramento
and the Delta

Sacramento is a thriving city and an enjoyable (and educational) tourist destination in its own right. At the top of the list is its fundamental role in California's hurly-burly history. It is also the hub of the state's leading industry—agriculture—and its role as the governmental headquarters for a state larger than Germany, with a population as diverse as Asia, provides basic lessons in democracy.

The city of Sacramento became the first non-native settlement in the Sacramento Valley in the late 1830s and grew quickly during the heady days of the gold rush after 1848. To the delight of Old West history buffs, much of that frontier heritage has been successfully preserved. Architecture and museums capture the spirit of early central valley life. Political figures and lobbyists huddle together as they have done since the state government set up shop here in the 1860s. Thanks to careful preservation and restoration, Old Sacramento looks much as it did when settlers began pouring into the state by the hundreds and thousands more than a century ago.

Sutter's Fort, in the blocks bounded by K, L, 26th, and 28th streets, stands as the symbol of Sacramento's Wild West origins. Its prime location at the confluence of the Sacramento and American rivers attracted the attention of the young Swiss immigrant, John Augustus Sutter. He established New Helvetia—New Switzerland—in 1839, enclosing it within whitewashed adobe walls as protection against presumably hostile tribes. The settlement and Sutter prospered, and Sutter's Fort became the destination of westward migrant parties throughout the 1840s. Then the historic discovery of gold at Sutter's Mill—his own property on the American River—ironically doomed Sutter's fortunes. Greedy miners and immigrants swindled Sutter out of his land, and he was forced to give up the fort and eventually his other property. He died a poor man. Bypassed and abandoned as California mushroomed and the city grew up, the fort was reconstructed in 1891 and restored to the look of the 1840s. The pioneers' living quarters, equipped with the cast-iron skillets and narrow beds of the time, give a sense of the frontier life of the 1840s and 1850s. The fort is open daily 10:00 A.M. to 5:00 P.M. Admission is $2. Call 916-324-0539.

The **Indian Museum,** adjoining Sutter's Fort, displays artifacts from the many tribes of Native Americans who inhabited California before the Spanish colonists and later the Americans. Although small, the museum is rich in tribal tradition. The tribal leaders themselves chose and supervised the displays, lending an authentic feel to the place. Many of the most interesting photographs are casual "family and friends" pictures donated by actual Indian families. The display of Native American handicrafts features a vast collection of intricately woven basketry, including the smallest basket in the world, as listed in the *Guinness Book of World Records*—so small that it could rest comfortably on the end of your pinky. Admission $2. Call 916-324-0539.

The **California State Capitol** stands in a palm-fringed park squarely in the center of the business district, occupying one oversize block bounded by L, N, 10th, and 15th streets. Its glittering dome and stately columns date back to 1860 when the peripatetic young California legislature, after several moves, settled on Sacramento as its permanent site. The legislature then secured the location by immediately appropriating $500,000 to construct the building, which took fourteen years to complete. Sit in the shaded park, lush with grass fields, for a picnic and a lazy afternoon of politician watching or walk over to the east end of the block to see the Vietnam Veteran's Memorial. Or venture inside to witness the California legislative process in action. Visitors' galleries in both the senate and assembly welcome public viewing. In 1972–1982 the legislative chambers were rebuilt and restored to their original 1900s decor, and several government offices became a small historic museum. Public tours of the museum and offices are conducted daily, 9:00 A.M. to 5:00 P.M. (10:00 A.M. to 5:00 P.M. weekends). Tours leave every hour on the hour until 4:00 P.M. They are free, but you should pick up a ticket in the basement Tour Office to reserve your spot. Call 916-324-0333.

Old Sacramento, along the Sacramento River, successfully captures the Old West feel of the early settlement days. You can easily imagine the Pony Express rider galloping through town on the last leg of the 1966-mile mail run that began in Missouri and ended less than ten days later at the B. F. Hastings Building on the corner of Second and J streets. The Old Sacramento restoration is so authentic that it has gone back to wood sidewalks and brick streets—good for walking, bad for driving. Parking is limited; use the public parking garage on Front Street.

The restored area houses the usual quota of restaurants and gift shops, but the real highlights are the museums—no less than eight of them within the five-block area. They range from displays of nineteenth-century hardware in the Big Four Building to Civil War artillery in the Citizen Soldier Museum—an excellent place to learn Sacramento history through a day of museum hopping. Buy a combination ticket for $11 which allows access to all the Old Sacramento museums.

The **California State Railroad Museum,** I Street, remains the most notable Old Sacramento museum. The collection of locomotives and rolling stock traces the history of the steam train—a revolutionary technology that determined the destiny and development of California. The state's cities, industries, crops, even political institutions have been shaped in large part by the railroads, especially the transcontinental link which joined the state to the rest of the country in 1869. The railroad museum pamphlet aptly sums it up, "The California State Railroad Museum exists to preserve the history of this vital industry," and that it does. The museum offers a film of railroad history, its development and importance to American transportation. Enter one of the passenger cars and get a glimpse of luxurious turn-of-the-century train travel or stand at the controls of the Santa Fe steam locomotive to relive the life of an engineer at the controls of a 6000-horsepower engine. Walk through the old sleeping and dining cars, watch how the mail was sorted on a hurtling train, or investigate the roundhouse, the train sheds, and the old passenger station. Museum admission is $5, including the film. For another $5, you can ride a steam-powered excursion train that chugs along the Sacramento River. Open daily, 10:00 A.M. to 5:00 P.M. For excursion information call 916-552-5252.

The **Towe Ford Museum,** Front Street outside Old Sacramento, boasts the largest collection of antique Fords in the country. More than 175 models represent almost every year dating back to 1903. Visitors of any generation can find Fords from their youth. And more than 90 percent of the exhibit cars actually run (although not in the museum). Besides Fords, the museum also displays some notable cars of other makes including former Governor Ronald Reagan's staff car, Governor Jerry Brown's infamous blue 1966 Plymouth, and a U.S. Treasury's 1976 armored Cadillac limousine. Each car is identified by name, price, and model year along with information on size and engine configuration and type of clutch or brake. An accompanying descriptive banner lists other significant events of each model year. Thus you learn that while people were driving the 1906 Model N Runabout, which sold for $500, the permanent wave had just been introduced—priced at $1000 and requiring eight to twelve hours to set. Open daily 10:00 A.M. to 5:00 P.M. Admission is $5 for adults, $4.50 for seniors.

The **Blue Diamond Exhibit** is for nuts—almonds, that is, one of California's major crops. The world's largest almond-processing plant, at 1701 C Street, north of Sutter's Fort, offers free tours that show how almonds (pronounced without the "l" in California) are grown, harvested, processed, and packaged. After a twenty-five-minute film, you follow the almonds through cracking, cleaning, grading, sorting, packaging, and finally tasting. There's a souvenir package and a small gift shop. Tours are Monday to Friday 10:00 A.M. and 1:00 P.M. by appointment. Admission free. For information call 916-446-8409.

Many elaborate Victorian homes can still be found in Sacramento. Nestled in tree-lined streets, these stately dwellings are largely concentrated from 7th to 16th streets, from E to I streets. The most notable homes are the Heilbron Home at 740 O Street and the Stanford Home at 800 N Street, residence of the railroad baron and state senator whose fortune founded Stanford University.

Special Events

The vast state of California varies dramatically from San Diego to the Oregon border, from the mighty Sierra Nevada to the sea. The nation's most populous state is home to farmers, scientists, entrepreneurs, movie stars, and manufacturers and has an ethnic diversity broader than any other state in the union. From mid-August through Labor Day all of these different cultures gather at the **California State**

SACRAMENTO RIVER DELTA

Below the state capital en route to the confluence with the north-flowing San Joaquin River, the Sacramento Valley widens into the Sacramento River Delta. It's a large rural basin lined with levees and dotted with small islands. From Sacramento, head south on State Highway 160 for a breath of pleasant landscape and an enjoyable drive. You drive along eucalyptus-lined roads atop a levee, then round a bend, cross a towering metallic drawbridge, and drop into lettuce fields where yachts and water skiers a few yards away in the wide and slow-moving waters parallel your course.

The meandering road zigzags back and forth across the river and its branches, passing through quiet riverside towns of a few hundred population, which offer little more than groceries, gasoline, and a few small restaurants. Keep driving until you reach Walnut Grove. Cross the bridge to **Locke**—and step back into rural China. Now largely deserted, the town was founded as a Chinese immigrant settlement by one Tin Sin Chan in 1912. Locke grew rapidly after the Chinese section of Walnut Grove burned in 1915. The buildings, constructed in traditional peasant Chinese style, still line the narrow main street today. A small Chinese population remains in the somewhat rundown buildings. A few stores operate largely on weekends.

You may also approach the Delta from the San Francisco area. From the East Bay, follow I-80 north (I-80 south from Benicia) to State Highway 4 east. Turn north on State Highway 160 at Antioch and follow it across the delta to Sacramento. From Sacramento, you may also head south on I-5, turn west on State Highway Route 12 to State Highway 160. Either direction is a pleasant afternoon's drive.

Fair for an eighteen-day celebration of the best of the Golden State. The gala event is held at the California State Fairgrounds on the western edge of Sacramento. Fair food vendors bring you the tastes of the world. Try spicy African chicken or soul burgers, or bite into zesty teriyaki beef. There are wine judgings and industrial exhibits, livestock shows and park rides. You'll see some of the richest agricultural displays in the world and learn about fruit- and vegetable-growing techniques. Spend a

PICK YOUR OWN LUNCH

California's central valley is known as the nation's fruit bowl. It is also the vegetable bin, rice supplier, and wine cellar. Many of the farms are giant agribusinesses, made prosperous by irrigation, but smaller farms survive, many of them delighted to welcome visitors or sell them produce directly, or if the visitors feel both nostalgic and energetic, to pick their own.

Watch for "Pick-Ur-Own" signs throughout the Sacramento area and other parts of the valley. They may be found on rural roads but also along major highways like I-5 and U.S. 99, which run north and south through the valley.

You can obtain a farmer-to-consumer directory by writing the Small Farm Center, University of California, Davis, California 95616-8699. Call 916-757-8579. The directory lists farmers throughout the state who offer ripe, freshly picked produce for sale to consumers in small quantities. You will also find unusual varieties—or old-time ones—that no longer make their way to supermarkets. (For instance, look for highly perishable, short-season Lambert cherries in late June, which many consider the sweetest of all black-cherry varieties.) You can make the farm visit an outing; some of the farms even have picnic areas and fishing ponds.

Be sure to bring your own container if you plan to do your own picking. Call in advance to see if fruits are in-season and ripe. Here are a few U-pick farms in the Sacramento area:

BP Ranch. Cherries, plums, peaches, and Asian pears. 2590 Elverta Road, Elverta. 916-331-2769.

Pocket Brand Farms. Tomatoes, pumpkins, gourds, sweet corn. Picnic area. 7801 Freeport Boulevard, Sacramento. 916-391-8689.

Silver Bend. All summer vegetables, including corn, popcorn, tomatoes, cucumbers, and okra. 34600 South River Road, Clarksburg. 916-665-1410 or 916-744-1409.

Gerry's Fruit Bowl. Many varieties of apricots, peaches, plums, nectarines, apples, and pears. "Come in the morning when it's cool!" 5450 Balfour Road, Brentwood. 415-634-4155.

day or more learning about the many sides of this giant state. For information, call 916-263-3000.

Restaurants ————————————————————

Sacramento restaurants cater to the political crowd as well as visitors. You can eat on a floating riverboat in Old Sacramento or dine among legislators and lobbyists near the capitol building. An abundance of quick, reasonably priced restaurants are found throughout the city.

- **Frank Fat's Restaurant**, 806 L Street, offers upscale Chinese dining and caters to the political crowd. Indeed it has been called the third chamber of the California legislature. Try the New York Steak Frank Style or the Peking Duck. 916-442-7092. Two other Frank Fat-operated restaurants are located in Old Sacramento. **California Fat's,** 1015 Front Street, serves California Pacific cuisine; 916-441-7960. **Fat City**'s art nouveau atmosphere includes a famous 100-year-old bar that adds a historic touch to the turn-of-the-century continental cafe. 1001 Front Street. Moderate. 916-446-6768.

- The *Delta King* offers formal dining on the Sacramento River, along the Old Sacramento waterfront. This stern-wheeler used to transport passengers between San Francisco and Sacramento, but now it remains fast to the dock. It serves as a deluxe hotel with a theater as well as an elegant restaurant. Old Sacramento waterfront. Expensive. 916-441-4440.

- The **Fire House** remains one of Sacramento's most famous restaurants. This Sacramento institution has been serving fine continental and international cuisine in the original Old Sacramento firehouse for thirty years. Lunch is served on the New Orleans-style courtyard, weather permitting. 1112 Second Street. Expensive. 916-442-4772.

- Inexpensive dining can be found at **Fanny Ann's** in Old Sacramento. It's not your typical burger joint. Antiques are dispersed throughout the dining room, creating a rustic atmosphere. A turn-of-the-century fire wagon hangs over the bar and carousel horses adorn the walls. This was one of the first restaurants in Old Sacramento. 1023 Second Street. 916-441-0505.

Lodging

At the intersection of two major east-west highways and Seattle–San Diego Interstate 5, plus the headquarters for state government and the popular state fair, Sacramento has a wide range of accommodations of all types and prices. They are concentrated along the three highway

WILL ROGERS STOPPED HERE

In 1921, a June heat wave hit Vacaville causing all the figs at the Allison fruit ranch to ripen at once. Desperately, Helen and Edwin Power set up a fruit stand along old U.S. Route 40, under a black walnut tree that had been planted years before by a pioneer ancestor—and happened to provide one of the few spots of cooling shade on the hot drive between San Francisco and Sacramento. The fruit stand, which they called "The Nut Tree," was successful enough to encourage them to continue and soon to open a small restaurant. It grew into a western institution that hosted the likes of Herbert Hoover and Will Rogers. The **Nut Tree** is still a favorite stopping place along the beeline San Francisco–Sacramento highway, but it now resembles a small city. The complex includes a scenic railway, an airport for private planes, dining rooms, gift shops, a bakery, ice cream stands, bookstalls, a wine shop, and toy shops. A satellite "Coffee Tree" was established across the highway. Recently, over fifty outlet stores have been added, catering to the bargain shopper and making this the largest of the factory store malls in northern California. Other shops, gas stations, and motels have sprung up nearby.

Scads of visitors come daily for refuge from the hot valley climate or to poke in the gift shops that still specialize in dried figs, fruits, and nut specialties. Take the Monte Vista Road exit off I-80.

corridors, downtown near the state fairgrounds. In general, rates are lower than in San Francisco or in popular tourist areas like Napa. "Expensive," by Sacramento standards, is $70 and up. An Accommodations Guide, including campgrounds, may be obtained from the Sacramento Convention and Visitors Bureau, 1421 K Street, N.W., Sacramento, California 95814. Or call 916-449-6711.

- **Amber House Bed and Breakfast,** seven rooms with private baths in a restored mansion downtown, is known for its gourmet breakfasts and friendly evenings around the fireplace. Moderate to expensive; senior discounts. 1315 22nd Street. 916-444-8085.

- **Aunt Abigail's Bed and Breakfast** is a Colonial Revival mansion a short walk from the State Capitol, downtown. Moderate. 2120 G Street. 916-441-5007.

- **Riverboat** *Delta King* is a home afloat—and old river steamer anchored at the Old Sacramento waterfront. Forty-four rooms, plus a restaurant, cocktail lounge, and live theater. Fun but not necessarily restful. Expensive; senior discounts. 1000 Front Street. 916-444-5464.

- **Days Inn,** just off I-5 near Old Sacramento, is part of the chain that caters to older travelers. 173 rooms. Moderate; senior discounts. 200 Jibboom Street. 916-448-8100.

- **Canterbury Inn,** near the fairgrounds, is an older full-service hotel with moderate rates and senior discounts. 1900 Canterbury Road. 916-927-3492.

- **Central Motel** is a small budget motel located next to the Governor's Mansion. Senior discounts. 818 16th Street. 916-446-6006.

- **Sierra Inn,** off Business Route 80 East, is a comfortable older motel whose pool is a welcome refuge in hot Sacramento summers. Moderate; senior discounts. 2600 Auburn Boulevard. 916-482-4770.

Chapter 15

North from Sacramento

The gold rush, the coming of the railroads, and the fertile soil attracted settlers to the Sacramento River Valley north of the state capital and to the surrounding mountain wilderness. Previously undeveloped regions sprouted small towns centered around the most lucrative mine sites. Today, however, the mountains no longer attract visitors in search of gold. Instead visitors come here for something that often seems more precious and harder to find in the 1990s. You will cry, "Nature!" in the same tones as lucky miners cried, "Gold!" some 150 years ago.

This is the country of scenic afternoon or all-day drives. Lush forests carpet the countryside as far as the eye can see. High mountains, sparkling lakes, and rushing waterfalls attract outdoors lovers from all over. Glimpsed from almost any point in the area, snowcapped Mount Shasta, 14,000 feet high, dominates the landscape. You can even see volcanic vents where heat from the core of the earth pushes minerals to the surface, forming boiling pools in the ground—side effects of the thermal activity that formed Shasta's sister volcano, Mount Lassen. Plan to put a good number of miles on your car. Nature is not only beautiful and complex but also vast.

Red Bluff

Red Bluff, the first major town above Sacramento as you head north on I-5, is a charming small town perched on the shores of the Sacramento River and boasting a large number of well-preserved Victorian mansions. The most notable is the **Kelly-Griggs House Museum,** renovated and completely furnished with antiques of the 1870s. Pick up a map here for a self-guided tour of other Victorians in Red Bluff. The museum is open September to June, Thursday to Sunday 2:00 P.M. to 5:00 P.M.; October to May, Thursday to Sunday 2:00 P.M. to 4:00 P.M. The museum is located at 311 Washington Avenue. A donation is suggested. Call 916-527-1129.

William B. Ide State Historic Park, north of Red Bluff, includes the restored home of the Bear Flag Republic's only president, William B. Ide. The republic was established when California declared itself independent of Mexico, with its own flag and government. The republic lasted about a month, whereupon California became a territory of the U.S. and eventually a state. Admission free. The home is open daily 11:00 A.M. to 4:00 P.M., the park, 8:00 A.M. to sunset.

Redding

Redding is a modern, bustling town, laid out in the north end of the Sacramento Valley and the gateway to the surrounding highlands. Like much of California's central valley, this area is very hot in summer, with temperatures often soaring over 100°. While protesting that low humidity makes the heat bearable, most locals escape into the cooler nearby mountains for relief—mountains are just a hop, skip, and a few gallons of gasoline away. Redding lies forty-eight miles from Lassen National Volcanic Park, sixty miles from Mount Shasta. Pleasant lakes and streams like Lake Shasta or Hat Creek are also found a short distance from Redding—great getaways for an afternoon picnic stop in the shade. And Redding boasts a large selection of hotels and restaurants, making it an ideal base for a couple of days of nature appreciation in the surrounding wilderness.

Redding is a child of the railroads. When gold was discovered near Mount Shasta in 1848, prospectors quickly flooded into the hills north and west of where Redding now stands. Slowly, the mines played out, and miners threw in their picks and shovels to start searching for other prospects. Then, in 1866 the Central Pacific Railroad (CP) decided to construct a line between San Francisco and Portland and chose Redding as the final rest stop before the arduous journey through the Oregon mountains. The railroad named the new town for its general land agent, B.B. Redding.

Redding's array of museums allows you to look back at the area's rustic past as well as its natural history. The **Redding Museum of Art and History** is the largest institution of its type north of Sacramento. It features regional art and exhibits on Native American culture and fine art shows that change every six to eight weeks. Located in Caldwell Park along the banks of the Sacramento River, the museum can be reached from North Market Street. It is open in summer Tuesday to Saturday, 10:00 A.M. to 5:00 P.M., Sundays 12:00 noon to 5:00 P.M.; off-season Tuesday to Sunday 12:00 noon to 5:00 P.M. Admission is free but a $1 donation is suggested. The museum is located at 56 Quartz Mill Road. For information call 916-225-4155.

Also located in Caldwell Park, the **Carter House Natural Science Museum** gives a good overview of the regional environment. The museum houses thirty-seven species of animals native to northern California, changing natural history exhibits and a dimly-lighted nocturnal room where you can watch the antics of screech owls, flying squirrels and other animals normally seen only at night. The museum is open year-round, Tuesday to Sunday 10:00 A.M. to 5:00 P.M. Admission is $1. For information call 916-225-4125.

Shasta State Historic Park is a short three-mile drive west of Redding on State Highway 299. A row of old brick buildings reminds you that the thriving town of Shasta once stood at this site (not to be confused with the current city of *Mount* Shasta). Shasta was known as the "Queen City" of the northern California gold rush in the 1850s. The park's **Courthouse Museum,** located in one of the original Shasta County courthouses, features memorabilia from the heyday of mining, especially the crime-and-punishment side, with a recreated courtroom, jail, and gallows. In addition, come here to see the large collection of California landscape art and a fine array of Pit River Indian basketry. The museum is open in the summer, daily 10:00 A.M. to 5:00 P.M.; from September to June, it is closed Tuesday and Wednesday. Admission is $2. Call 916-243-8194.

Across the street, the **Litsch Store Museum** recreates an old-time Wild West general store that was actually in operation from the 1850s to 1960. Although its cash register is now closed, you can still view the various products available to the miner. Shelves are packed with canned goods, yard goods, and derby hats. Barrels that held pickles and grain line the floor. Storekeeper Litsch never put any wares on sale. If an item didn't sell, he simply tucked it away in the warehouse, bequeathing park curators a treasure trove of yesterday's merchandise ranging from plug tobacco to high-button shoes to whiskey barrels. The museum is open on spring, summer, and fall weekends, 10:00 A.M. to 5:00 P.M. Free with park admission. 916-243-8194.

Touring and Sightseeing

To get the most out of a visit to the northern Sacramento Valley and its surrounding splendors, head out of Redding on the winding highways into the mountains. Here are several natural—and quite different—loop trips, each departing from and leading back to Redding. You will probably want to stay in Redding. See Restaurants and Lodging at the end of this chapter.

NORTH LOOP: The North Loop covers the high country north of the Sacramento Valley all the way up to snowcapped Mount Shasta. It includes a long stretch through lightly populated forest land, passing many interesting museums but emphasizing the beautiful countryside.

Head north from Redding on I-5. This route takes you directly over man-made **Lake Shasta,** the deep blue of its water contrasting with the tanned hillside. Shasta is a major recreation center where houseboating, waterskiing, fishing, and just relaxing in lakeside cottage communities are the main activities. Spreading out in a spiderweb of drowned canyons, the monster lake was formed by Shasta Dam, the second largest dam in the United States, which now produces enough hydroelectric power to supply the city of Sacramento.

For a peaceful interlude in scenic backcountry, rent a houseboat and drift lazily around the lake or poke into its remote corners for fishing and exploration ashore. No maritime experience is required to operate the slow-moving vessels; you can check out as a skipper with a half-hour's orientation. The fully equipped houseboats can sleep up to ten persons and can be rented for three, four, or seven days. Summer rates are $825 for seven days and maximum of six persons; $1600 for a ten-person boat. Off-season rates are $425 to $1000. For information call

Trinity Lake Houseboating, 800-286-2225 or Trinity Alps Marina, 800-286-2286.

On the lake's east bank are the **Lake Shasta Caverns,** an intricate set of caves nestled into the mountainside. The caves are honeycombed with stalagmites and stalactites in spectacular formations, surrounded by miniature waterfalls and embedded with sparkling crystal. A two-hour tour starts with a fifteen-minute boat ride from Government Docks across Lake Shasta connecting to a special bus that carries visitors 800 feet up the mountain to the cave entrance. Like most caverns, the caves are cool; bring a light jacket or wrap. For information call 916-238-2341 or write Box 801, O'Brien, California 96070. Afterwards, you can seek your fortune in the adjoining gold-panning park, prospecting for the precious metal in the once lucrative streams leading into the lake.

Beyond Lake Shasta, drive north another twenty-five miles to **Castle Crags State Park.** Far above the highway, sharp, pointed granite outcrops jut from the mountain in rugged profiles, some 6,000 feet above sea level—looking (or so the early settlers thought) like the mountaintop redoubt of some medieval monarch. Best points for viewing the geological sculptures are from scenic turnouts along the roadside. It takes a strenuous climb of several hours to reach the top where you are awarded with an impressive panorama of the surrounding countryside. The hike is suggested for those athletic types with a surplus of energy only.

At the base of Castle Crags State Park, along I-5, the **Railroad Park Resort** offers a different and fun place to see and stay overnight. You sleep in your own refurbished antique caboose and dine in antique dining cars. The park holds many relics from the area's railroad past, integrated into the resort atmosphere. From the pool you can examine a variety of Southern Pacific rolling stock, both freight and passenger. The cost is $60 single for a private caboose; $5 additional for second occupant. For reservations call 916-235-4440.

Dunsmuir, north of Castle Crags, is a quaint rustic town that developed around the railroad much as Redding did. In its early history Dunsmuir served as the area's central railroad dispatch point, and it still claims fame as home of one of the last roundhouses leftover from the steam train era. The **Dunsmuir Museum** recounts the area's history with yesterday's artifacts—a 1919 Western Electric telephone switchboard and women's fashions of the 1900s. The museum is open daily

10:00 A.M. to 4:00 P.M. Admission is free, but a donation is suggested. The museum is located at 4101 Pine Street (between Dunsmuir Avenue and Sacramento Street). Call 916-235-0733.

The **city of Mount Shasta** is another small alpine community that grew up as a mining center. Its strategic location at the base of Mount Shasta provides grand views of the huge, presumably dormant volcano. The city's other major claim to fame is the headwaters of the Sacramento River. You can see the river emerge from underground springs in a city parklike setting off Mount Shasta Boulevard, where it begins its long southern journey through the fertile heart of California to feed eventually into San Francisco Bay and the Pacific Ocean. The headwaters park provides a cool and pleasant spot for an afternoon picnic before sightseeing.

Mount Shasta has two informative attractions in one central location—the **Sisson Museum** and **Mount Shasta Fish Hatchery.** The museum features a series of exhibits that tell about the area's weather as well as the history and geology of the mountain. In the connected hatchery you can walk among the hatching and rearing ponds and see trout in all stages of development. Admission is free. The museum and hatchery are located at 1 North Old Stage Road. Open 12:00 noon to 4:00 P.M. daily, 1:00 P.M. to 4:00 P.M. Sundays. Call 916-926-5508.

Mount Shasta itself is the dominant feature of the entire northern California landscape, visible for fifty miles. Rising abruptly out of the surrounding foothills and towering over them, Shasta is a spectacular sight in good weather, outlined against the vibrant blue California sky. Shasta is one of a chain of volcanic cones that includes the giant pyramid of Mount Rainier in Washington and the more recently active Mount Lassen and Mount Saint Helens. It has been dormant since before the white man discovered it in 1827. A mantle of snow adorns the 14,612-foot peak winter and summer for it is ringed with five glaciers year-round.

Winter athletes should note that Mount Shasta has recently opened a ski resort on some of its slopes. The small hill caters to beginners and advanced intermediate skiers—a great place to learn or practice your technique. The resort boasts two high-speed triple chair lifts, twenty-two runs, and a large novice area. The resort is ten miles east of the city of Mount Shasta, on State Highway 89. Lessons are available. Lift tickets cost $25 on weekends, $20 on weekdays. Lifts also operate in summer to ferry sightseers, photographers, or mountain bikers up the mountain for $7.

You can get a different and dramatic view of Mount Shasta as you head back south. Follow I-5 south for a few miles, then turn east on State Highway 89 south. The small mountain community of **McCloud** sits directly south of Mount Shasta offering the most scenic Shasta vistas. McCloud is a one-time company town, developed in the heady days of northern California logging. The boom is long over and the mills have closed, but the memory lives on in the **Heritage Junction** of McCloud Historic Center. Go there and see logging-industry memorabilia such as early fire-fighting gear and a Corliss engine from the 1903 Steam Log Mill, larger than a similar one at the Smithsonian Institution. The center is open Tuesday to Saturday, 11:00 A.M. to 3:00 P.M., Sunday 1:00 P.M. to 3:00 P.M. It is located at 320 Main Street.

Continue down State Highway 89 to **McArthur Burney Falls Memorial State Park,** a small state park that features short hikes and a large waterfall. (Note that McArthur Burney Falls can also be included on the East Loop—see below—if either time or energy has been used up for the day.) A short walk from the parking area takes you up close to the 129-foot plunge of Burney Falls. Two lone trees on a rock outcropping divide the wide lip of the falls. The water races around the little island and cascades over a moss-covered cliff into the pool below. A short but downhill one-mile hike will take you to the base of the falls (but remember, you have to hike back up). Burney Falls' 3,000-foot elevation and dense forest shade make for pleasantly cool temperatures.

State Highway 89 connects with State Highway 299. Head west for a pleasant scenic drive back to Redding. Note that this stretch overlaps the East Loop.

EAST LOOP: Both the nature lover and the fisherman (or a combination thereof) will appreciate the East Loop. It offers caves and forests, small towns, and large fish. It's a short day's drive around the edge of the Shasta-Trinity National Forest. From Redding, head east on State Highway 44 toward Shingletown. This stretch of road has been designated a scenic highway, its path winding through lush evergreen forest and rippling meadows nearly untouched by man. Turn north on State Route 89, past Subway Caves and Hat Creek toward Burney Falls to pick up the loop.

Subway Caves is an unusual and interesting stop. A series of tubes or tunnels were formed when molten lava on the surface cooled and hardened while other lava still flowed beneath. The whole structure solidified, leaving tubes in the rocks. You can walk into and explore the large tunnels but bring a jacket and a flashlight. There is no admission and all tours are self-guided. The caves are just off State Highways 44 and 89, about fifteen miles northeast of Manzanita Lake. For information call Redding Visitor and Convention Bureau at 916-225-4106.

Hat Creek has been called a fisherman's delight by both visitors and local anglers. The picturesque, rushing mountain stream is very accessible, lying just off State Highway 89. Hat Creek boasts a vigorous population of rainbow and brown trout. Take a lunch and stop at one of the numerous picnic areas along the stream. Or catch your meal.

The **Hat Creek Radio Astrological Observatory,** operated by the University of California, offers a technical reprieve from nature watching. The observatory scans signals from outer space and also measures movement of the tectonic plate. The surrounding mountains help the scientific observation by blocking out all man-made radiation. Six new telescopes supplemented the observatory's three twenty-foot telescopes and one eighty-five-foot model in 1993. The observatory offers casual tours daily 9:00 A.M. to 4:00 P.M. To get there, turn off State Highway 89 to Bidwell Road to Doty Road, following the well-placed signs.

Burney Falls (also included in the North Loop) is easily reached from the East Loop. Simply continue on State Highway 89 five miles past the State Highway 299 junction. For information see the Burney Falls section in the North Loop segment.

To pick up local fishing hints, return to State Highway 299 and head east to **Fall River Mills,** a small town that developed around one of the many water-powered flour and lumber mills that once operated along Hat Creek. Today, fishing enthusiasts can stock up on bait, learn which flies are attracting trout, and get the lowdown on fishing hot spots in the upper region of Hat Creek. Nonfishermen can browse through the arts and crafts studios where local artisans display their wares. Over the years, Fall River Mills has become a center for local artists and craftspeople.

Return to Redding by State Highway 299, a pleasant seventy-mile drive through the dense forests and into the rambling golden hills. The North Loop can be combined with the East Loop to make a very full-day trip through the north country. From Fall River Mills or Burney Falls simply continue north on State Highway 89 to McCloud. Allow at least eight hours for the journey.

TRINITY HERITAGE SCENIC BYWAY: This loop takes you north in the beautiful wilderness of the Shasta-Trinity National Forest, passing through a number of small mountain towns for a full day's trip. Take the entire loop or break it into shorter sections. You can choose to wind through a variety of old mining settlements, see panoramic views, or hit great fishing holes. Or all of the above.

To start the tour, drive from Redding west on State Highway 299 to Weaverville. You should pick up the free, very detailed, and well laid-out Trinity Heritage Scenic Byway Self-Guided Auto Tour Map available at the Trinity County Chamber of Commerce, 317 Main Street, Weaverville. The map traces the route in detail and also gives information on historic and nature sites.

From Weaverville, the loop follows State Highway 3 north all the way up to Yreka where you connect with I-5. Here are some of the highlights.

Weaverville is a quaint mountain community, its main street lined with well-preserved buildings from its mining past. Visit the **Joss House,** a Chinese place of worship (open daily 10:00 A.M. to 5:00 P.M.; admission and twenty-minute tour $2; closed in winter), and the **Jake Jackson Museum** (open in summer, daily 10:00 A.M. to 5:00 P.M.; November through April 12:00 noon to 4:00 P.M.; admission free). Up the road, catch the Lewiston Vista where you look out over the valley to view bald eagles and ospreys fishing in Lewiston Lake in the early evenings. Farther north on Highway 3 you will reach Trinity Center, a small mountain community whose original site now lies far beneath the waters of Trinity Lake. Construction of Trinity Dam was going to flood the valley floor so its citizens simply moved the town, rebuilding it where it stands today. You should pick up some fuel here if your tank is low.

The **North Shore Vista** offers a dramatic and disturbing sight left-over from the last days of heavy mining. Much dredging and mine tailings filled this stretch of the Trinity River with islands of residue gravel. The area was abandoned when gold mining became unprofitable. Continue north to Carrville Pond, another remnant of the area's mining past. The pond was created by one of the last bucket-line dredges in Trinity

County that worked the rich Trinity River bottom from 1939 to 1946. The dredge is gone but the pond remains, full of fish, thanks to the California Department of Fish and Game. Stop here to join the locals fishing for trout dinners.

Farther, **Coffee Creek** is yet another quaint mountain community born and raised on gold, but today its main industry is tourism. It's a quiet getaway set deep in the forested mountains, full of family-type resorts so popular that reservations are a must. The Trinity Heritage Byway Map includes a full list of resorts and B&Bs. A typical resort, Ripple Creek Cabins is $69 per night, double occupancy. Call 916-266-3505.

Coffee Creek residents give a variety of explanations for its unusual name. Some say a flood washed away a supply boat, and the coffee in its cargo turned the water a deep brown. Others claim that mud in the spring runoff was responsible for the color and the name. Whatever the explanation, Coffee Creek sparkles clearly today. And the streamside community has a lot to offer, including the last gas station before I-5. Pick up some fuel for the last thirty-nine miles.

Drive up and over **Mount Eddy,** 9,025 feet above sea level, and get spectacular views of Mount Shasta from across the valley. From here you can truly appreciate the sheer magnitude of this monstrous mountain. Continue to I-5, which will take you south back to Redding.

Lassen Volcanic National Park

Lassen Volcanic National Park, a series of glaciated canyons dotted and threaded with lakes and streams, lies forty-six miles southwest of Redding via State Highway 44. The area is best known for its many sites of thermal activity—a great place for short hikes through the wilderness or around volcanic ground vents. Bring a jacket because park temperatures drop as the cool breeze blows through the mountains.

Long thought to be an extinct volcano, Lassen Peak erupted in 1914 in the first of a series of blasts that destroyed the surrounding forest landscape. The finale came in 1915 when the peak shot an enormous mushroom cloud seven miles skyward, blowing away the upper half of its peak. Until Mount Saint Helens took away its steam with its eruption in 1984, Lassen Peak was the most recent volcanic outburst in the contiguous forty-eight states.

Entering the park from Redding via the northwest entrance, you immediately start climbing up the mountain pass on State Highway 89. (This road is closed by snow during winter and sometimes in other seasons, depending on the weather.) Look to the east as you cross Emigrant Pass and notice the barren gravel-covered hillside. This stretch of landscape, called the **Devastated Area,** was once a thick forest. The forest was leveled during the 1915 eruption when lava flowed out of the volcano and rapidly melted all the surrounding snow. Huge mud slides, some twenty feet deep, swept away the forest, leaving the gravel layer exposed. At the heart of the devastated area you can see the Crescent Crater, the vent primarily responsible for the lava flow.

Kings Creek and Upper Kings Creek Meadow make pleasant rest stops on your way toward the southwest end of the park. Small streams wind through the tall grass of the meadow where a wide variety of wildlife gathers. This is a good place to watch for deer that come for a late afternoon drink. Across the road is Kings Creek picnic area where you can lunch in the shade after meandering through the open meadow. Note that the site and trail markers are small, brown wooden posts alongside the road, easy to miss.

Terrace Lake and Summit Lake trails offer beautiful and easy hikes of .5 miles and .8 miles respectively. The hikes quickly take you from the world of automobile noises into wilderness to enjoy an hour or two of relaxation around the cool alpine waters of the two lakes.

The best hikes and all the continuing thermal activity lie at the southwestern end of the park. This portion of the park is a compact laboratory of volcanic phenomena. Steam hisses from cracks in the earth, and mud pots and sulfur pits boil and gurgle, spewing aromatic sulfur into the clear mountain air. Nose plugs are not necessary, although the sulfur fumes are strong and can be smelled well before you come to the pits. A small visitor center, open in summer, provides explanations of the volcano's past and present.

Bumpass Hell lies to the east of State Highway 89 in the southwest end of the park. To reach the volcanic vent you must pass a tough and treacherous downhill hike of 2.2 miles—and then you have to hike back up! This hike is advised for the adventurous and young at heart. However, this area is Lassen's most spectacular and diversified hydro-

SCENIC DETOUR: FEATHER RIVER CANYON

The Feather River Canyon is out of the way but well worth the trip. State Highway 70 follows the rushing river that carved this deep, tree-lined canyon through the Plumas National Forest—a pleasant afternoon drive. The most scenic section covers fifty miles between the junction of state highways 89 and 70 (northwest of Quincy and south of the Mount Lassen Volcanic National Park southwest entrance) to State Highway 149 at Oroville in the central valley. As you drive through the canyon you will wish you could cut off the roof of the car (or at least have a convertible with the top down) for a better view of the towering canyon walls. Instead, take advantage of the numerous turnouts and scenic overlooks for great views and photo opportunities. Giant rock faces jut from the lush vegetation above you while the river hurtles over and around smooth river stones set in the river bed 100 feet below. Although the road clings to the river's twisting course, it is not a taxing drive. But for a driving break and refreshments and to absorb what you've just seen, stop at **Belden,** twenty miles into the canyon from the state highways 89 and 70 junction, across a one-lane bridge. The small population center consists of a motor-home park, a campsite, and a general store. Pick up some picnic food at the general store. Or take a longer rest in the motor-home park at the Belden Saloon, whose patio is right over the rushing water.

The western end of the trip boasts panoramic views of the Sacramento Valley, whose golden hills spread for many miles into the distance and make the valley look like a vast sandy desert. Be sure to use one of the turnouts to admire the view.

thermal area with hot springs, mud pots, and fumaroles, and it may be worth braving the hike. Some call it a "Little Yellowstone." Colorful wildflowers bloom along its steaming borders. Bumpass Hell was named for Kendall Vanhook Bumpass, who discovered it only to lose a leg after falling into one of the thermal pools. Learn from Bumpass's example: Step carefully because pool temperatures can reach 240°.

Thermal activity can be seen right along the roadside. Continue down State Highway 89 to the **Sulfur Works** where hot gases rise out of the earth into a group of steaming sulfur pits. Take the boardwalk that runs around and over this ancient vent of Mount Tehama for easy viewing up close. The water has a high content of sulfuric acid so avoid getting it on your skin or clothes.

Restaurants ————————————————————

A wide variety of food is available in Redding, from prime steak in a casual atmosphere to Cajun cuisine to fresh seafood.

• **Jack's Grill** is a very deceptive local favorite. Anyone passing the unpretentious white façade or entering the small, almost bare, dining room might justifiably consider Jack's a "hole-in-the-wall." But Jack's atmosphere does not reflect its food quality. The two-word neon sign says it all: Choice Steaks. Insiders say Jack's serves the best and thickest steaks in this cattle-ranching region (they actually say the best in the world, but that may be simply local pride), but you must be prepared to wait for them. Jack's follows a strict no-reservations policy, and some evenings the waiting line can be two hours long. One possibly apochryphal story tells of then President George Bush stopping to eat at Jack's on a visit to northern California. The president's tight schedule allowed forty-three minutes for dinner; the wait at Jack's was longer. Bush left hungry. If your schedule is less crowded than the president's, try to fit in a meal at Jack's. (Hint: Come at 5:00 P.M. and you will probably be served within fifteen or twenty minutes.) Moderate. 1743 California Street. 916-241-9705.

Other Redding restaurants cannot match the character and the fame of Jack's but offer tasty meals in a variety of settings.

• Add a little spice to your life at **River City Bar and Grill** which serves American cuisine with a cajun influence. Moderate. 2151 Market Street. 916-243-9003.

• **Kenny's Seafood Grill** features fresh seafood and steak. The decor features photographs of the owner displaying his own prize catches. Moderate. 2705 Churn Creek Road. 916-222-1405.

- For seafood with a view, try the **Hatch Cover.** The restaurant perches high on bluffs overlooking the Sacramento River and Redding. As a bonus, you get a view of Mount Shasta. It includes a salad bar. Moderate. 202 Hemsted Drive. 916-223-5606.

Lodging

Redding offers a range of bed and breakfasts in a variety of decors. Luxury hotels and budget accommodations are also available. (Note: A 10 percent hotel-room tax is tacked onto your bill in Redding.)

- The **Tiffany House** is a B&B shaded by large oak trees. The late Victorian house sits on a hilltop with a panoramic view of the Mount Lassen range. Here you can cool off in the pool or sit in an old-fashioned porch swing on the shady deck and enjoy the colorful countryside. Included in the price are breakfast and refreshments with hors d'oeuvres. Reservations are recommended. Moderate. 1510 Barbara Road. 916-244-3225.

- For a taste of the more recent past go to the **Cabral House B&B** which is decorated in the style of the 1920s to 1940s. It is set in a quiet, relaxing residential neighborhood. Reservations are recommended. Expensive. 1752 Chestnut Street. 916-244-3766.

- The convenient hilltop location of **Palisades Paradise** affords a view across the city and Sacramento River. Relax in the garden spa after a day of sightseeing. Reservations recommended. Moderate. 1200 Palisades Avenue. 916-223-5305.

- The **Best Western Hilltop Inn** is a luxurious hotel with easy access to I-5. Take the East Cypress Avenue exit, then turn north on Hilltop Drive. Moderate; 10 percent senior discount. 2300 Hilltop Drive. 916-221-6100.

- **Oxford Suites,** a few blocks from the Hilltop Inn, offers full breakfast and has a pool. Inexpensive to moderate; 10 percent senior discount. 1967 Hilltop Drive. 916-221-0100.

- **Motel 6,** just off West Cypress Avenue, falls into the budget category. Easy access to I-5. Inexpensive. 2385 Bechelli Lane. 916-221-0562.

Chapter 16
Around Lake Tahoe

An immense blue alpine lake containing enough water to cover the entire state of California to a depth of fourteen and one-half inches, Lake Tahoe has always left visitors awestruck. Take Mark Twain, for example: "With the shadows of mountains brilliantly photographed upon its still surface," he wrote of this "noble sheet of blue water" in *Roughing It,* "I thought it must surely be the fairest picture the whole earth affords." Mere words, in short, cannot do Tahoe justice. Go and see it for yourself.

Between its twelve by twenty-two miles of water and its surrounding 10,000-foot peaks, Tahoe is a playground winter and summer. Tahoe's north shore is said to have the greatest concentration of ski areas in the U.S.—twelve for downhill, seven for cross-country. On sunny summer days, roads teem with bikers, roller bladers, joggers, and casual strollers. Their vibrant day-glow pinks, yellows, and green streak past lakeside cabins and keep car drivers on their toes. The lake hums with jet skis, water skiers, powerboats, and sailboats. Yet there's also room for those who prefer the slow lane. The hillsides are laced with hiking trails; shopping remains a favorite spectator sport and eating a participant activity; and Tahoe has recently expanded its cultural horizons with a Summer Music Festival, operatic performances, and Shakespeare on the beach at Sand Harbor. And, despite all the hectic activity and the heavily developed lakeshore, you can still stand at the water's edge, look across at the opposite shore and appreciate Tahoe as Twain and the Washoe Indians did.

The North Shore

Truckee, at the intersection of transcontinental I-80 and state highways 89 and 267, is the most common entry point for the Tahoe area. It's a small old western logging and railroad town that has grown into a hub for skiers and summer visitors. The town's colorful history dates back to 1844 when the Murphy-Stevens-Townsend pioneer party was migrating west and trying to cross the forbidding Sierra before winter set in. A friendly Paiute offered to guide them through the high passes. To the settlers, their scout's name sounded like "Tro-kay." They dubbed him "Truckee," and the name stuck to the town.

As the gateway to a major pass to the West, the area played a key role during the stampede that followed the gold rush. Then, in 1868 the Central Pacific Railroad, in a heroic engineering feat comparable to building the Pyramids, rammed its section of the transcontinental railroad through the high, avalanche-prone pass. Truckee became the main switching point for crews and special locomotives to move trains over the Sierra Nevada. It also developed a well-deserved reputation as a wide-open town where railroaders kept the saloons and brothels busy all night long. The railroaders have moved on, but Southern Pacific freights and Amtrak passenger service continue to rumble right along Commercial Row, the town's main street, causing hideous traffic jams at grade crossings. Trains often reach more than 100 cars long—nightmares for locals, but fun for visitors who like to count cars. And the town retains one other souvenir from its rip-roaring past. The old **Truckee Jail** housed more than its share of drunks and other miscreants between 1875 and 1964. It has been spruced up a bit to receive visitors, but it's still unmistakably a jail, and a cramped one at that. The bleak stone walls and tiny cells may be viewed on weekends 10:00 A.M. to 4:00 P.M. You'll find the jail behind Commercial Row at Jibboom and Spring streets. Open 10:00 A.M. to 4:00 P.M. weekends.

Commercial Row, appropriately, faces the railroad and the old passsenger station (now a tourist information center). It's a line of nineteenth-century buildings that have been transformed into a stroll-and-browse strip of restaurants, bars, and specialty shops selling sports clothing, outdoor equipment, antiques, and sheepskin jackets. The Capitol Building, vintage 1870, is the oldest structure and centerpiece. Once its upstairs theater played host to stage companies and entertainers who straggled through town; today it's the Local Artists Gallery Fair. Downstairs is Sierra Shirts.

Donner Memorial State Park, on Donner Lake at the western edge of Truckee, commemorates the fate of the famous (and infamous) Donner Party, which gave its name to the lake, the challenging pass, and the mountain summit, as well as providing one of the grimmest tales in pioneer history. The Donners were part of the great westward migration of 1846. Naive midwestern farmers, they had little conception of the hardships of cross-country travel and were persuaded to deviate from the established Emigrant Trail in hopes of reducing their travel time. Far from a shortcut, the route took longer, and they reached the Sierra Nevada rampart late in October as winter was closing in. Already starving and exhausted, they chose to rest for a week before the last push over the mountains—a fatal error. A harsh early snowstorm swept in, making travel impossible and limiting their efforts to supplement dwindling food supplies by hunting or fishing. Snowbound by immense drifts and confined to crude cabins as their food ran out, many perished; others resorted to cannibalism to survive. Of eighty-nine men, women, and children who set out from Missouri for a better life, only forty-seven lived to reach California's central valley.

The **Donner Memorial Monument,** a short walk from the park entrance, memorializes the tragic expedition. The monument stands twenty-two feet tall, the estimated height of the Sierra Nevada snowpack during that disastrous winter, one of the worst ever recorded in the mountains.

The Emigrant Trail Museum, honoring all pioneers, tells the whole grisly Donner story in a twenty-five-minute slide show. A special exhibit displays original Donner-party artifacts, from salt and pepper shakers to parasols and shawls and including a replica of a doll carried throughout by Patty Reed, whose family was one of two to survive intact. The museum is open daily 10:00 A.M. to 5:00 P.M. Admission is $2.

Donner Lake has been called the "Gem of the Sierra." Three miles long and three-quarters of a mile wide, it is tucked in the lee of the redoubtable Donner Pass; from its southern shore you can look up to the tunnels and snowsheds that enabled the Central Pacific to conquer the worst of the Sierra Nevada winters. Popular with boaters and fishermen, the lake also has a beach recreation area at its western end.

The **Western Ski and Sport Museum** traces ski mountaineering history from its California beginnings. Look with awe at the twenty-foot skis used by the fearless Norwegian, John "Snowshoe" Thompson, to carry the mail over the Sierra Nevada between 1856 and 1876—free of charge. Or admire photos of the early downhillers when skis were simple wooden boards strapped to the feet. Then there's the fashion photographs—women of the late 1800s gliding more or less gracefully down the slopes in voluminous skirts. It's a must-see for skiers. It is open in summer, Tuesday to Sunday 11:00 A.M. to 5:00 P.M., in winter Wednesday to Sunday 11:00 A.M. to 5:00 P.M. Admission is free. You'll find the museum in the Boreal Ridge Ski Area lodge at Donner Summit (Castle Peak exit from I-80). Call 916-426-3313.

Squaw Valley USA made its name as the site of the 1960 Winter Olympics and of course as one of America's premier ski resorts. Drive south from Truckee on State Highway 89 until the familiar five interlocking rings of the Olympic symbol welcome you. Turn right, wind past ski chalets, and suddenly you are overwhelmed by the towering peaks that dwarf the valley. Squaw Peak, Emigrant Peak, KT-22, and Granite Chief all rise beyond 8,000 feet. Crane your neck to see how in summer greenery edges up the mountain, gradually giving way to rugged splashes of granite. In winter the same scene is draped in white, interrupted by rock faces jutting out of the snow—an incredibly scenic sight in all seasons.

To truly appreciate the grand scale of Squaw Valley, which has thirty-three ski lifts and 4,000 acres of skiing terrain, climb aboard the 150-passenger cable car aerial tramway and soar 2,000 vertical feet to High Camp, 8,200 feet above sea level. In winter High Camp serves as a base for skiing the snowfields at Squaw's higher elevations; in summer you can swim in a heated lagoon, skate on an Olympic-size rink, watch bungee jumpers free-fall from a man-made tower, hike into the high mountains, ride horseback ($15 an hour, including guide) into the little-known backcountry behind Squaw Peak, or just enjoy the sweeping views far across the valley and into the Nevada desert. The cable car ride ($10 round-trip summer and winter for sightseers, included in skiers' lift ticket in winter), while not recommended for those with vertigo, offers similar bird's-eye views. Cable-car operators happily point out the old Olympic sites and other landmark features. Be warned, however: even on hot days in the valley, bring a jacket. High Camp is breezy and likely to be at least ten degrees cooler.

SCENIC DRIVES

Two state highways connect Truckee with the north shore of Lake Tahoe, each with its own dramatically different vistas.

State Highway 267 is your choice if you're planning a day at the beach. Turn south at the end of Truckee's Commercial Row and you're on your way. The highway passes the Truckee Airport (private planes only), the meadows of the Martis Valley, and Northstar-at-Tahoe (a golf, tennis and ski resort and second-home development). Then the two-lane highway climbs steadily upward to the 7000-foot-plus Brockway Summit. As you wind downhill beyond the summit, the lake plays peekaboo, great swatches of blue appearing suddenly through the trees, then disappearing again around the next curve, until you reach the settlement of Kings Beach, where state highways 267 and 28 join. Truckee to Kings Beach is a thirty- to forty-five-minute drive.

State Highway 89 follows the Truckee River from the town of Truckee to Tahoe City on the lake, passing the ski resorts of Squaw Valley USA and Alpine Meadows en route. Beyond Squaw Valley, the road narrows and clings to the river, with fine views of the stream. The river hurries along in winter, with kayakers challenging the foaming waters; in summer, however, you may see large flotillas of river rafters drifting lazily downstream. State highways 89 and 28 join at Tahoe City.

Squaw Valley, incidentally, is one of the great skiing bargains for seniors: for $5, those over sixty-five can ski all day, including weekends.

On The Lake

Several fine beaches lie within a short distance of the intersection of state highways 267 and 28. Turn left from State Highway 267 onto State Highway 28; the public recreation area of **Kings Beach** is about a mile on your right. It's a popular sunning and bathing spot, since (fig-

CALL ON THE CARTWRIGHTS

Remember "Bonanza," the most-watched television series of the late 1960s and 1970s? Ponderosa Ranch, the original location for the series about the ranching Cartwright family, father and grown sons, lies between Incline Village and Sand Harbor on State Highway 28. You can tour the Cartwrights' house and corral where Little Joe and Hoss ducked in and out in their ten-gallon hats or wander around a recreated Old West town (not part of the "Bonanza" set), or even be photographed in borrowed cowboy attire. From 8:00 A.M. to 9:30 A.M. the Hay Wagon breakfast takes you two miles into the hills for an all-you-can-eat cookout of eggs, bacon, and sausage. Ranch admission is $7.50, $9.50 with breakfast. For information call 702-831-0691.

ures show) the chances of sunshine are 80 percent. And because parking space is limited, there's usually plenty of room for beach blankets. (Beach entry is free, but there is a small parking fee.) A point to remember, however, before plunging in: Tahoe is the second deepest lake in the U.S. (1,645 feet at the deepest point), and water temperatures can be described as moderate to chilly.

Sand Harbor Park lies beyond Kings Beach on State Highway 28, across the state line in Nevada. Connoisseurs call it the ultimate Tahoe beach experience. Sand Harbor actually has two well-kept sand beaches washed by clear blue water. The beaches are divided by wooded Sand Point, a spot to picnic or retreat into the shade. Arrive early on weekends; the small parking area fills quickly and entry is limited to parkers. The fee is $4 per car.

Tahoe City is a bustling lakeside community, full of shops and restaurants doing a brisk business year-round. It was not always so. The town's landmark is "The Big Tree," a giant set in the middle of State Highway 28, which serves as Tahoe City's Main Street. Opposite the tree, the **Watson Cabin** portrays lake life as it was at the turn of the century. Robert Montgomery Watson built the cabin in 1909 for his son, Robert H., and the son's bride, Stella Tong, who were one of only five families to live on the lake year-round. Registered as a national historic site, the cabin offers guided tours by docents dressed in costumes of the period. Go and see the Watsons' original handmade furnishings, and admire the lilacs planted beneath the sunroom window nearly a century ago. The cabin is open June 15 to Labor Day, daily 12:00 noon to 4:00 P.M. Admission is free.

The Boatworks is Tahoe City's favorite window-shopping, browsing, and spending spot. One of several shopping clusters along State Highway 28, it is easily the most dramatic, perched on a bluff above the lake and designed around an atrium with spectacular views. The shops run heavily to sports attire and equipment, with craft shops and specialty stores thrown in. And, if you can't find what you like, in Tahoe City there's always another store across the street.

Tahoe's West Shore

Fanny Bridge got its nickname because townsfolk decided its true name, Butt Bridge, was too crude. The bridge spans the Truckee River, the lake's only outlet. Giant rainbow trout panhandle under the bridge, making it a favorite spot for tourists to toss bread crumbs. Beyond the bridge, State Highway 89 runs twenty miles to Tahoe's south shore, another series of postcard views.

Sugar Pine Point State Park, nine miles south of Tahoe City, is a wilderness area with camping, picnicking, and a network of hiking trails reaching into the backcountry. The park nature trail, a fairly level and easy walk, has markers telling the story of Tahoe and its natural history. (A full list of hiking trails in the Lake Tahoe basin, graded according to difficulty, may be obtained from Lake Tahoe Basin Management Unit, 870 Emerald Bay Road, Suite 1, South Lake Tahoe, California 95610. 916-573-2600.) Two man-made landmarks highlight the park: the Ehrmann Mansion, one-time vacation retreat of a wealthy San Francisco family, and the original log cabin of the old Indian fighter, General William Phipps. The parking/entry fee is $5.

Emerald Bay, about twelve miles farther south, is one of the true jewels of the Tahoe landscape and may be one of the most photographed places on earth. The highway here threads up a promontory high above the lake. Pull off at the Emerald Bay sign, walk across the parking lot and look down, down to the sparkling deep-green water that gave the glacially scoured bay its name. You can only reach the waterside via a steep one-mile hike, but it may be worth it for a visit to Vikingsholm.

This thirty-eight-room lakefront mansion was built by a wealthy San Franciscan after an inspiring trip to Scandinavia. It is open mid-June to Labor Day for tours only, 10:00 A.M. to 4:00 P.M. daily, tours every half hour. Admission is $2. This section of the highway is sometimes closed in winter.

The South Shore

The city of **South Lake Tahoe** huddles up against the Nevada border and is a bedroom for tourists who wish to walk a few steps to the gambling tables at Stateline, Nevada. But it has attractive features in its own right. Like the north shore, it is a winter hub for skiers and is the home of the Heavenly Valley ski resort whose slopes extend into both states. In summer, its beaches and waterfront bustle with activity from Memorial Day to Labor Day.

The **Forest Service Visitor Center,** on Highway 89 on the South Shore (916-573-2674), houses an exhibit hall and snow-measuring instruments. Its outstanding feature is the Stream Profile Chamber where you can view Kokanee trout in their native habitat through underwater windows.

TEE-UP TIME

The Lake Tahoe area offers a large selection of challenging golf courses. In fact, you can play eighteen holes a day for a week and never play the same course twice. Pine-tree-lined greens and fairways and interesting terrain, to say the least, can make for challenging hazards. A few suggestions: **Squaw Creek** in Squaw Valley Meadow, 800-4-GOLF-TE; **Tahoe Donner** on the western edge of Truckee, 916-583-1516; **Northstar** on State Highway 267, 916-562-2490; and **Incline Executive Course,** 702-832-1150. All courses except Incline have driving ranges; see if the thin mountain air improves your distance.

TRY YOUR LUCK

Gambling casinos are illegal in California, but the tables are just a throw-of-the-dice away in Nevada. On the north shore, at Crystal Bay, Nevada, adjoining Kings Beach, California, the **Cal Neva** casino actually straddles the state line, with gambling rooms on the Nevada side and food and drink purveyed in California. Next door, **Crystal Bay Lodge,** with lower-budget tables, stands four square in Nevada. Farther along the lake on State Highway 28 are the casinos of Incline Village. At South Lake Tahoe, visitors have only to walk a few feet down U.S. 50, the main street, to enter Stateline, Nevada, and try their luck at **Harvey's, Harrah's,** and other neon-lighted establishments. The largest concentration of casinos is at Reno, thirty minutes northeast of Truckee on I-80. Floor shows vie with crap tables and roulette wheels at **Harrah's, Circus Circus,** and the **Hilton.**

The *Tahoe Queen,* a glass-bottomed lake paddle-wheeler, pushes off from the Ski Run Marina, off U.S. 50, on a regular schedule. Cruises allow close-up views of Emerald Bay, Vikingsholm, Eagle Falls, and Cave Rock while allowing remarkable views of underwater scenery. Departures June to September daily at 11:00 A.M., 1:30 P.M., and 3:55 P.M.; October to May, 12:30 P.M. only. A sunset dinner-dance cruise departs in summer at 7:00 P.M., in winter at 6:30 P.M. Day cruises cost $14; the dinner cruise is $18 plus meals, which start at $14. Reservations are recommended. During January through March, *Tahoe Queen* provides a ski shuttle service across the lake, to and from Squaw Valley and Alpine Meadows ski areas: $18. For information about all *Tahoe Queen* rates and services, write P.O. Box 14327, South Lake Tahoe, California 95702, or call 916-541-3364.

Special Events

Tahoe's calendar of specials ranges from the cultural to the lively. Here are a few.

Bard on the Beach, Recently, over fifty outlet stores have been added, catering to the bargain shopper and making this the largest of the factory store malls in northern California. Shakespeare at Sand Harbor presents three plays during August from a stage set in the dunes with Lake Tahoe as a backdrop. Two of the three are usually from the Bard's works. Admission is $15 for seats in the sand; bring a blanket to keep sand out of your back pocket and a jacket for protection against lake breezes. 916-583-9048.

Tunes in the Dunes, the music festival, is held in the same beachside open-air theater at Sand Harbor during a long weekend in mid-July. Programs range from California rock'n'roll to modern jazz to Broadway show tunes. Tickets for individual events are under $20. 916-583-9048.

The **Lake Tahoe Summer Music Festival** brings in musical groups of many types from around the U.S. during July. Performances are held throughout the Tahoe basin, including an ensemble performance at 8200-foot High Camp at Squaw Valley. Prices vary. 916-583-3101.

The **Tahoe Snowfest** celebrates the magic of winter in one of the nation's premier winter sports centers. Beginning in late February, more than 130 events cater to skiers and nonskiers alike. Even includes parades, ice, and snow-sculpture contests, and a few zanies such as the napkin hat contest, a Hawaiian luau, a dress-your-dog contest, and a wild game and fish cookoff. Events are held throughout the Tahoe basin. 916-583-7625.

Restaurants ————————————————————————

Exercise with the knife and fork is a favorite pastime in the Tahoe basin. Cuisine varies almost as much as the scenery and ski terrain.

- **Le Petit Pier** introduced fine French cuisine to Tahoe some twenty years ago. The specialty is pheasant for two. The fifteen appetizers on the menu change daily. The dining room extends over the water with spectacular views from every table. It is extremely popular, and reservations are essential and must be made two days in advance for summer weekends. Dinner only. Expensive. 7238 North Lake Boulevard on State Highway 28 between Tahoe City and Kings Beach. 916-546-4464.

- **Jake's** looks out on a marina and across the lake. Appropriately, it specializes in fresh seafood, led by a fine king salmon baked with citrus juices and ginger. Also try the afternoon seafood bar. Moderate to expensive. 760 North Lake Boulevard, Tahoe City. 916-583-0188.

- The **Bridgetender** adjoins Fanny Bridge and is one of several inexpensive breakfast-lunch places along the lake. It is said to serve the best burgers in the Tahoe basin; people are said to travel from as far as Reno for a taste. 30 West Lake Boulevard, Tahoe City. 916-583-3342.

- **Rosie's Cafe** is located across from The Big Tree; from its deck, you can see both the tree and lake. Decorated eclectically with Tahoe antiques, including a moosehead over the fireplace, old wooden skis, and a 1950s bicycle suspended from the ceiling. Rosie's serves breakfast all day. Inexpensive. 571 North Lake Boulevard, Tahoe City. 916-583-8504.

Lodging ——————————————————————————

The Tahoe basin offers a wide variety of accommodations for every taste and budget. A computerized reservation system helps locate lodgings in all price ranges. Rates usually vary by the season. Call 800-TAHOE-4-U.

- The **Resort at Squaw Creek,** dominating the valley, is a 405-room all-seasons resort and conference site with three swimming pools, an ice rink, a tennis court, six restaurants, shops, and a championship golf course. This is not exactly a get-away-from-it-all spot but worth a walk-through. Expensive. P.O. Box 3333, Olympic Valley, California 96146. 800-327-3353.

- **River Ranch Lodge** sits on the edge of the Truckee River at the entrance of Alpine Meadows ski area. Rooms with balconies overlook the river; the cocktail lounge is cantilevered over the Truckee rapids. Continental breakfast is included. Moderate to expensive. State Highway 89 at Alpine Meadows Road. 916-583-4264.

- **Truckee Hotel** is an old hotel from the railroad days recently refurnished for winter and summer guests. Breakfast included. Moderate. Downtown Truckee. 916-587-4444.

- **Donner Country Inn** is a small, cozy B&B a few steps from the shores of Donner Lake. It serves a sumptuous breakfast. Moderate. 916-587-5574.

- **Timber Cove Lodge** sits directly on the beach; most rooms have a view of the lake. Full American breakfast is included. There are special weekday rates. Moderate. 3411 Lake Tahoe Boulevard, South Lake Tahoe. 916-541-6722.

Chapter 17

Yosemite
National Park

The natural architecture of the Yosemite Valley reduces the most jaded traveler to a state of awe. The sheer massiveness of the steep granite faces, rising abruptly from the valley floor, makes a mere human being feel like an insignificant ant, dominated by Mother Nature. The great naturalist John Muir called Yosemite "the grandest of all temples of nature." Few of the three million visitors who come to the park each year would disagree with his lyrical description.

The national park encompasses more territory than the state of Rhode Island, 95 percent of it lofty wilderness. Yosemite Valley is the central jewel and primary tourist destination. U-shaped, six miles long, and a mile wide, the valley evolved into its present dramatic form by a complicated series of geologic actions. An estimated 200 million years ago, tremendous heat and pressure caused part of the Pacific plate to melt into what is called magma, which slowly rose to the surface and cooled over the next 10 million years, forming into a granite layer. The upthrusting of the Sierra Nevada tipped the layer so that a fast-running river carved a V-shaped canyon. Then, a mere million years ago, glaciers filled the canyon, widening it into a vertically walled U shape as they lumbered through. Ice scoured and polished the granite faces, knocking off the weaker sections of rock and leaving behind the stronger solid portions before the glaciers melted away 250,000 years ago. Glaciers are probably responsible for the unique hemispherical shape of Yosemite's most distinctive formation, Half Dome, which stands at the eastern edge of the valley and rises to an elevation of 8,842 feet. The moving ice apparently sliced away half the huge dome, so that it now stands with one abruptly vertical face and a neatly rounded shape behind, as though someone had taken a knife and cut a tennis ball in two. Half Dome began as an immense piece of forest-covered granite that, after years of erosion, shed its rocky outer layers and developed a natural curvature at the summit.

The valley lay "undiscovered" by European colonists until the mid-nineteenth century. On March 27, 1851, the Mariposa Battalion of the U.S. Army entered the valley in search of the Native Americans who allegedly were harassing miners and settlers along the lower Merced River. The battalion found only one old Ahwahnee woman, but more importantly they discovered the Yosemite Valley. Word of Yosemite's beauty spread quickly, and in 1855, the first party of tourists arrived. In 1864, President Abraham Lincoln deeded the valley and the "Big Trees" groves to the state of California to protect its beauty. Then, in 1890, John Muir, the noted naturalist, and Robert John, editor of *Century* magazine, lobbied together to put the park under the protection of the federal government. Their efforts paid off on October 1, 1890, when the U.S. Congress authorized Yosemite National Park.

Four routes lead into the park, all converging into a one-way loop road that circles the valley, roughly following the course of the Merced River. The route leads you past, one by one, Yosemite's wonders, each of which carries its own distinctive character and descriptive name. As you enter from the west, a large, almost rectangular rock face protrudes into the north side of the valley, on your left. This is the infamous **El Capitan** (the captain), the largest monolith, or single solid chunk of rock, in the world. "El Cap" stands about three Empire State Buildings high, or 3,593 feet above the valley floor. Bold rock climbers constantly challenge their skills and tackle the six-day ascent. Look for tiny, slow-moving specks on the granite face.

The **Cathedral Spires** stand opposite the grand monolith, on the valley's south side. They are identifiable by the natural two-granite outcroppings that rise out of the ridge and resemble the towers of a Gothic church. East of the Cathedral Spires, **Sentinel Rock** rises like the tower of a huge protecting fortress overlooking the center of the valley. Near the head of the valley, on the north side, the **Royal Arches** look like a series of arcs etched into the granite rock face. The arches were actually formed by the joining of granite sheets. As the granite cooled, bits of the outer layer flaked off to form the curved cracks.

The Park's Mighty "Voices"

When the glaciers retreated, mountain streams that had once fed into the Merced River were left in hanging canyons, with no outlet except to spill over the rock faces into the valley below. The result is one of the most spectacular displays of waterfalls anywhere in the world. The white water of the falls seems almost to defy gravity, floating down the cliffs in slow-moving sheets of mist.

Bridalveil Falls, on the south side of the valley, are the first falls you see as you enter the valley. Yosemite's original residents, the Ahwahnee Indians, called the falls Pohno, "spirit of the puffing wind." On some afternoons the wind swirls around the cliff and blows the water into billows of mist at the base of the falls. It often looks as if the water is moving in reverse, actually rising up the mountainside. Seen from a distance against the surrounding canyon walls, Bridalveil may appear as a thin gossamer trickle. The water actually falls 620 feet, the height of a sixty-two-story building, in a single plunge to the valley floor. To fully appreciate its splendor, walk to its base on an easy trail from a roadside parking lot.

Yosemite Falls, on the north side of the valley east of El Capitan, is the most famous and dramatic waterfall in the park. John Muir called

BUT ISN'T IT CROWDED? YES AND NO

Don't come to Yosemite without a reservation, whether for a campsite, housekeeping cabin, or hotel/motel room. The park is full to the last tent peg in summers; on holiday weekends, cars may be turned away.

But the joy of Yosemite is the way its massiveness overcomes the congestion. No matter how many tourist heads poke up between you and El Capitan, the great monolith towers over them all. On the most crowded day, you can lift your eyes and see Upper Yosemite Falls sparkling in the sun, or awake early and see mule deer loping across the meadow. Don't be frightened by stories of vacationing crowds. Go, look up, and feast your eyes.

it "the richest, most powerful voice of all the falls in the Valley." It is also the largest waterfall in North America, cascading 2,325 feet in three continuous plunges, and the fifth tallest in the world. The base of 320-foot Lower Yosemite Falls is a short walk from the parking lot and decidedly worth it, if only to feel the cooling spray on a hot day. From the walk itself, you can see both upper and lower falls.

For the best waterfall performance, visit Yosemite in spring. Then the melting snow in the mountains pours down the rock faces in torrents, creating impromptu waterfalls all around the valley; the voices of Bridalveil and Yosemite Falls become a full-throated roar. Later in the year some of these high-altitude streams dry up and the waterfalls disappear. Bridalveil and Yosemite Falls, although diminished, keep right on flowing, as do Nevada and Vernal Falls, above the valley.

Down in the Valley

Yosemite's original residents, the Ahwahnee Indians, made their home in the heart of the valley. That is still the center of activity, the location of **Yosemite Village** with its full array of tourist services, including a grocery, a bank, a post office and a service station. It's also the best starting place for a visit.

The **Yosemite Visitors Center** provides a wide variety of information about the park trails, including nature talks and a desk full of rangers to answer any questions. Its small museum shows the geological history of the rock formations using pictures and diagrams to explain the scientific evolution. A multimedia orientation program about the park is presented throughout the day in the west auditorium behind the visitors center. A shorter video program, "One Day in Yosemite," gives basic information on how to get the most out of a shorter visit.

Next to the visitors center, the **Indian Museum** displays Ahwahnee artifacts such as a feather ceremonial dress and a squaw's buckskin dress. Go outside the museum and see the Ahwahnee village that was reconstructed to show the huts of the original valley inhabitants. Both the visitors center and museums are free.

The **Ahwahnee Hotel** has hosted presidents and royalty, and its 123 rooms are often booked a year in advance. Whether or not you have that much foresight, the Ahwahnee is definitely a must-see walk-

THE BAD NEWS BEARS

Black bears, native to the Sierra Nevada, have become conditioned to human food and can cause considerable damage and injury in trying to obtain it. Hungry bears have been known to smash car windows and peel off car doors in their strenuous quest for food. Do not leave food in the passenger section of your car or in an unattended ice chest; store it in a locked car trunk. If you are camping, use food storage lockers or suspend food from a high tree branch, beyond bears' reach. Bears are frequently seen around campgrounds; if you spot one, give it a wide berth, and by no means attempt to feed it. Feeding any wildlife in Yosemite is a violation subject to fine.

through. Built in 1927, allegedly because a titled Englishwoman complained that the park's primitive accommodations were unworthy of such a beauty spot, the luxury hotel beneath the Royal Arches has won numerous architectural awards and has been designated a national historic site. Its towering Great Lounge stands three stories high, surrounded by public rooms displaying priceless Native American baskets, paintings, photographs, and Persian rugs. The floor-to-ceiling windows of the chandeliered dining room look out on some of the park's most magnificent sights. Looking about you, you can only marvel at the challenge of such an imposing construction project in such an isolated site.

Getting Around

Car travel is discouraged within the valley because fumes and congestion harm the mountain atmosphere. Fortunately, parking space is plentiful, and the National Park Service offers alternative (and considerably more enjoyable) transportation. Free shuttle buses circle the valley on a regular schedule. The shuttle system services most low-level trailheads, the visitor centers, campgrounds, Yosemite Lodge, and Curry Village, and other destinations within the valley. Buses run frequently and are easy to catch at well-marked bus stops throughout the park.

To see the valley the easy way, sign up for a guided tour offered by the Yosemite Park and Curry Company, the park's main concessionaire. The tours traverse the valley in an open-air tram (a truck towed trailer with seats) complete with a tour guide who points out the various points of interest and describes the connected history, including mystic Ahwahnee legends. In offseason and bad weather, tours are given in enclosed buses. Try to take the open tram. The valley floor tour is an excellent introduction to the park. It takes two hours, covers the main sites in the valley, and costs $13.75 for adults, $12.75 for seniors. Reserve in advance and bring a light jacket even on warm days. Other, longer tours take you to the Wawona Hotel 27 miles from the valley, to Glacier Point, and into the sequoia groves. For information call 209-372-1240.

The best way to enjoy Yosemite's pristine wilderness is on foot. The park is laced with hiking trails, some easy, some more challenging. Among the most popular hikes is the **Mist Trail,** a moderately difficult one-mile hike. The trail starts at Happy Isles (at the edge of Curry Village, easily reached by shuttle bus) and climbs alongside the Merced River to Vernal Falls. From the footbridge spanning the rushing river you get a dramatic, close-up view of the 317 feet of free-falling water. Then, if you're feeling bold and athletic, continue on through the mist, along a trail of steps cut into the rock, to the larger Nevada Falls, a dramatic 594-foot drop.

For good waterside picnicking, take a short walk to **Happy Isles** or go a longer but easy mile to **Mirror Lake.** Happy Isles, near Curry Village, is a pleasant hike through the valley from Yosemite Lodge or a few steps from shuttle stop 16. The Merced River rushes around two little islands that are connected to shore by bridges. At Mirror Lake during spring you will see impressive views of Tenaya Canyon and an upside-down reflection of Mount Watkins. In fall, Mirror Lake is more grass than glass. In line with National Park Service policy of restoring the valley to a more natural state, the lake is gradually being allowed to fill in and form a meadow. The Mirror Lake trail hike starts at shuttle stop 17.

Another more adventuresome way to see Yosemite is on horseback. **Saddle Tours** offer rugged and scenic routes through the park. Take a two-hour ride through the wooded valley and along rocky paths

SCENIC DETOUR

An enjoyable if winding drive up to **Tunnel View** and on to Glacier Point affords the visitor dramatic views of the valley. From the valley, follow the one-way road toward the west exit. When the road forks, take the left fork across the river, then follow the signs to State Highway 41, your next right. The road climbs for less than half a mile before the Tunnel View parking lot. Stop at this overlook to enjoy a lengthwise aerial view of the valley. Then continue through the tunnel and follow State Highway 41 for another fifteen to twenty minutes to Chinquapin. Turn left on Glacier Point Road toward Badger Pass for another sixteen miles. Even those prone to car sickness should attempt the rough ride. The views from the top are well worth it.

Glacier Point, a short walk from the parking lot, looks over the Ahwahnee meadow from 3,214 feet. Some call it the most exhilarating overlook on earth. From your perch on the rim of the Yosemite Valley, you get an eagle's-eye view of the entire eastern part of the valley including Yosemite Falls, the Royal Arches, and the Merced River. A placard points out the various sites.

to Mirror Lake or take a longer half-day trip up to Vernal and Nevada falls. The horse rides are not as informative as the valley tour so rides should be taken to supplement the tram tour. No equestrian experience is necessary, but note that riding can be uncomfortable for rear ends unaccustomed to the saddle. The horses know the way so little steering is necessary and experienced guides help you along the way. The two-hour ride costs under $30; reserve in advance. For more information call 209-372-1248.

The Big Trees

The sequoia trees of the Sierra Nevada are different from California's coastal redwoods. They're bigger, for one thing, and older, for another. Some were already giants in the days of Julius Caesar. Yosemite National Park contains three monumental groves of *Sequoia gigantea*—all outside Yosemite Valley. The **Mariposa Grove,** just north of the park's south entrance, is the largest of the three; it has been protected since 1864, when Abraham Lincoln signed the Yosemite Grant, deeding the grove and Yosemite Valley to the state of California. Some of the trees in the Mariposa Grove are taller than a thirty-story skyscraper, with trunks more than twenty-five feet in diameter. The Grizzly Giant tree is thought to be more than 2,700 years old and the granddaddy of all sequoias. You will crane your neck in vain to see its crown.

Auto traffic is prohibited in the grove beyond the parking area. However, from May to October, a one-hour tram tour is conducted through the grove, including a stop at the **Mariposa Grove Museum,** with exhibits explaining the natural history of the trees. Hiking and cross-country skiing are permitted in the grove in winter.

The smaller **Tuolomne and Merced groves** are at Crane Flat, near the intersection of State Highway 120 and Tioga Pass Road, east of the Big Oak Flat entrance station. The Dead Giant tree, which was tunneled in 1878, is the only tree in Yosemite that you can still drive through. The road through the grove is a one-way, six-mile loop. Or you can leave the car in the parking lot and take the easy half-mile hike into the grove.

Winter in the Valley

Although a million visitors a month flock to Yosemite in midsummer, the park is relatively empty in winter with fewer than 150,000 visitors in January (many of them skiers in for a day.) Tioga Pass Road is closed by snow, and the high country is limited to cross-country skiers. The 8,000-foot peaks surrounding the valley are snow mantled, but the valley itself, at 3000 feet, is mainly snow free, hushed, and peaceful. Many facilities, including certain campgrounds, are open, as are the hiking trails.

This is the time to visit the waterfalls in more solitude for they tumble exuberantly down the cliff faces during the winter months. But there's a difference. Spray freezes quickly on the rocky walls, in the case of Yosemite Falls building up a "snow cone" at the base that stands forty feet high.

The 7,000-foot Badger Pass was the first ski area in a national park and one of the first in the West. Relatively tame by more challenging Sierra ski standards, it is a pleasant day's outing for older downhillers. If you're a cross-country devotee (or want to try), be sure to head across Summit Meadow to Glacier Point for an even more spectacular view than in summer. Better yet, join a snowshoeing tour led by a park ranger. Snowshoeing is little more strenuous than walking, requires virtually no instruction, and can open up fascinating untracked areas of the high-altitude forest. The snowshoeing tour includes a nature talk. Equipment for downhill, cross-country, and snowshoeing can be rented at Badger Pass. Shuttle buses to the winter sports area depart regularly from valley points.

At **Curry Village** you can imitate Brian Boitano (or Sonja Henie, if your memory goes back that far) at an outdoor ice rink set in the shadow of Glacier Point. The rink operates December to February; rental skates are available.

The three main roads into the park—state highways 120 and 140 from the west and State Highway 41 from the south—are kept open during winter, as are the roads on the valley floor. At times, however, chains or snow tires (or four-wheel-drive vehicles) may be required. Check road conditions before your visit.

Renaissance Christmas, Pioneer Christmas

The **Bracebridge Dinner** at the Ahwahnee Hotel is a one-of-a-kind holiday event that is about as easy to crash as a private party at Buckingham Palace. Thirty thousand persons a year vie for a spot at one of the five Christmas-season seatings—two on December 22, one on December 24 and two on December 25. But only 1,800 persons win the annual lottery for the coveted seats. Still, everyone has an equal chance. All you have to do is submit your application between December 15 and January 15 for the next year's drawing. 5410 E. Home Avenue, Fresno, California 93727.

The Bracebridge dinner recreates "a Christmas that never was, but lives in everyone's hearts," in the words of its producer, Andrea Fulton. Loosely based on Washington Irving's tale of an Elizabethan-era celebration at an English country manor, it was instituted for the Ahwahnee Hotel's first Christmas in 1927 and has been a fancy-dress tradition ever since. Dressed in a plumed hat and embroidered jerkin, the "squire" of Bracebridge sits at a high table and greets his guests, while a chorus carols, a dancing bear performs, and lackeys bring in each gourmet dish of a seven-course meal for the squire to taste and approve. This three hours of pageantry and gourmandizing doesn't come cheap, of course. The 1992 tab was $135 per person, plus wine and tip. Few complain about the price, however.

Christmas at the 100-plus-year-old Wawona Hotel, eight miles from the park's south entrance, is open to everyone. The seasonal hotel reopens for the holidays with a **Pioneer Christmas.** The adjoining Pioneer Village features a sleigh, Santa, and carolers in costumes of the post-gold rush years.

Restaurants

Reservations at the following restaurants can be made through the Yosemite Reservations office, 209-252-4848, which also handles lodging reservations.

- The **Ahwahnee Hotel** dining room is casual for breakfast and lunch, but formal for dinner. Jacket and tie are required for men, dresses or evening pantsuits for women; no shorts or sweatsuits allowed. The restaurant is noted for elegant meals to go with its elegant setting. Sunday brunch is especially popular. Expensive. 209-372-1489.

- **Yosemite Lodge** offers a variety of eating places, including a broiler room, a family dining room, and a cafeteria. Other cafeterias and fast-food service are available in Curry Village and Yosemite Village. Inexpensive to moderate.

Lodging

Bed space at Yosemite runs the gamut from campsites to the elegant Ahwahnee Hotel. For hotel reservations, call the centralized number for all lodging, 209-252-4848, or write Yosemite Reservations, 5410 East Home Avenue, Fresno, California 93727. In addition, lodging is available at a number of locations outside the park boundaries, most of them at least thirty minutes' drive from the valley.

- The **Ahwahnee Hotel** has recently undergone renovation in its spacious and colorfully decorated guest rooms. In addition to the main hotel, you can rent cottages accommodating up to twelve persons. Expensive. 209-372-1489.

- **Yosemite Lodge** offers deluxe rooms with balconies or patios, standard rooms, rooms without bath, and rustic cabins with and without bath. Moderate.

- **Curry Village,** in the shadow of Glacier Point, is budget hospitality. Established nearly 100 years ago, it offers inexpensive tent cabins, cabins, and moderately priced hotel rooms. It is also known as the coolest place in the valley. The village includes a camp store, mountain shop, and restaurants.

- **Wawona Hotel,** near the park's south entrance, 27 miles from the valley, is a wide-verandaed Victorian charmer that has recently been refurbished. Built in the 1870s, its restored lobby received recognition from the California Trust for Historic Preservation. Open Easter week through Thanksgiving, during the Christmas holidays, and on weekends year-round. Moderate to expensive.

- **Campgrounds** are spaced throughout the park; those in the valley, Hodgdon Meadows, and Wawona are open all year. Reservations are a must. They may be obtained through Mistix; for more information call 800-365-2267. Utility hookups are not available at Yosemite campgrounds, but all have toilets and running water.

Chapter 18

The High Country and Eastern Sierra Nevada

The eastern Sierra Nevada is a secluded, seldom-visited treasure nestling on the eastern border of California where the Nevada desert overlaps the Sierra Nevada Mountains. This relatively untouched region keeps its rustic Wild West atmosphere while remaining a summer escape for lovers of nature and for adventuresome tourists. A few small towns, separated by large expanses of sagebrush-covered foothills, doze alongside the eastern Sierra Nevada's many lakes where you can swim in the summer and ice fish in the winter. The region is blanketed by snow in the winter and bakes in the spring and summer, and fall can be any combination (or sequence) of the two. Locals say that the weather has a tendency to do whatever it pleases regardless of the season. The bizarre climate is matched by some of the diverse attractions of the region, specifically the alien habitat of Mono Lake, the eerie ghost town of Bodie, and the other-worldly rock formation of Devil's Postpile.

Tioga Pass

Tioga Pass Road, State Highway 120, cuts through the little-known yet extraordinarily beautiful high country of **Yosemite National Park.** The road climbs quickly, rising 3,000 feet in twelve miles as it threads upward toward the 13,000-foot Clark Range on the edge of Yosemite. Granite mountain tops, some of them splashed with snow even in July, and deep lush valleys spread out as far as the eye can see. Its empty spaces are a far cry from the densely populated regions of California. But except for a small number of hardy mountaineers, they are accessible only during summer. Like other trans-Sierra Nevada routes, Tioga Pass is closed by snow from about mid-October to mid-May.

Pick up the Tioga Pass Road a few miles after you enter the western Yosemite Park gateway at Big Oak Flat. The road starts its upward climb almost immediately as it swings northeast across the park. The narrow road runs briefly through dense forest before emerging onto a high plateau flanked by ramparts of solid rock and backdropped by the rugged peaks. Take advantage of turnouts here to enjoy the magnificent scenery spread before you.

The road skirts **Lake Tenaya,** an alpine lake set into the rocky mountain slopes and a particular beauty spot. Smooth lake water reflects the surrounding mountain ranges—a good place for wish-you-were-here photographs or a quick rest stop. Continuing along the ridge high above a deep canyon, the road suddenly curves onto a large, level, grassy meadow. **Tuolumne Meadows,** 8,800 feet above sea level, is the largest subalpine meadow in the Sierra Nevada. You can walk through the tall grass out into the middle of what was once a collecting basin for the surrounding glaciers before they melted away.

Wildlife roams freely in the meadow. You can often see mule deer peacefully drinking from one of the many streams that thread through the fields, or a coyote loping through the grass; if you have sharp eyes (or high-powered binoculars) you may spot bighorn sheep on the high crags. Brilliant wildflowers of all descriptions burst into bloom and carpet the meadow in early summer. Stick to the paths as you walk through, however; the meadow ecology is very delicate. Visit the **Tuolumne Meadow Visitors Center,** which displays geological information about the area as well as providing details about its wildlife. The center is located on the south side of the road, directly opposite the meadow.

The Tioga Pass Road rises to nearly 10,000 feet just as you exit the Yosemite Park eastern boundary. It is the highest automobile pass in California. You'll notice that the type of vegetation changes rapidly as you cross the pass and begin your descent from the crest of the Sierra Nevada. Instead of dense green coniferous forests, a dull gray, low-lying sagebrush covers the rolling landscape—a barren, desolate backdrop

TAKE IT EASY!

Yosemite's high country ranges from 7,000 to 13,000 feet. That means less oxygen; that, in turn, means you may find yourself tiring easily and short of breath, especially when climbing hills, running, or engaging in vigorous exercise. Those with heart or respiratory conditions should be especially cautious. Watch for signs of nausea, headache, fatigue, dizziness, or disorientation. Slow your pace, walk easily, rest frequently if you feel tired, and avoid alcohol. The mandatory slow pace is actually a blessing in disguise; it gives you more time to enjoy the wonders around you.

suited to TV westerns. Welcome to the stark world of the eastern Sierra Nevada.

Mono Lake

The eastern Sierra Nevada is underpopulated, to say the least, with only a few widely separated towns. **Lee Vining,** the first settlement you encounter after leaving Yosemite, is a rustic community built on the edge of Mono Lake, with a small number of restaurants and hotels catering to visitors seeking accommodations outside the crowded Yosemite Valley as well as to intrepid souls who have come to explore the strange world of Mono Lake.

Mono Lake's odd geological and ecological formations result from the unusual composition of the water. Having no outlet, the lake developed into a settling pool for debris from mountain streams. Some people call it an inland sea like Utah's Great Salt Lake or Israel's Dead Sea. The water is two and a half times saltier and a thousand times more alkaline than the ocean—good for washing clothes but bad for swimming.

The two large islands that rise out of the water in the middle of the lake serve as a way stop for migratory birds who touch down en route from Canada and the northern United States to their winter quarters in Argentina, Chile, and other South American countries. During the fall huge flocks of avocet and killdeer mingle with the seagulls who inhabit the lake in great numbers. The lake is a major gull breeding place. For birdwatchers, a visit to Mono Lake is a must.

Strange towers of calcium carbonate, called tufa towers, stand like little castles protecting the shoreline. These 200- to 900-year-old towers formed above the many underground springs around the lake. Through a chemical reaction, the alkaline water of the lake combined with the calcium in the spring water as it gurgled up through the earth to form limestonelike deposits that have grown into structures resembling upside-down icicles or stalagmites. Some of these weirdly shaped towers stand sixty feet tall. The northern edge of the lake has a large collection of tufa towers that you can walk through and explore for yourself.

The Mono Lake basin is a geologist's and volcanologist's delight, a hotbed of seismic activity where minor earth tremors may be felt several times a day. Nestling into the dark volcanic landscape at the southern end of the lake, a young volcanic cone complete with crater rises out of the earth. Barren and lifeless, the volcanic area contrasts sharply with the vegetation of the surrounding foothills.

Much controversy surrounds the threatened future of Mono Lake. Many of the streams that feed into the lake have been diverted to supply water for the lawns and faucets of Los Angeles, lowering the lake water level and threatening its fragile ecology. Local environmentalists have been fighting in court to maintain the water level, but the situation remains unresolved because the streams are a vital water resource for dry southern California. For information about the environmental movement, go to the Mono Lake Committee Information Center and Bookstore in Lee Vining on the east side of U.S. 395. This committee leads the fight to protect the lake and offers a free twenty-five-minute slide show about the movement.

The **Mono Basin National Forest Scenic Area Visitors Center,** located just off U.S. 395 on the west side of the lake, captures the essence of the entire region with its well-thought-out evening slide shows and informative museum displays. The center's rear observation deck overlooks the whole area. You can see the volcanic crater, the tufa towers, and the birds flying around the islands. Informative placards point out the various sites while the museum describes the lake ecology with visual displays, models, and interesting tidbits of information about the lake. The center offers a canoe tour of the lake, a walking tour around the tufa towers, and a sightseeing tour of the volcanic area.

Bodie

The ghost town of Bodie lies hidden in the barren foothills northeast of Mono Lake, filled with memories of its notorious past. More than 100 weathered buildings remain from its mining heyday, a mere 5 percent of the original town but enough to capture the feel of the rough frontier lifestyle that flourished here a century and more ago. Now incorporated into a state historic park, Bodie's small cabins remain in a state of arrested decay. The unpainted exteriors have turned gray, beaten by the changing seasons; whole houses lean over, propped up by supporting beams; and the interiors still hold piles of clothes, kitchen utensils, and bedding abandoned by the miners during Bodie's last years. Today, you can safely wander the dirt streets of Bodie and peer into the dusty building windows and try to imagine the wild life of its citizens.

And life was wild in Bodie. Its outlandish reputation spread across the Sierra Nevada. One frightened little girl, who was moving from Truckee to Bodie, supposedly wrote in her diary the infamous words that beautifully sum up Bodie's reputation: "Goodbye God, I'm going to Bodie!" Far from being ashamed of its reputation, the town gloried in it, and her words became its boastful catch phrase.

Bodie came late to the gold rush, one reason for its lawless reputation. Waterman S. Bodey discovered a rich deposit of gold here in 1859 that attracted hard-up miners from all over, just as the other mines were playing out. Its citizens changed the spelling to "Bodie," rhyming with Cody, ensuring the correct pronunciation of the name that was to become synonymous with a violent and abusive population. Bad men, bad whiskey, and bad weather proved to be a bad combination as bar brawls and street shootouts were daily hazards in the isolated town that, at its height, housed sixty-five saloons.

The Reverend F. M. Warrington visited Bodie in 1881 and called it "a sea of sin, lashed by the tempests of lust and passion." Today, however, the sea and the tempests have subsided, and all Bodie's baddies are in their graves so you can calmly revisit its past. Follow U.S. 395 north from Mono Lake, then turn east on State Highway 270. (Note that State Highway 167 also goes to Bodie, but much of the road is unpaved, whereas only the last three miles of State Highway 270 are unpaved.) Entry fee to the park is $5 per car. Pick up the Bodie walking guide for $1 more. It explains in detail each of the various buildings, providing the history and color of the once bustling town. The **Bodie Museum,** located on Main Street, boasts a pair of much-used funeral coaches, evidence of Bodie's violent past. You can see a thirty-minute film on Bodie in the County Barn, just off Main Street, Saturdays and Sundays at 2:15 P.M., and you can take a tour of the mill (normally closed to visitors) Monday, Wednesday, Friday, and weekends 11:00 A.M. to 4:00 P.M.

Other Eastern Sierra Nevada Sites

Plenty of freshwater lakes dot the eastern Sierra Nevada south of Mono Lake just off U.S. 395. Swim in the clear waters to cool off or spend an afternoon fishing. The string of lakes that comprise the **June Lake Loop**—June, Gull, Silver, and Grant lakes—offer some of the best fishing in the region. (Mono Lake itself contains no fish.) These lakes lie just west of U.S. 395 on State Highway 158. Farther south on U.S. 395, Mammoth Lakes holds a wide variety of recreational opportunities. The **Mammoth Lake Basin** is a mecca for sightseers, day hikers, and photographers. Cascading waterfalls, old abandoned gold mines, and mammoth rock formations are spread over the area.

The **Mammoth Museum and Historical Preserve** sits on the edge of a meadow alongside Mammoth Creek and Old Mammoth Road, with the expansive Sherwin Range as a backdrop. The museum displays artifacts, photographs, and other memorabilia from Mammoth Lake's early days. The town of Mammoth Lakes offers a number of interpretive programs, including day hikes around Mammoth Lake Basin. For information call the Park and Recreation Department, 619-934-8983.

Mammoth Lake is also the headquarters for **Mammoth Mountain Ski Area,** one of the largest and most challenging ski resorts in the western United States, crowded on weekends with skiers from southern California. Call 619-934-2571.

Devil's Postpile

West of Mammoth Lake, along State Highway 203, a strange and eerie rock formation rises from the countryside—the **Devil's Postpile National Monument,** formed when a basaltic lava flow hit glacier ice and fractured into symmetrical columns of rock more than sixty feet tall. An easy half-mile trail leads to the base of the Postpile, and a more strenuous trail takes you to the top of the sheer cliff. The Devil's Post-pile can also be reached via a shuttle bus that boards in the parking lot of Mammoth Mountain Ski Area.

Restaurants

Don't go to the eastern Sierra Nevada for the cuisine. **White Wolf** and **Tuolumne Meadows Lodge** both have small restaurants serving nothing-fancy meals at modest prices. The **Sierra Inn** in June Lake serves chicken, steaks, and seafood and offers a senior discount. Simple coffee shops and diners are found along U.S. 395.

Lodging

The eastern Sierra Nevada is not exactly Motel Row. Two basic lodging places operate in the Yosemite high country; motels, sports lodges, and a few B&Bs are scattered along U.S. 395.

- **White Wolf Lodge,** in the high country of Yosemite National Park, is a popular jumping-off place for one-day hikes into the wilderness. It is open in summer only. Cabins and tent cabins with central bath are available. Reservations are essential. Moderate. Reserve through Mistix: 800-365-2267.

- **Tuolumne Meadows Lodge,** in Yosemite at 8600 feet, has sixty-nine tent cabins, a restaurant, and a store. Popular with hikers and backpackers, it is open June to September. Reservations are very important, especially at the height of the season. Moderate. Reserve through Mistix: 800-365-2267.

- **Cain House** is a historic restored home with an antique decor. Full breakfast is served. Wine and hor d'oeuvres are offered in the evening. Moderate. Route 395, Bridgeport, north of Lee Vining. 619-932-7040.

- **Best Western Lakeview Lodge** is on Mono Lake. Some units have kitchens. Rates are lower in off-season. Moderate. U.S. 395, Lee Vining, near the State Highway 120 and U.S. 395 junction. 619-647-6543.

- **Boulder Lodge** overlooks June Lake. It is secluded with mountain views and some housekeeping cabins. Senior discount. Moderate. On State Highway 158. 619-648-7533.

- **Campsites** are available at both White Wolf and Tuolumne Meadows and at parks along U.S. 395.

Chapter 19

Sequoia and Kings Canyon

The giant sequoia trees of Kings Canyon and Sequoia national parks have long been known as the largest and oldest living things on earth. Some scientists now insist that a monster fungus growing under several midwestern states is larger, and certain species of lichen are older. If they're not the oldest and the largest, California's biggies are beyond question the most awesome specimens in the plant kingdom.

Besides trees, the adjoining parks have mountains to match. The highest mountain peak in the contiguous forty-eight states, Mount Whitney (14,495 feet), is here, joined by many other peaks towering over 13,000 feet to make up this rugged rampart of the Sierra Nevada. The parks contain some of the nation's most spectacular alpine scenery of lakes, canyons, rushing rivers, and varied wildlife—mule deer, bears, fox, bighorn sheep, marmots, and 150 species of birds, including the golden eagle. And fish. The streams and alpine lakes are full of them, including the golden trout, found only at high altitude. It's a nature-lover's, hiker's, backpacker's dream—but there's plenty to attract a seasoned traveler who's less energetic.

First, the trees. Yosemite (Chapter 17) and Calaveras Big Trees State Park (Chapter 20) have their groves of giants, but Kings Canyon and Sequoia have the greatest concentration and the largest examples. Some date back nearly 3,000 years; they may reach more than 200 feet upward and measure 25 feet in diameter. They're readily accessible by auto and short, not-too-difficult hikes. Anyway, when they're the height of a twenty-five-story building, you can scarcely miss them.

The usual route into the parks for northern California travelers is

State Highway 180, fifty-two miles east from State Highway 99, the Central Valley Highway, at Fresno. That brings you to the Big Stump gate to **Kings Canyon.** (There are no eastern entrances to the park, nor trans-Sierra Nevada roadways. Most of the unpaved roads into the wilderness areas are closed in winter and some do not reopen until July 1.)

The **General's Highway** links the two parks, a forty-six-mile all-season scenic highway between the Big Stump entrance to Kings Canyon and the Ash Mountain entrance to Sequoia. The road passes near or through most of the forested groves and points of interest, spreading one spectacular landscape after another in front of you. The sixteen-mile stretch of narrow road between Giant Forest and the Ash Mountain gate twists and climbs and is not made for RVs and large trailers. But the road is not a problem for careful auto drivers.

Grant Grove is just inside the Big Stump entrance. This area was unfortunately heavily logged before being protected in 1890 as General Grant National Park (and eventually, with the addition of backcountry, expanded into Kings Canyon National Park.) "Big Stump" and other stumps (including the "Centennial Stump," remains of a sequoia cut for display at the 1876 Philadelphia exhibition) mutely testify to the ravages of early timbering. Some of the stumps are broad enough for a dance floor.

A short, easy, half-mile trail known as the "The Trail for All People" (wheelchair accessible) leads to the **General Grant Tree,** a.k.a. "The Nation's Christmas Tree." General Grant is the world's third largest known sequoia. Nearby and slightly smaller is the second largest tree in the grove. Appropriately, it is named for General Lee.

The **Grant Grove Visitor Center** at Grant Grove Village explains the natural history of the sequoias as well as that of the humans who found them and logged them.

Redwood Mountain Grove, four miles beyond Grant Grove and also in Kings Canyon, is the largest grove of sequoias in the world. Directly accessible only on foot by rather rugged trails, the route rewards you with several scenic overlooks from which you can gaze into the grove and the surrounding country. **Kings Canyon Overlook,** two miles farther, allows dramatic views into the Kings Canyon backcountry, including the deep chasms cut by the south and middle forks of the Kings River.

Lodgepole, in Sequoia National Park, has tall trees, too—but they are lodgepole pines, better suited to the cooler and windier miniclimate

SCENIC DETOUR

State Highway 180 turns away from the General's Highway and the popular park attractions just inside the Big Stump Gate. It leads to **Hume Lake,** a sparkling jewel of an alpine lake, and then follows the canyon of the south fork of the Kings River to Cedar Grove, where it dead-ends. Here, too, are tall trees, but these are fragrant incense cedars. The two-lane road is steep at times, but not too challenging if you're careful. It passes through the logged-over areas and clings to cliffs high above the river, with views into the primitive wilderness beyond. Take a picnic lunch or snack at the small Cedar Grove cafeteria before turning back. State Highway 180 is closed for the winter at Hume Lake Road; usually the closure is from October to May. Most of the road is actually outside the two parks, in the Sequoia National Forest; only the Grant Grove portions and Cedar Grove are within the park boundaries.

here. The visitor center not only has excellent exhibits about the trees but shows several short films about the park.

The **Giant Forest,** in Sequoia, is the home of the largest tree of all, this one named for General Sherman. The tree is 274 feet tall and 102 feet in circumference. Several other trees in the two parks are actually taller, but the General Sherman surpasses the others in sheer bulk. This one can be reached by a short, level walk, scarcely requiring any output of energy at all, and it is surrounded by benches, where you can rest, pay your respects to the monster, and try to imagine what the world was like when the tree was a sapling, twenty-five or more centuries ago.

The **Congress Trail** is one of several well-marked relatively easy trails in the Giant Forest area that wind through the groves where you can get a real feeling for the immensity of the trees. Some of the trails are as short as a mile, others longer, but none terribly difficult. You can obtain a map of the trails at any of the visitor centers or at the campstore at Giant Forest Village. If you visit in July, take the short trail to **Round Meadow** or the longer ones to **Crescent Meadow** or **Log Meadow** for the brilliant displays of wildflowers. You can also get a breathtaking perspective on the giant trees.

The **Tunnel Tree** is for cameras. It's reached from the General's Highway at Giant Forest by a short spur road that passes right through the tree's base (a low bridge for RVs, however, which must detour around it). But of course you'll want a picture of the family sedan chugging through. Auto Tree is a fallen tree; you can drive your car onto it for a photograph to show the folks back home. **Tharp's Log,** at Log Meadow near Giant Forest, is a pioneer cabin built in a fallen sequoia.

Restaurants

Cafeterias and snack bars are found at Grant Grove, Lodgepole, Cedar Grove, and Giant Forest Village. The food is basic, nothing fancy. Giant Forest Village also includes a more formal restaurant. Prices are moderate.

Lodging

- **Campgrounds** are scattered throughout both parks (and in the adjoining Sequoia National Forest). Reservations are accepted only at Lodgepole. They may be made through the National Forest Service at 800-283-2267.

- The **Montecito-Sequoia Lodge** is the most luxurious place in the two parks. Located on a small lake, it offers canoeing, sailing, and paddleboats and has a heated pool and tennis courts and cross-country ski trails in winter. There are lodge rooms and cabins with a central bath. There is a dining room. It is open all year. Modified American Plan. Expensive. On the General's Highway ten miles south of Grant Grove. 800-227-9900.

- The **Giant Forest Lodge**, Giant Forest Village, includes motel units, one- and two-room cottages with bath, and canvas-roofed tent cabins with a central bath. Some of the cabins have wood-burning stoves and outdoor patios. There is a senior discount. Reservations are strongly recommended, especially during summer. Write Sequoia Guest Services, P.O. Box 789, Three Rivers, California 93271. Moderate. 209-561-3314.

- The **Cedar Grove Lodge,** operating mid-May to mid-September, offers small, basic facilities along the Kings River. Some rooms have bunk beds. There is a coffee shop. Moderate. Write P.O. Box 789, Three Rivers, California 93271. 209-561-3314.

Chapter 20

The Gold Rush Country: North and South

When the cry of "Gold!" went up a century and a half ago, Americans by the hundreds of thousands flocked to the low-lying hills of the Mother Lode. Visitors still head for the Gold Rush Country, but no longer to seek their fortunes. The gold rush and its brawling mining camps petered out around 1859, leaving behind tiny towns and villages frozen in time whose clapboard houses and flowered dooryards have changed little since the days of Lola Montez and Black Bart. For antiques lovers, history buffs, and seekers of the nostalgic, the crafts shops, little theaters, compact museums, winding streets, sleepy settlements, and near ghost towns offer a charming step backward into a fabled past.

The Gold Rush Country strings out for 300 miles along the foothills of the mighty Sierra Nevada, stitched together by the (mainly) two-lane Mother Lode Highway, appropriately designated State Highway 49 for the year of the Forty-niners. Smaller branching roads lead to villages tucked into remote canyons or buried among the tall trees. (Be warned, however, that some country roads may end abruptly at a riverbank or be closed completely during winter.)

North-south State Highway 49 is bisected by two major east-west freeways—I-80 and the parallel U.S. 50. Although the Forty-niners classified the Mother Lode diggings into the northern mines, the central mines, and the southern mines, the two highways effectively divide the Mother Lode into northern and southern sections. Each segment is worth several days' exploration, including fascinating swings off the beaten track.

THE NORTHERN MINES: COLOMA
TO WASHINGTON

Coloma, on State Highway 49 fifteen miles north of Placerville, is where it all started. James Marshall, a carpenter, was building a sawmill for Captain John Sutter on the American River in 1848 when he spotted a gleaming pebble in the mill's tailrace. "Boys, I think I've found gold!" he announced to his fellow workers, and the stampede was on.

Coloma was the largest city in the state for a few years, but it was quickly eclipsed by other richer sites. A large portion of the original town is preserved in the **Marshall Gold Discovery State Historic Park.** Sutter's Mill has been rebuilt on the banks of the American River—not on the original spot, however, because the river has changed course. The electrically powered replica operates for tourists on weekends. The restored village includes a blacksmith shop, miners' dwellings, the Chinese store, and Marshall's own cabin. An excellent small museum displays artifacts from mining's early days. A short film tells the story of Marshall and Sutter, both of whom died broke. Drive up the winding road to Marshall's hilltop gravesite, marked by a larger-than-life statue pointing to the spot where he made his dramatic discovery. For information, write Marshall Gold Discovery State Historic Park, P.O. Box 265, Coloma, California 95613. Or call 916-622-3470.

Auburn, on I-80, is a modern community on the hilltop, but the original gold rush settlement, restored and designated Old Town, still thrives in the valley. Auburn was less a mining camp than a commercial center where miners brought their gold dust to be assayed, to buy supplies for more prospecting, and to meet the stage from San Francisco. Old Town clusters around the red-brick edifice housing the post office (service began in 1852) and the original Wells Fargo office, a firehouse said to be the home of the oldest fire-fighting company in California and an 1860s vintage livery stable. Restaurants with Old West names like Awful Annie's prosper among a plentitude of antique emporia. Awnings shade the old sidewalks; here and there a hitching post still waits for rider and steed.

Grass Valley, site of the Mother Lode's greatest single bonanza, teaches a basic lesson in mining history. Early prospectors panned for

SCENIC DETOUR

Two miles north of Placerville, turn north on State Highway 193 for spring's most spectacular drive. March roadsides are a sea of brilliant yellow Scotch broom. State Highway 193 winds past the almost ghost towns of Chili Bar and Kelsey, through the verdant truck farms and horse pastures of Garden Valley to **Georgetown,** one of the best preserved of the gold rush towns. Many of Georgetown's buildings date from the 1860s; the Shannon Knox House, still standing on Main Street, for instance, was constructed in 1864 of timbers shipped around Cape Horn. Known as Growlersburg before it was destroyed in one of the Mother Lode's many disastrous fires, Georgetown was rebuilt along the 100-foot-wide hilltop Main Street, which served as a fire break and helped the renamed Georgetown survive. Today the shaded sidewalks are lined with craft and antique shops; afternoon tea—a drink the miners might have scorned—is served on the veranda at the 100-year-old Georgetown Hotel, known as the Nevada House in the miners' heyday.

---

gold by sloshing water and streambed gravel in a shallow pan until the heavier gold settled to the bottom. Placer mining, using a series of sluices, applied the same principle on a larger scale. Hard-rock miners took the diggings underground. The Empire Mine, preserved as the **Empire Mine State Historic Park,** was the most lucrative underground (and industrialized) mine. Miners rode skip cars down mile-deep shafts to a 367-mile honeycomb of workings and tunnels. Mined rock was transported to the surface and crushed in a huge stamping mill with eighty one-ton pulverizers used to separate gold from quartz. The pulverizers thumped 100 times a minute and shook the earth for miles.

An excellent museum at the visitor center traces the impact of the search for gold throughout world history, as well as its role in civilization and in the arts. The museum also tells the history of the mine, which operated until 1956, and of its various owners. There's a fascinating, intricately detailed model of the mine itself, updated by the model maker as the mine extended and modernized. At the gold room vault—look through the barred windows, don't touch—displays show representative stacks of the precious stuff.

You can't enter the mine shaft (assuming you'd want to), but the surface buildings give a picture of the vastness of the enterprise. Docents conduct regular tours of the remains of the stamping mill, sorting mill, carts, smithy and repair shops, and the English manor house where mine owner William Bourn, Jr., lived. The showplace 1893 "cottage" is paneled in clear-heart redwood and was California's first electrified house. The formal gardens blossom in spring with rare, pre-1929 roses. Despite the grandeur of the cottage, Bourn spent most of his time at Filoli (see Chapter 3), his estate south of San Francisco where he presided over even more elaborate gardens. He couldn't sleep at Grass Valley, he complained, what with the stamping mill hammering around the clock a few feet away. For information write Empire Mine State Historic Park, 10791 E. Empire Street, Grass Valley, California 95945, or call 916-273-8522.

According to the kind of farfetched legend that abounds in gold rush history, a miner named George McKnight literally stumbled on the Grass Valley mines. Looking for a lost cow one night, McKnight stubbed his toe on a rock, inspected the rock and forgot the cow. The quartz outcrop was the tip of the largest, richest vein of ore in gold rush history. In 106 years, the Empire Mine alone produced 5.8 million ounces of gold, worth more than $2 billion in today's prices. The spot off Jenkins Street where McKnight allegedly made his briefly painful discovery is now commemorated by a marker.

The **Nevada County Museum** in the old Northstar Mine Power Station on lower Mill Street houses two floors of gold rush artifacts, including a thirty-foot Pelton wheel. This giant contraption, eight times more efficient than traditional paddle wheels, harnessed water power to operate the compressors that pumped air into the mines and pumped out water, making underground mining both practical and profitable. The museum also displays a working model of a stamp mill and—its latest proud acquisition—a machine used to pack explosive charges after Alfred Nobel's discovery of dynamite.

For another side of gold rush history, visit the Chamber of Commerce headquarters at 248 Mill Street, 916-273-4667, housed in the one-time home of Lola Montez. Lola, one of the outrageous characters for whom the Mother Lode was famous, was the ex-mistress of mad King Ludwig of Bavaria. She kept a bear in her front yard, once horse-whipped a newsman who disparaged her spider dance, and held soirees that wowed the locals. According to a plaque on the building, she "brought culture and refinement" to the Mother Lode, and was "a mistress of international intrigue and a feminist before her time," which may qualify as gilding the Lola. Eventually Lola tired of the Mother Lode and moved on. Her bear is gone, but a few of the house's original furnishings remain.

Nevada City spills down a hillside to a white-spired church and may remind you of a New England village. The most lovingly preserved of Mother Lode settlements, Nevada City's gaslit downtown was declared a national historic landmark in 1985. Nevada City was also the most sophisticated of gold rush towns and retains that air. The **Nevada Theater** at 401 Broad Street (916-265-6161), the oldest theater in California, has been operating continuously since 1865; Mark Twain and Lillian Russell performed here as did Shakespeare companies straight from London. The theater still offers a year-round repertory. Across Broad Street, brick-red **Firehouse Number 2** was built in 1861 to protect against the highly flammable Gold Country's devastating arch-enemy, fire; it is still a working firehouse, and its Victorian belltower and gingerbread trim make it the most photographed building in Nevada City. **Firehouse Number 1** houses the **Nevada City Museum,** good for a quick visit into the city's past; 214 Main Street. Call 916-265-5468. The verandaed **National Hotel,** little changed since Mark Twain slept there, anchors Broad Street, where it is slipping into shabby gentility. 211 Broad Street; 916-265-4551.

Like most gold rush towns, Nevada City is best savored on foot. Obtain a self-guided walking-tour map from the Chamber of Commerce at 132 Main Street, 916-265-2692, or join the Sunday morning two-hour guided tour ($10). You may also view Nevada City from the elegance of a horse-drawn carriage ($10 for two.) The chamber itself is an ideal starting point because it is housed in the town's oldest building, once the home of the South Yuba Canal office and John Ott's assay office where miners came to have their gold weighed. Follow the walking route up Broad Street, but explore Pine, Commercial, and Main streets with their array of galleries and gift and craft shops. And poke into Nevada City's cobblestoned, hilly lanes with their classic Victorian houses, picket-fenced gardens, gazebos, and verandas. The elite lived on Aristocracy

Hill, one of seven hills on which the city is built; many of the city's proudest Victorian mansions still stand there, gingerbread trimming their rooflines. The **American Victorian Museum** has merged into the Teddy Bear Castle at 431 Broad Street. Here you can see life-size bears relaxing on antique furniture from the Victorian period. Visits are by appointment only. Admission is free, but donations are welcome. Call 916-265-5804. An open house tour of old Nevada City homes is conducted each spring.

Downieville, nestled in a river canyon amid rugged, steep mountains, maintains the air of the roaring, wide-open, get-rich-quick days; it even has a gallows. Its dubious claim to fame is that it was the first community to execute a woman. Buildings date as far back as the 1850s, one of them a former Chinese store and gambling den now more prosaically housing a fine small museum. Stroll Downieville's wooden sidewalks and peer into the old storefronts—some of them still selling shovels and miners' pans—and you can imagine the stage about to come rumbling into town. You may, in fact, see prospectors themselves—some using high-tech equipment to dredge in the north fork of the Yuba River, others backpacking into the hills toward some secret lode. Downieville, site of a huge strike in the early 1850s, remains the mecca for those convinced that more gold remains in the earth than was taken out of it. If you want to try your own luck, you can hire a guide or buy prospecting supplies at the local grocery store.

Sierra City lies twelve miles east and more than 1000 feet higher than Downieville as the Mother Lode Highway (State Highway 49) sweeps upward toward the high Sierra passes. It has the scars to prove it. Three times the settlement was obliterated by avalanches and each time painstakingly rebuilt. Today the few buildings cling to the steep hillsides. Sierra City is a winter sports center; the remaining 200 residents, ironically, make their living from snow.

The spectacular rock formations called the Sierra Buttes, more than 8000 feet high, tower over the small community. On the buttes' flanks miners found a rich, if quickly depleted, gold strike. The second largest nugget ever found in California, said to weigh an incredible 141 pounds, was found here. The **Kentucky Mine** east of town exploited the gold until 1944. Tours of its restored stamp mill are conducted daily, and there is a small county museum. A natural bowl at the mine forms an amphitheater, where a summer program of concerts is performed. Closed during the winter. For information call 916-862-1310.

SCENIC DETOUR

Between Nevada City and Downieville, a web of old logging and mining roads, some unpaved and some barely paved, leads to some of the Mother Lode's most tucked-away communities. Turn east off State Highway 49, just north of Nevada City, on the two-lane Ridge Road.

Alleghany, which clings to a hillside like the cliff dwellings of Arizona, is one of the last of the working-mine communities. Its Sixteen to One Mine (named for presidential candidate William Jennings Bryan's famous Cross of Gold speech) operated continuously between 1896 and 1967, producing $28 million in what was considered the richest ore in the Mother Lode. It was reopened in 1992 after prospectors using metal detectors found a new strike. Sorry, no tours.

North Bloomfield, even more deeply tucked into the wilderness on the middle fork of the Yuba, is a monument to the most destructive of the mining methods. The hydraulic method blasted the hillsides with high-pressure hoses powerful enough to propel fifty-pound rocks 100 feet in the air. The water and loosened gravel were directed through a series of sluices where the heavier elements settled out. The waste gravel was washed downstream where it choked rivers and overwhelmed farmers' fields until finally a court decision put an end to the practice.

Left behind was the charming village of North Bloomfield. It survived until World War II, when the village closed up and left everything just as it was. Now part of **Malakoff Diggins State Park,** the general store is complete with miners' boots, dynamite, picks, and shovels and mail waiting to be picked up. Even books and desks are still intact in the old schoolhouse. A small museum displays the monitor nozzles used in hydraulic mining and explains the method. A small cadre of sixteen full-time residents leads tours and talks about the town.

A short drive below the town are the "diggins" themselves, a surreal landscape of orange and red twisted cliffs and minarets, sculptured by the water's powerful force. Ironically, they are now one of the Mother Lode's beauty spots.

Within sight of North Bloomfield—but across the white-water Yuba—is another sleepy and remote village. **Washington** lies at the foot of a twisting canyon road off State Highway 20, east of Nevada City. Now only a handful of retirees and dropouts from society live in the picturesque spot where general stores and a clapboard church still carry the flavor of 1900.

Restaurants ————————————————————————

Cornish miners whose forebears had worked tin mines for 1000 years were brought to the Mother Lode in the 1850s and are credited with developing the deep mines. At one time, more than 85 percent of miners were Cornish. The Cornishmen brought with them a special meat and vegetable pie, the Cornish pasty (pronounced to rhyme with nasty), which they carried to underground lunches in metal buckets. Pasties can be found on menus throughout the Mother Lode.

The Hangtown Fry originated in Placerville, allegedly when a miner flush with gold dust ordered a dish made of the two most expensive items on the menu—oysters and eggs. The combination omelet (most chefs throw in onions, too) is now served not only in Placerville but also in other Mother Lode restaurants.

Among the earliest immigrants were Chinese, and Chinese restaurants, some of them dating back 100 years or more, dot the Mother Lode. They were followed in the late 1800s by Italians; Italian dishes are another Mother Lode specialty.

Here are restaurant recommendations in the northern mine communities.

- **Owl Tavern** dates back to 1852. It offers basic seafood, steak, and beef dishes along with plenty of atmosphere. Moderate. 134 Mill Street, Grass Valley. 916-274-3737.

- **Michael's Garden,** on a creekside, serves lunches and dinners in an outdoor, flower-bedecked setting. Moderate to expensive. 216 Main Street, Nevada City. 916-265-6660.

- **Cirino's** is a classic Italian restaurant. At the Forks, Downieville. (Another Cirino's can be found at 309 Broad Street, Nevada City.) Moderate. 916-289-3479.

- **Butterworth's** is popular with skiers, despite its elegant setting. It offers new cuisine. Moderate to expensive. Adjoining the Placer County Court House in Auburn, just off I-80. 916-885-0249.

- **Selaya's** attracts theatergoers and is a traditional favorite. Moderate to expensive. 320 Broad Street, Nevada City. 916-265-5697.

Lodging

The Mother Lode abounds in quaint old inns and charming bed and breakfasts, many with history and legends of their own. Here are a few, with price ranges. For more information, contact Bed and Breakfast Inns of the Gold Country, P.O. Box 462, Sonora, California 95370; or Historic Country Inns of the Mother Lode, P.O. Box 106, Placerville, California 95667. Or write for the free folder, Historic Bed and Breakfast Inns of the Grass Valley–Nevada City Area, Box 2060, Nevada City, California 95959.

- The **Red Castle Inn** overlooks the town from Prospect Hill. Decorated in antiques and arranged around terraced gardens. It was one of California's first B&Bs. Moderate. 109 Prospect Street, Nevada City. 916-265-5135.

- **Grandmere's Inn,** built in 1856, is on the National Register of Historic Places and has been restored as a B&B. It is in the central district. Moderate. 449 Broad Street, Nevada City. 916-265-4660.

- **Flume's End** is built around waterfalls on three wooded acres and is a short walk to downtown Nevada City. Moderate. 317 South Pine Street, Nevada City. 916-265-9665.

- **Herrington's Sierra Pines** is a comfortable resort/motel on a riverside, west of Sierra City. Inexpensive to moderate. Sierra City. 916-862-1151.

- **Holbrooke House** is a classic old hotel, completely refurbished, in the heart of town. Moderate. Main Street, Grass Valley. 916-273-1353.

SOUTHERN MINES

The southern section of the Mother Lode Highway (State Highway 49) between Placerville and Mariposa winds through country that is less rugged and more pastoral than the northern portion. Charming villages (and two or three bustling modern communities) are found along its route; turn east from State Highway 49 to discover even smaller picturesque hamlets snoozing in the sun. The southern area is also freckled with small wineries and tasting rooms, some of them dating back more than 100 years. For a list and map of those affiliated with the Calaveras Wine Association, call 800-999-9039.

Placerville on U.S. 50 at State Highway 49 is one of the larger, modern towns in the Gold Rush Country. Once upon a time, it was known as "Hangtown" following a series of lynchings. Understandably, the good folk in town didn't care for the grisly name and changed it to today's more prosaic title, but history persists in the town's food specialty, the Hangtown Fry, an extravagant omelette of oysters and eggs. Not much else remains from the gold rush days except the **Gold Bug Mine in Gold Bug Park**, perhaps the only municipal gold mine in the country. A guided trail takes you through two underground shafts, one of which highlights a vein with streaks of gold ore. Located on Bedford Avenue, nine-tenths of a mile north of Highway 50. Call 916-622-0832.

Fiddletown's main claim to fame is its name, on which it has capitalized. There's a huge cutout of a violin on the town hall, and a fiddlin' contest, attracting bowmen from all over, is held each spring. Actually, the name of this sleepy little spot, six miles east of State Highway 49 at Plymouth, has nothing to do with Stradivari; it was named because the young people in town were said to be "always fiddlin'." Bret Harte picked up the name and made it famous in "An Episode in Fiddletown."

When antique shoppers die, they will probably go to **Sutter Creek**. Main Street, a sweeping curve in State Highway 49, is wall-to-wall antique shops. Store after store offers oak bureaus, Tiffany lamps, dog-eared books, 1920s posters, patinaed jewelry, crockery, linens— whatever a collector might desire. Antique Row not only stretches from border to border in Sutter Creek but spills over into the hamlets to the north, Amador City and Drytown.

Sutter Creek bills itself as "the nicest town in the Mother Lode." It may also be one of the oldest. In 1844, Captain John Sutter sent workmen out from his fort at Sacramento to gather timber for construction projects. The crew found what they were looking for along a creek they eventually named for Sutter. They also put up a large tent camp which Sutter made a headquarters. The temporary settlement was at first bypassed by the gold rush, but the later discovery of a hard-rock vein made the town a mining center until the last mines closed in the 1940s. Water-powered foundries, one of which still operates, produced hardrock mining equipment.

Most of the antique shops are housed in Main Street buildings dating from that era, each with its own piece of history. An excellent walking-tour map, available at many of the stores in Sutter Creek, illustrates each structure and explains its heritage. Locals have been zealous in retaining the "nicest town" atmosphere. A campaign is now on to purchase and preserve several old buildings, including the 1870s grammar school.

Jackson, two miles south of Sutter Creek, has evolved from an old mining center to a modern community. But it still retains some of its old, picturesquely balconied buildings along the main streets. On a hilltop overlooking the town, the **Amador County Museum** is one of the finest small museums in the Mother Lode. Originally built by Armistead Brown for his family of nine children, its kitchen and living quarters continue a lived-in look, right down to the drying petticoats. An excellent exhibit presents the California-or-bust rush itself, describing the overland, Cape Horn, and Panama routes the gold seekers followed in heading west. There were "three ways to get there," the miners said, "and all of them were hell." The museum is open Wednesday to Sunday 10:00 A.M. to 4:00 P.M. North of town, the head frame of the Kennedy Mine is open for guided tours, along with the huge tailing wheels built to carry away waste gravel from the mine. The wheels are found in a small park, with well-marked trails, off Jackson Gate Road.

Mokelumne Hill, or "Moke Hill," on historic State Highway 49 off the main highway between San Andreas and Jackson, had a reputation as one of the most violent of the gold rush encampments, which is quite an achievement. There was supposed to have been at least one fatal shooting for seventeen consecutive weekends. Not only that, Moke Hillers fought an international war. It wasn't just Americans who flocked to California during the gold rush; so did Chinese, French, Chileans, and Germans. When French miners made a big strike, they raised a tricolor over their diggings. Moke Hill's Americans, claiming the French were thumbing their noses at the U.S. government, swarmed up French Hill and drove the French out—claiming the mines, of course, as war booty.

It's a bit different now. You could fire a cannon down the sleepy, dusty Main Street and not hit anyone beyond a stray tourist or two, at least on weekdays. Moke Hill's architecture and winding streets survived the bloodshed and make it a charming town to visit. The town's

SCENIC DETOUR: VOLCANO AND DAFFODILS

Volcano isn't really in the bottom of a crater, but you might believe it as you corkscrew down the steep grade of the Volcano-Pine Grove Road leading to this most picturesque of tiny gold rush towns. To get there, turn off State Highway 49 onto State Highway 88 east, travel twelve miles uphill to Pine Grove, then turn left onto a well-marked but unnumbered route to Volcano.

The town has a colorful history, as several plaques along the two-block Main Street remind you. Pointing right down the street, for instance, is Old Abe, a Civil War cannon that (according to legend) won the war's westernmost battle without firing a shot. It was said a group of southern sympathizers wanted to take over the town and its mines to provide gold to the Confederate cause. But a group of Union volunteers smuggled the cannon into town, faced down the incipient takeover, and ended the rebellion.

Many of the old stone buildings still stand, housing a general store, a few craft studios, and a wine shop; others, unoccupied, are slowly crumbling to ruin. The Wells Fargo office and the assay office are mostly façades. The 1857, three-story, balconied St. George Hotel has been refurbished several times and still welcomes visitors. But it is more mood and atmosphere than history and architecture that sets the quiet isolated town apart from other Mother Lode settlements. Walk its few streets, picnic in its creekside park, browse in the craft shops, or sip coffee at the venerable Jug and Rose, and catch the Volcano flavor.

Continue beyond Volcano on Ram's Horn Grade, a marked road, to **Daffodil Hill.** In a setting that would have delighted the poet Wordsworth, the hill is covered with a "host of golden daffodils" each spring. More than 300,000 flowers lift their heads on the hill, which is neither a formal garden nor a commercial enterprise but part of a working ranch whose owners (and their ancestors) simply love flowers. You are free to walk among them for about six weeks, usually (depending on weather) from about mid-March until May 1. After that, horses and sheep graze on the hill. For information call 209-296-7048.

Return through Volcano to State Highway 49 at Sutter Creek, following the Volcano-Sutter Creek Road (marked) along the sparsely populated canyon of Sutter Creek.

centerpiece, the balconied, 1850s Leger Hotel, once housed the county courthouse; when the county seat moved to San Andreas, hotel keeper George Leger incorporated that part of the building as a restaurant. Look at the old I.O.O.F. building with its iron shutters as a classic example of gold rush fireproof construction. It's one of several Moke Hill structures built of a richly colored light-brown stone.

Read Bret Harte and Mark Twain before you visit **Angels Camp,** about twenty miles south of Moke Hill. Harte thinly disguised the brawling, wide-open collection of shacks and tents in "The Luck of Roaring Camp"; Twain immortalized it in "The Celebrated Jumping Frog of Calaveras County." Twain, who came west in 1861 and settled on Jackass Hill near Columbia, won his initial fame with this tall tale about how a scam artist dethroned Jim Smiley's champion leaper by the rascally trick of filling Smiley's frog up with quail shot. A monster bronze frog stands in the center of Angels Camp to commemorate the story. And each mid-May, the frog jump highlights the **Calaveras County Fair.** For a mere $3 you can rent a frog and strive for the $1,500 first prize. No experience is necessary, but some people train their entries for months before the big day and come from as far off as Oregon. Your frog is allowed three jumps, and you're permitted all kinds of vocal encouragement, from swear words to whistling to "Go! Go!" You can even pound the floor behind him, but touching is not permitted. The world's record jump, by the way, is 21 feet, 5½ inches, held by the frog world's Carl Lewis, "Rosie the Ribbiter." For more information, call 209-736-2561.

Oh, yes, you might also want to pay homage to the man who started all this foolishness. There's an imposing statue of Twain, a.k.a. Samuel Clemens, in the city park. The Angels Hotel, on Main Street, is said to be where he first heard the story. Twain's cabin, where he lived for several months in 1861, is off State Highway 49, north of Columbia.

Columbia was known as the gem of the southern mines, and with reason. It was the largest and richest of the gold-mining towns, yielding $87 million worth of the stuff in its heyday. And it may have been the most wide open: at one time it had twenty-one grocery stores, a public school—and twenty saloons.

During the 1850s, two devastating fires, back to back, swept the flourishing town. The townsfolk learned their lesson. They rebuilt in brick and stone, with heavy metal fire doors. Consequently, Columbia is

SCENIC DETOUR

Turn east from Angels Camp on State Highway 4 to **Murphys.** It's a small town, slumbering under the elms, but with a lively past. The now-spruced-up Murphys Hotel, on Main Street, once played host to the likes of President U.S. Grant, John Pierpont Morgan, John Jacob Astor, and Horatio Alger. The register for January 10, 1880, with the signature, "U.S. Grant—Washington," is proudly displayed in the lobby.

Murphys had a rich gold strike, but it wasn't precious metal that attracted the big-name visitors. About twenty miles northeast of Murphys, along what is now State Highway 4, a hunter named A. T. Dowd had discovered the most enormous trees anyone had ever seen. Dowd proclaimed the 2,000-year-old sequoias one of the wonders of the world and had the bark stripped from one and sent to London for the Crystal Palace exhibition of 1855. After that, the "Calaveras Big Trees" were a must on every traveler's grand tour of the American West.

The mammoth specimens, now incorporated into **Calaveras Big Trees State Park,** no longer attract the ranking celebrities, but they're well worth an open-mouthed, look-at-the-size-of-that-one visit. It's a pleasant place for a shady picnic. There is a $3 entry fee. Call 209-795-2334.

Return on State Highway 4 to State Highway 49 or continue east on State Highway 4 through Ebbetts Pass to the playgrounds of Lake Tahoe.

---

one of the best preserved of gold rush towns. In 1945, the state took it over as the **Columbia State Historic Park,** refurbished some buildings and restored others to the look of the 1870s. For general information, call 209-532-4301.

To walk down Columbia's Main Street is to step back a century or more. Sip a sarsaparilla at Jack Douglas's 1857 saloon, and imagine what things were like when the stage rumbled through on its daily run to Stockton or grizzled prospectors carried their precious dust to the assay office, then headed for the fandango halls to spend it all. It's a working town, too, with the blacksmith at his anvil, the carpenter turning out handcrafted toys (under a sign that reads "Coffins and Fine Furniture"), and the Cheap Cash store offering bargains in 1870s fashion. *The Columbia Gazette* still publishes as it has since the 1850s. You can even pan for gold at the old Hildreth's Diggins and take a bus ride and subterranean guided tour to a hard-rock mine. (The tour is $7, $6 for seniors.) Don't be crushed, however, if you don't come home with one of those legendary lemon-size nuggets.

Although you may dodge a rumbling Wells Fargo stagecoach (sightseeing rides: $4, $3.50 for seniors; riding shotgun $4.50) or an occasional horse and carriage filled with happy sightseers, no automobiles are permitted in town. For information call 209-532-0663. The state park headquarters, near the parking area on the fringe of the town, distributes a free map that charts a ninety-minute strolling tour. Don't miss the two small Main Street museums by the Sons of the Golden West, the

TRY YOUR LUCK

You don't need a pan, pick, or metal detector to try your own luck at gold prospecting in the Mother Lode. Panning sites and instruction are available throughout the area, although no nuggets are guaranteed. There are three gold prospecting sites in Jamestown alone, others in Angels Camp and Columbia. A good spot for beginners is the **Matelot Gulch Mine Supply Store** (Main and Washington streets, Columbia; 209-532-9693), which teaches the technique of sloshing water and gravel in a shallow pan until the gravel has been washed away and only the heavier gold remains. Customers are usually rewarded with one or more pinpoint flecks. Jensen's Pick and Shovel Ranch at Vallecito offers overnight prospecting trips of a hardier nature; some are made by helicopter or river rafting. Rates are $20 an hour for basic training, $75 a day for more extended trips. Old-timers insist there's plenty of gold left in the hills, waiting to be taken, and some lucky person is going to strike it rich: "Why, only last month a dude from New York reached into a stream bed just down the road here and found a nugget as big as your fist." The dream of 1849 goes on.

restored livery stable, and by all means pay your respects to "Papeete." This 1850-model pumper was bound for Tahiti via San Francisco when the twice-burned Columbians shanghaied it and brought it home to combat their old enemy. The fire engine, now in retirement, is kept in tip-top repair and enshrined in a place of honor. Columbia rolls it out and proudly parades it at Fireman's Muster in early May, the social event of the Columbia year.

Jamestown—Jimtown to the locals—lies just off State Highway 49 along State Highway 120, the main highway west to the San Francisco Bay Area and eastward to Yosemite National Park. Its four-block Main Street is a colonnade of well-kept 1890s balconied buildings, almost every one of which seems to house a craft or antique shop or

THE THEATER

The miners loved theater—everything from Shakespeare to girlie revues. The gold rush towns of the southern mines maintain this tradition. Virtually every one has a repertory company operating during summer. Some perform year-round.

Fallon House Theater, home of the Columbia Actors Repertory, offers drama and musical productions all year. Some of the performances are by drama students from nearby Columbia College. Columbia. Call 209-532-1470.

The **Claypipers** have been bringing the scoundrels and villains and pure-hearted heroes of old-fashioned melodrama to the Mother Lode each summer for thirty-five years. The audience is encouraged to boo, hiss and cheer. Between acts, there's a chorus-line girlie show the miners would have liked. For information write P.O. Box 155, Drytown, California 95699. Call 209-245-4604.

Volcano Theater Company performs in an outdoor amphitheater in summer (a sweater and insect repellent are advised) and indoors in the Cobblestone Theater later in the year. Volcano. Call 209-223-4663.

Sierra Repertory Company offers a full schedule of dramatic productions four days a week that range from drama to musical comedy to classics. Sonora. Call 209-532-3120.

twelve-table restaurant. Hence it is one of the most popular destinations for day-trippers, shoppers, and browsers.

Railtown 1897 State Historic Park just east of Jamestown tells you everything you ever wanted to know about steam railroads—and offers a weekend excursion to illustrate its lessons. This collection of railroad lore includes locomotives and rolling stocks, a station, a round-house, and maintenance facilities. It is open spring to fall. Admission is $2. The fee for train rides is $7. 209-984-3953.

Restaurants

You can still whoop it up miner-style in some of the local bars and eateries, many of which offer music and floor shows. For more sedate dining, however, try the following.

- **Bellotti Inn** is an old-time, family-style Italian restaurant serving all the traditional pasta dishes in quantities that would overstuff Luciano Pavarotti. Moderate to expensive. 53 Main Street, Sutter Creek. 209-267-5211.

- The **Miners' Shack** claims to serve thirty-five different varieties of omelettes, including the Mother Lode tradition, Hangtown Fry. Inexpensive. 157 Washington Street, Sonora. 209-532-5252.

- **City Hotel** offers candlelight formal dining and Sunday champagne brunch. The emphasis is on fresh ingredients. Expensive. Main Street, Columbia. 209-532-1479.

- **Les Chanterelles** prides itself on award-winning French cuisine. Expensive. 1090 Utica Lane, Angels Camp. 209-736-4209.

- **The Peppermint Stick,** an old-fashioned ice cream parlor, serves miners' bowls of soup, chili, or beef stew, and also ice cream specialties and old-fashioned candies. Inexpensive. Main Street, Murphys. 209-728-3570.

- **Calaveras Cattle Company** is the home of beef ribs and

other hearty dishes. They offer a senior discount. Moderate. 570 N. Main Street, Angels Camp. 209-736-6996.

Lodging

A few modern motels with all the 1990s motel amenities welcome guests in the larger Mother Lode towns, such as San Andreas and Jackson. Campgrounds are available at state parks throughout the area. To really soak up the atmosphere, however, stay in one of the small, refurbished 1870s hotels, or a B&B in a converted Victorian.

- **City Hotel,** in the restored area of Columbia, has ten rooms with half-baths and bath*robes*—the showers are down the hall. The three choice rooms have balconies overlooking Main Street; others open on an interior salon. Antique furnishings capture the flavor of the past. Moderate to expensive. Its sister hotel, the **Fallon House,** has recently been redecorated and spruced up. Moderate to expensive. Main Street, Columbia. 209-532-1479.

- **Sutter Creek Inn**, in a handsome old New England-style mansion on Main Street in Sutter Creek, claims to have been the first B&B west of the Mississippi, established in 1966. It is certainly one of the most unusual. Rooms are furnished with antiques, have wood-burning fireplaces and swinging beds. Outbuildings have been revamped into cozy cottages; how'd you like to sleep in the "Lower Washhouse"? It is renowned for its lavish breakfasts. Sutter Creek. 209-267-5606.

- **St. George Hotel** is the most prominent building in the sleepy town of Volcano and one of the most atmospheric lodging places in the Mother Lode. Established in 1852, it's three stories high, balconied, with large rooms furnished in antiques. There's a cozy bar and dining room that serves a fixed meal nightly; reservations are necessary. Moderate. Box 275, Volcano, California 95689. 209-296-4458.

- **Black Bart Inn,** named for the area's favorite stage robber (and worst poet), is an up-to-date two-story motel in the heart of one of the Mother Lode's most modern towns. It is complete with swimming pool—a refreshing escape in Mother Lode summer heat. 55 St. Charles Street, San Andreas, California 95249. 209-754-3808.

- **Murphys Hotel** is the place to sleep in General Grant's bed or occupy his entire suite or any of several other historic rooms in the 1850s structure. There's also a modern motel wing. Moderate. P.O. Box 329, Murphys, California 95247. 800-532-7684.

- **Leger Hotel** has recently been repainted and redecorated although its main selling point remains its history and atmosphere. Moderate. 8304 Main Street, Mokelumne Hill. 209-286-1401.

- **National Hotel** has been in continual operation since 1859. Its eleven rooms feature brass beds and pull-chain toilets right out of the 1800s but also boast air-conditioning, showers, and television sets on request. A continental breakfast is served outdoors under the grape arbor. Main Street. Moderate. P.O. Box 502, Jamestown, California 95327. 209-984-3446.

Index

251

N